Mathematics for economists

An integrated approach

E. Roy Weintraub
Professor of Economics
Duke University

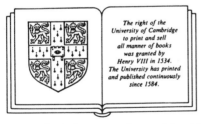

The right of the
University of Cambridge
to print and sell
all manner of books
was granted by
Henry VIII in 1534.
The University has printed
and published continuously
since 1584.

Cambridge University Press

Cambridge
New York   Port Chester
Melbourne   Sydney

Published by the Press Syndicate of the University of Cambridge
The Pitt Building, Trumpington Street, Cambridge CB2 1RP
40 West 20th Street, New York, NY 10011, USA
10 Stamford Road, Oakleigh, Melbourne 3166, Australia

HB
135
.W44
1982

First published 1982
Reprinted 1985, 1986, 1988, 1990

Printed in the United States of America

Library of Congress Cataloging in Publication Data

Weintraub, E. Roy.
Mathematics for economists.
Bibliography: p.
Includes index.
1. Economics, Mathematical. I. Title.
HB135.W44 1983 510′.24339 82-4244
                          AACR2

ISBN 0 521 24535 4 hard covers
ISBN 0 521 28769 3 paperback

Contents

v

Preface

*...a training in mathematics is helpful
by giving command over a marvellously
terse and exact language for expressing
clearly some general relations and some
short processes of economic reasoning.*
Alfred Marshall

Once upon a time, science or natural history studied "causation": What
causes the sun to rise? What caused the battle to be lost? What caused the
wealth of nations? Explanation of a phenomenon was equivalent to dis-
covery of the cause of that phenomenon. Hume's criticism of the concept
of causality, his analysis that suggested the causality could mean no more,
but no less, than a relationship between events, led gradually to a different
approach to the growth of knowledge. Specifically, the focus of science
became "explanation," and, epistemological issues aside, explanation
came to depend on the construction of mathematical arguments in which
laws or assumptions entailed conclusions that were potentially falsifiable.
The assumptions explained the conclusions; the theory or model explained
the phenomena.

In economics, this mode of reasoning may begin with a question, such as
"What causes the unemployment rate to rise?" This is transformed into
"What is the explanation of changes in the unemployment rate?" Given
the question in such a form, most economists would profess themselves
satisfied with an argument in which various economic hypotheses are
joined together to model the employment decisions. Analysis of the model
would then entail that the unemployment rate depend on, or be related to,
other economic variables, *assuming the hypotheses are correct.* This dependence might be expressed as "the unemployment rate is a function of gross
private domestic investment, government expenditures, the supply of real
money balances, etc." Thus, the answer to an explanation request frequently involves the presentation of a mathematical relationship, a function, that relates one set of variables to another set of variables. It should
be apparent that as one's understanding of functions and relationships and
variables becomes richer and more detailed, one's ability to provide explanations for economic phenomena becomes stronger and more sophisticated.

For better or worse (although I believe it is much better than the alternatives), explanation requires creating mathematical models. Fortunately, the ability to be an intelligent consumer of mathematical models is an ability that is not difficult to develop.

This book is written out of the belief that a student's *intuition* should be involved in the study of mathematical techniques in economics. This intuition does not develop so much from *solving* problems as from *visualizing* them. A picture is worth not only a thousand words but also at least two hundred problems at the end of a chapter on determinants. This book is written for the student who asks: "The guy who created the concept of positive definite matrices, whatever was he thinking of?" This objective has determined the selection and organization of topics.

The economics student must, at a minimum, be able to follow an optimization argument. Therefore, this book concludes with two chapters on classical programming and nonlinear and linear programming. The 10 preceding chapters (with the possible exception of Chapter 8) take the reader from real numbers through those topics necessary to understand optimization analysis. The topics are developed from the basic idea of linearity. Linear functions have simple properties, and the differential calculus represents an attempt to study complicated relationships by using locally linear functions. This approach requires that matrix algebra be developed naturally from properties of linear functions. Such a treatment is common, these days, in mathematics books, but it has not had much impact on the mathematical training economists provide their students. Because courses in "Math for Economists" (in American universities especially) presuppose, at either the graduate level or undergraduate level, that the student has studied calculus for a year in college and has seen a matrix somewhere, this book also presupposes that experience.

I have deliberately avoided stating and proving theorems. Gaining an understanding of the Implicit Function Theorem, for example, is a complicated process, and in my 15 years of teaching math to economists I have never found a student whose insight into the use of the theorem was aided by an understanding of its proof. As a consequence of this expository choice, I have had to restrict the generality of the exposition somewhat. I have presented a chapter on R^n, not a chapter on real vector spaces of finite dimension. I have linked the discussion of square matrices with the Hessians so useful to economists, so that symmetric matrices are emphasized over general nonsymmetric matrices.

The examples are drawn from the economic theory that the student probably is studying simultaneously. Each major concept is illustrated by an example from economics at the time it is introduced. The exercises at the end of each chapter, and the additional set of exercises at the end of the book, should test the reader's understanding of the material.

This book has been influenced by those who have influenced me. David Rosen, of Swarthmore College, and Jerry Kazdan, of the University of Pennsylvania, helped form my mathematical taste. My Duke University colleague, Dan Graham, by sharing my mathematical predilections and prejudices, has been a sustaining support for this book. Ann Davis typed the manuscript, Sue Havrilesky drew the figures, and Michael Alexeev developed a number of the exercises. Colin Day, of Cambridge University Press, has been my editor, taskmaster, cheerleader, and friend. To all of these, and to my special students at Duke, I say "thanks."

Durham, North Carolina   E. R. W.
June, 1982

CHAPTER 1

Real numbers

Mathematicians, ever since they began
to apply arithmetic to geometry, became
alive to the fact that it was convenient
to represent points on a straight line by
numbers, and numbers on a straight line
by points.
Philip E. B. Jourdain (1879–1919)

Mathematics facilitates economic explanation. The idea of a function, which links some variables to other variables, can express relationships among economic phenomena. The richer the language that expresses propositions about economic variables, the greater the explanatory reach. In a phrase, economic variables frequently are identified with real numbers. This chapter presents a variety of facts about real numbers and the properties of real numbers.

There are several paths to understanding a complicated notion. A mathematical construction such as the real numbers may be developed formally as an abstract system that satisfies several properties. For example, a noted text defines a real number "as a residue class modulo η in the domain of fundamental sequences of rational numbers."[1]

Such a definition is hardly useful to an economist. As René Thom has written: "I am certain that the human mind would not be fully satisfied with a universe in which all phenomena were governed by a mathematical process that was coherent but totally abstract."[2] Consequently, one approach to understanding that will be exploited both now and later is picture thinking. Ideas can be identified with geometric entities. The picture can be a model of the abstraction. Another way of presenting a "big" idea is to develop it as a construction out of simpler ideas. Understanding the constructing can lead to understanding the construction. In the case of real numbers, both pictures and constructions are available.

The starting place is the integers, or whole numbers, for, as the nineteenth-century mathematician Richard Dedekind remarked, "God created the

[1] B. L. van der Waerden, *Modern Algebra, Vol. 1* (New York: Ungar, 1953), pp. 217–18.
[2] René Thom, *Structural Stability and Morphogenesis* (Reading, Mass.: W. A. Benjamin, 1975), p. 5.

integers. All the rest is man's work." There is one useful picture to think of when someone says "real numbers." That picture is Figure 1.1. Define the set of positive integers[3] to be $Z^+ = \{1, 2, 3, \ldots\}$; then Z^+ is as represented in Figure 1.2. This construct identifies the elements of a set with points on a line. Thus the collection $\{1, 2, 3, \ldots\}$ has a representation as a concrete set at some place.

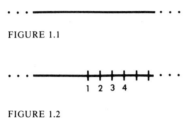

FIGURE 1.1

FIGURE 1.2

Consider two other sets: $Z = \{\ldots -2, -1, 0, 1, 2, \ldots\}$, called the *integers*, and $Q = \{p/q\}$ (p and q are integers with no common divisors), called *rational numbers*. Integers need no introduction. Rational numbers are simply fractions (proper or improper) in lowest terms, fractions with no common divisor for both numerator and denominator. These sets appear in Figures 1.3 and 1.4. To anticipate the conclusion of the story, real numbers will be identified with points on the line. Thus integers, and rational numbers, are certainly real numbers. The question that remains is whether or not there are points on the line, real numbers, that are not identified as elements of Q.

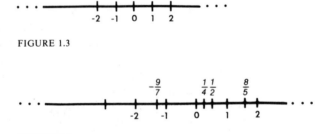

FIGURE 1.3

FIGURE 1.4

Figure 1.4 gets very messy. There are lots of rational numbers to fit on the line. Intuitively it would seem that rational numbers could "cover" the line: (a) a rational number is assigned a point on the line (that's easy), and (b) every point on the line is assigned a rational number. The Greeks found out, to their dismay, that (b) is false.

---

[3] Z stands for *Zahlen*, the German word for "numbers."

To see this, take a number. The square root of 2 will work. If (b) were true, then $\sqrt{2}=p/q$, and p and q have no common divisors. But then $2=p^2/q^2$ (squaring both sides); so $2q^2=p^2$ (cross-multiplication), so that p^2 is even (p^2 is divisible, evenly, by 2). Hence p is even (this is easy to believe, but difficult to show; see Exercise 1.1). Thus $p=2s$, for some s. But then $2q^2=(2s)^2=4s^2$. Thus $q^2=2s^2$, so that q^2 and also q are even. But then p and q have a common divisor of 2, so that $\sqrt{2}$ cannot be equal to a quotient of integers with no common divisors. This means that $\sqrt{2}$ is not a rational number. This also means that at least one object, $\sqrt{2}$, that is larger than 1 but smaller than 2, is on the line but is not a rational number. Thus there are more points on the line than there are rational numbers.

EXAMPLE

Economists use the number-line representation, without explicit reference to its construction, every time a graph is drawn. If q is to stand for units of output, and only outputs greater than zero can be produced, economists generally draw a diagram like Figure 1.5.

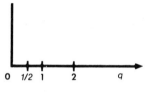

0   1/2 1   2 q

FIGURE 1.5

Another way to understand real numbers is to appreciate some of their attributes. When they are considered as a collection, or set, of objects, it is natural to ask "How many are there?" Certainly there are more real numbers than integers.

How many integers are there? There is, it should be clear, an infinite number of them. The set $\{1, 2, 3, 4, 6\}$ has five elements in it. That set has cardinality equal to 5. By convention, the cardinality of Z^+, the set of positive integers, has the special name $\aleph_0$, aleph-null (aleph is the first letter of the Hebrew alphabet).

What is the cardinality of Z? It is a fact that Z also has cardinality $\aleph_0$. This is shown by counting the elements in Z^+ and in Z and determining if they have the same cardinality. Use Figure 1.6. Each arrow attaches a posi-

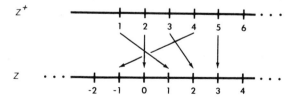

FIGURE 1.6

tive integer to an integer via the rule that odd integers get attached to positive integers and even integers get attached to nonpositive integers. Every element of Z^+ is attached to exactly one element of Z. The sets are in a one-to-one correspondence. Thus the sets Z and Z^+ have the same cardinality, because the idea that two sets have the same number of elements is embodied in the notion that they have the same cardinality; that is, their elements can be made to correspond each to each, one to one.

Consequently, even though one set, Z, properly contains another set, Z^+, they have the same number of elements, namely $\aleph_0$.

What is the cardinality of Q, the set of rational numbers? If they are countable, that is, if Q is in a one-to-one correspondence with Z, then Q must have cardinality $\aleph_0$ also. Count the elements of Q as follows: First, write out all fractions with 1 in the numerator:

$$\frac{1}{1} \quad \frac{1}{2} \quad \frac{1}{3} \quad \frac{1}{4} \quad \frac{1}{5} \quad \cdots$$

Next, write out all fractions with -1 in the numerator, and so on, creating the array

$$\frac{1}{1} \quad \frac{1}{2} \quad \frac{1}{3} \quad \frac{1}{4} \quad \frac{1}{5} \quad \cdots$$

$$-\frac{1}{1} \quad -\frac{1}{2} \quad -\frac{1}{3} \quad -\frac{1}{4} \quad -\frac{1}{5} \quad \cdots$$

$$\frac{2}{1} \quad \frac{2}{2} \quad \frac{2}{3} \quad \frac{2}{4} \quad \frac{2}{5} \quad \cdots$$

$$-\frac{2}{1} \quad -\frac{2}{2} \quad -\frac{2}{3} \quad -\frac{2}{4} \quad -\frac{2}{5} \quad \cdots$$

$$\vdots \quad \vdots \quad \vdots \quad \vdots \quad \vdots$$

Every element of Q appears in this infinite array. Now follow the arrows to count the array (Figure 1.7). Skipping duplicates ($\frac{1}{1} = \frac{2}{2}$), every element in Q corresponds to an element in Z^+, and conversely. Thus Q has the same cardinality as Z^+.

What is the cardinality of R, the set of real numbers? By now it may seem that all infinite sets have the same cardinality. That is not true. R cannot be counted. It is an uncountably infinite set, as opposed to Z or Q, which are countably infinite.[4] The cardinality of R is denoted $\aleph_1$.

---

[4] This idea, that not all sets with infinite numbers of elements have the same cardinality, is a profound one. It also leads to a variety of enchanting paradoxes, or propositions, that, although true, seem false. For example, consider von Neumann's hotel. Take a hotel with an infinite number of rooms, numbered 1, 2, 3, etc.

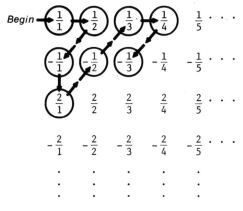

FIGURE 1.7

The set of real numbers contains many more elements than does the set of rational numbers. Representing the rational numbers on the real-number line leaves an uncountably infinite number of gaps on the line, despite what Figure 1.4 seems to suggest. Drawing in all the points of R makes the line sort of continuous; R is a continuum. The first property of real numbers is that there are lots of them.

EXAMPLE

The cardinality of the real numbers, the fact that the reals are a continuum, makes a surprising appearance in the theory of resource allocation, specifically general-equilibrium theory. Suppose there is a market with a finite number of traders, say n traders of m goods. This kind of trading problem is posed to analyze the equilibrium pattern, or allocation, of goods to traders once trading rules are devised. Notions of competition appear in this model when traders "take prices as given" or when "each trader is too small to influence market prices." In his important 1964 article,[5] however, Robert Aumann wrote that "though writers on economic equilibrium have traditionally assumed perfect competition, they have, paradoxically, adopted a mathematical model that does not fit this assumption. Indeed,

Suppose all rooms are full. A weary traveler arrives and asks for a room. Does the clerk say "There's no room at the inn"? Not at all. He simply shifts the person in room 1 to room 2, the person in room 2 to room 3, etc. Room 1 is thus empty, and the traveler can rest.

[5] R. J. Aumann, "Markets with a Continuum of Traders." *Econometrica* 32:39–50, 1964.

the influence of an individual on an economy cannot be mathematically negligible, as long as there are only finitely many participants. Thus *a mathematical model appropriate to the intuitive notion of perfect competition must contain infinitely many participants.* We submit that the most natural model for this purpose contains a continuum of participants [so] the actions of a single individual are negligible [p. 39]."

There is a significant point at issue here. If any one of a finite number of traders has an effect on the market, why not simply use a set like Z, of cardinality $\aleph_0$, to represent the traders? Why go all the way to R, with cardinality $\aleph_1$, for the representation?

The answer goes beyond the coverage of this book, to the foundations of the ideas of measure and integration. Nevertheless, some partial answer can perhaps be sketched. Briefly, the problem is to add up the effects of market participants. This adding up, or summing, involves integration over the set of traders. Suppose the problem is to integrate over the set of rational numbers between 0 and 1 (a set of cardinality $\aleph_0$). It is impossible to approximate smoothly the area over that set on the line (to integrate) because that set has too many holes in it. Integration must be over a continuum to have "length" in the "area" concept, for it is a continuum that is essentially holeless. Consequently, the appropriate representation of insignificant traders is as a continuum of points on the line, or *real numbers*.

Order

So far, the real numbers are an abstract set. As such, the only interesting question is "How many are there?" But real numbers are much more structured. They have many interesting properties. For instance, the set of real numbers is *ordered*. There is a relationship between any two real numbers, denoted $\leq$, that is read as "less than or equal to." Specifically, if x and y are reals, then (1) it is true that either $x\leq y$ or $y\leq x$ (or both statements are true). This order relationship has the additional properties that (2) for any real number x, $x\leq x$; also, (3) for x, y, and z real numbers, if $x\leq y$ and $y\leq z$, then $x\leq z$. Property (1) is sometimes called the completeness property of the ordering, whereas (2) is the symmetry property and (3) is the transitivity property.

Using the geometric picture of the reals, the real-number line, $x\leq y$ means that "x does not lie to the right of y." From the "$\leq$" relationship, the relationship "$=$" is defined by "$x=y$ if $x\leq y$ *and* $y\leq x$." Thus x and y

coincide on the line. Further, if it is true that $x \leq y$ *and* it is false that $x = y$, then $x < y$. This has the interpretation that x lies to the left of y.

EXAMPLE

In consumption theory, economists assume that the household has preferences for bundles of goods. Those preferences satisfy certain properties. If x and y are goods bundles, a preference relationship exists. Write $x \precsim y$ to mean that "bundle y is at least as desirable as bundle x." Assume that the relation "$\precsim$" satisfies the properties of completeness, symmetry, and transitivity. The relation "$\precsim$" induces the relationships $x \sim y$ ("x and y are in the same indifference class") and $x \prec y$ ("y is preferred to x"). As a consequence, bundles are ranked like real numbers – "better" or "more preferred" works like "more."

Topology of R

Real numbers are points on the number line that contains standard subsets of R, like Z^+, Z, and Q. R, as a set, has a continuum of elements. Other kinds of sets contained in R are distinguished by their geometric properties. Consider an infinite (countable) set of real numbers. Denote the elements $a_1, a_2, \ldots$. Define $s = \{a_i\}_{i=1,2,\ldots}$ to be this set, called a *sequence*. This is shown in Figure 1.8. Call a the *limit* of the sequence $\{a_i\}$ if, eventually, all the a_i points get close, and stay close, to a. Formally, for any positive number ϵ, is it true that there exists an N such that for $n > N$, $a_n - \epsilon < a < a_n + \epsilon$?

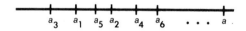

FIGURE 1.8

What does this formalism mean? Certainly $a_n - \epsilon < a < a_n + \epsilon$ means that a_n is at most a distance of ϵ away from a on the line. If a is to be the limit of the $\{a_i\}$ sequence, going far enough out in the sequence, past N (for some N), forces later terms like a_n (for $n > N$) to lie within ϵ distance of a. To get closer than ϵ to a, such as distance $\epsilon/2$ from a, requires a larger N; that is, to get closer, it is necessary to go out farther in the sequence.

A *limit point* of a set S of real numbers is the limit of any sequence formed from that set S. If $S = \{1, \frac{1}{2}, \frac{1}{4}, \ldots\}$, then 0 is a limit point of S (see Exercise 1.2). A subset S of real numbers, written $S \subset R$, is *closed* if S contains all its limit points. Thus, there is an easy test to determine if a set of numbers is closed: Simply locate that set on the number line and see if any sequence of its points tends, in the limit, to a point not in the set. Given a set $S \subset R$, the set S^c (the complement of S in R) is the set of all real numbers not in S. A set $S \subset R$ is *open* if its complement is closed.

It is not necessary in most economic models to worry about arbitrary subsets of R. In fact, almost any interesting set in R can be constructed out of some very simple subsets of R, namely the intervals. Some standard notation is needed:

$$[a,b] = \{x \in R : a \le x \le b, \quad \text{for} \quad a \in R, b \in R, a < b\}$$

$$(a,b) = \{x \in R : a < x < b, \quad \text{for} \quad a \in R, b \in R, a < b\}$$

$$[a,b) = \{x \in R : a \le x < b, \quad \text{for} \quad a \in R, b \in R, a < b\}$$

$$(a,b] = \{x \in R : a < x \le b, \quad \text{for} \quad a \in R, b \in R, a < b\}.$$

In words, $[a,b]$ is a closed interval, (a,b) is an open interval, $[a,b)$ is closed on the left and open on the right, and $(a,b]$ is open on the left and closed on the right. The intervals are the basic subsets of the real numbers. When economists need to model a variable, they usually choose an interval of real numbers to model the potential behaviors of that variable.

EXAMPLE

Price is an important economic variable. It is usually modeled on, or represented by, the interval $[0, \infty)$. This is the half-number line including zero and going to the right. Frequently, picturesque language is heard to the effect that "prices live in $[0, \infty)$." If a zero price is ruled out, then prices live in $(0, \infty)$, or, if p is a price, $p \in (0, \infty)$. Those who don't want to take the trouble to write horizontal "eights" to indicate infinity just write "$p > 0$."

Intervals are the important subsets of R. They can be categorized by asking whether or not a limit of a sequence of points in an interval escapes from that interval. However, there is something strange about an interval like $[a, \infty)$. The sequence $a+1, a+2, a+3, \ldots$ represents points moving out, a unit at a time, along the line rightwards from a. Does it escape to the right? Formally it does, because it sort of has infinity as a limit, and ∞ is not in the set. To rule out such strange behavior, a set $S \subset R$ is called *bounded* if there exists a finite real number r such that, for any $s \in S$, $-r \le s \le r$. Thus, a bounded interval is one in which neither a nor b is equal to ∞.

A closed and bounded subset of R (or a closed and bounded interval) is thus guaranteed to contain all its limit points as finite numbers. A subset of R is _compact_ if it is closed and bounded; thus compact sets are effectively finite sets, not because of the number of elements in the set but rather because of the way in which infinity or "escape" has been ruled out. It is for this reason that many important economic variables are modeled on, or live in, compact sets in R.

EXAMPLE

Economists use probabilities with great frequency. A probability lives in $[0,1]$.

Algebra on R

This subsection will be very short. Every economist can add, subtract, multiply, and divide real numbers. Further, if $a \in R$ and $b \in R$, then (1) $ab \in R$, (2) $a+b \in R$, (3) $a-b \in R$, and (4) $a/b \in R$, unless $b=0$. One is never allowed to divide by zero.

There is a way to do algebra geometrically, using, of course, the number line. To add 3 to 2, first locate 2 on the line. Then locate 3 on the line. Take the segment from 0 to 3 and place it at 2, as in Figure 1.9. The segment now ends at 5, which expresses the geometric addition of two numbers. Subtraction is easy also. To subtract 3 from 2, take the segment from 0 to 3 and flip it over so that it goes left from 2, as in Figure 1.10. The answer, $2-3=-1$, is immediate.

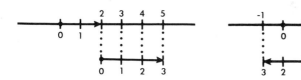

FIGURE 1.9   FIGURE 1.10

Multiplying a positive real number, a, by another positive real number, b, greater than 1 has the interpretation of "stretching" the segment from 0 to a by a factor of b, whereas if $b \in (0,1)$, the stretching is actually a shrinking. If $b<0$, there is a stretch or shrink in the opposite direction (i.e., leftward from 0, not rightward).

Although this number-line picture representation of the algebraic operations of addition and multiplication may seem unwieldy and unhelpful, these pictures guide sensible definitions of addition and multiplication in higher dimensions (see Chapter 3). The geometry adds little to understanding $2+3$, but it actually shapes the proper meaning of addition in sets that are more complicated than the real numbers.

Convex subsets of R

There is another concept associated with the real-number line that ought to be noted. A set $S \subset R$ is *convex* if for any two points s_1 and s_2 in S, and $\lambda \in [0,1]$, the point $\lambda s_1 + (1-\lambda)s_2$ is also in S. Certainly, if s_1 and s_2 are real numbers, and $\lambda \in [0,1]$, λs_1 is a real number, as is $(1-\lambda)s_2$, and thus $\lambda s_1 + (1-\lambda)s_2$ is a real number. The question is whether or not that resulting number is also in S. Intuitively, if $\lambda = \frac{1}{2}$, then $\lambda s_1 + (1-\lambda)s_2$ is $\frac{1}{2}s_1 + \frac{1}{2}s_2$, or an arithmetic average of the points s_1 and s_2.

Using the geometric interpretation of addition and multiplication of the preceding section, a convex combination of s_1 and s_2, that is, the set of points of the form $\lambda s_1 + (1-\lambda)s_2$ for $\lambda \in [0,1]$, is just the line segment connecting s_1 and s_2, as in Figure 1.11. That is, for some $\lambda \in [0,1]$, $x = \lambda s_1 + (1-\lambda)s_2$. Thus a subset S of R is convex if for any two points in S the line segment connecting those two points lies entirely in S.

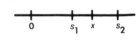

FIGURE 1.11

EXAMPLE

Most economic variables live in intervals. Compact sets that are also convex are really indistinguishable from intervals like $[a,b]$ for a and b infinite. Such intervals are the basic compact and convex sets on the real line.

FURTHER READING[6]

Most advanced calculus books or real analysis books present a rigorous discussion of real numbers. *Mathematical Analysis* by Apostol and *Real Analysis* by Royden are traditional references. A classic reference for the ideas of cardinality of infinite sets is Kamke's *Theory of Sets*.

The issue of interest to economists is related to the usefulness of real numbers as the set on which economic variables are modeled. How, for instance, does this representation restrict economic discourse? Some interesting remarks on "arithmomorphism" have been sketched by Georgescu-

---

[6] A detailed bibliography can be found at the end of this book.

Roegen in Part I of *Analytical Economics*. See also Katzner's *Analysis without Measurement* for an extended discussion of how to model economic variables on *abstract* sets.

EXERCISES

1.1 Show that $\sqrt{3}$ is irrational.

If $\sqrt{3}$ is rational, then $\sqrt{3} = p/q$, where p and q have no common factors. Then $3 = p^2/q^2$, and $3q^2 = p^2$; so p^2 is divisible by 3. The problem turns on whether or not this entails that p is divisible by 3. If p is divisible by 3, then $p = 3s$ for some s; so $p^2 = 9s^2$. Then $3q^2 = 9s^2$ and $q^2 = 3s^2$. Thus q^2 has a divisor. Does this entail that q has 3 as a divisor? If it does, then p and q have a common factor of 3; so $\sqrt{3}$ cannot be rational.

The problem thus reduces to showing that if p^2 is divisible by 3, then p is divisible by 3 (where p is an integer). The simplest way to show this involves the introduction of the idea of prime numbers: An integer, π, is a prime if it has only 1 and π as its divisors. Thus, $2, 3, 5, 7, 11, 13, 17, 19$, etc. are prime numbers.

If the number p is a prime, then $p^2 = p \cdot p$ and p^2 divisible by 3 means that $p \cdot p$ is divisible by 3. But p is only divisible by itself (and 1). Thus p^2 divisible by 3 requires p to be divisible by 3, which can be the case only if p equals 3. Thus p^2 divisible by 3, and p a prime, entails that p is divisible by 3.

If p is not a prime, it is divisible by factors that themselves, ultimately, must be primes. This factorization theorem states that any integer $p = \pi_1^{a_1} \pi_2^{a_2} \ldots$, where the π_i are primes and the a_i are integer powers (e.g., $100 = 2^2 \cdot 5^2$). Further, the factorization is unique. Thus if p is not prime, $p = \pi_1^{a_1} \pi_2^{a_2} \ldots$. Then $p^2 = \pi_1^{2a_1} \pi_2^{2a_2} \ldots$. The divisors of p^2 include π_1, π_2, etc. If p^2 is divisible by 3 (a prime), then the unique factorization shows that p must be divisible by 3.

I do not know of any applications of prime numbers, or the prime factorization theorem, to economic problems, although prime numbers do play a role in some computational problems in integer programming and time-series analysis.

1.2 Show that if $s = \{1, \frac{1}{2}, \frac{1}{4}, \ldots, \frac{1}{2^n}, \ldots\}$, then 0 is a limit point of s.

It is necessary to show that given an $\epsilon > 0$, there is some N such that going far enough "out" in the sequence, past N, gets subsequent terms to within ϵ of 0. The nth term in the sequence is, of course, $1/2^n$. Pick an $\epsilon > 0$. Is $0 - \epsilon < 1/2^n < 0 + \epsilon$? Because $1/2^n$ is always positive, the left inequality is always satisfied. The problem is to ensure that $1/2^n < 0 + \epsilon = \epsilon$. But if $1/2^n < \epsilon$, then $1/\epsilon < 2^n$, so that $\log(1/\epsilon) < n \log 2$ (logarithms are natural logs). Because $\log(1/\epsilon) = -\log \epsilon$, $1/2^n < \epsilon$ whenever $-\log \epsilon / \log 2 < n$.

If N is the first integer larger than $-\log \epsilon / \log 2$, then, for $n > N$, $1/2^n < \epsilon$, or 0 is a limit point of S.

CHAPTER 2

Functions from *R* to *R*

And what are these [derivatives]? The velocities of evanescent increments. And what are these same evanescent increments? They are neither finite quantities, nor quantities infinitely small, nor yet nothing. May we not call them the ghosts of departed quantities?
                          Bishop Berkeley (1734)

The idea that some phenomena, represented by elements of a set of real numbers, are associated with other phenomena, also represented by real numbers, leads to the important concept of a *function*. If an economic variable lives in one set, and changes in that variable help to explain changes in another economic variable, the two variables are related. There is a correspondence between the two sets of variables. If the first set is denoted S_1 and the second is denoted S_2, the correspondence (which is denoted by f) is written

$$f: S_1 \to S_2$$

to suggest that f associates elements in S_1 with elements in S_2. Think of the diagram shown in Figure 2.1. Here, f "sends" or "transforms" x in S_1 into y and z in S_2. If each element in S_1 gets sent to precisely one element of S_2, then f is called a function. See Figure 2.2. Notice that more than one ele-

FIGURE 2.1   FIGURE 2.2

ment in S_1 may go to a single element of S_2. This, however, is too abstract. The sets of interest usually are sets of real numbers; so functions can be pictured as in Figure 2.3.

13

FIGURE 2.3

EXAMPLES

1. Let S_1 be a set of real numbers that represent quantities of a particular commodity such as apples. Let S_2 be a set of real numbers that represents "utils" of utility. A utility function, denoted U, may be described by $U: S_1 \rightarrow S_2$ to suggest that different amounts of apples produce different levels of utility.

2. Let S_1 contain two elements, s_{11} and s_{12}, where s_{11} is the state of the world tomorrow in which it rains and s_{12} is the state of the world tomorrow in which it does not rain. Let S_2 be the set of two real numbers $\{\frac{1}{3}, \frac{2}{3}\}$. Then $p: S_1 \rightarrow S_2$ defined by $p(s_{12}) = \frac{1}{3}$ and $p(s_{22}) = \frac{2}{3}$ can represent the idea that the "probability of rain tomorrow equals $\frac{1}{3}$."

If the language of explanation is the language of functions, it is of some importance to develop a rich grammar of functions. The problem is to create ways of combining functions and describing their properties. How can functions be classified to facilitate the drawing of nontrivial inferences about the relationships they model? The basic approach to answering this question is suggested by Figure 2.3. Simply stated, a function transforms a set of real numbers into another set of real numbers. But a set of real numbers may have a certain coherence or structure. The set may be open, or compact, or convex, etc. Because that set is transformed by a rule or function representing an explanation or theory, the structure of the set S_1 ought to have an analogue in the structure of the set S_2.

Thus the important question to ask is whether or not a function preserves the relevant structure of the set being transformed. *Functions are appropriately classified by the kinds of structures they preserve under the transformations they represent.* In Chapter 1, a set of real numbers had a topological structure, an algebraic structure, and an order structure. The categorization of functions proceeds by investigating the preservation of those structures.

Continuous functions

One standard classification device involves the idea of *continuity*. Intuitively, a function is continuous if it transforms "nearby" points into "nearby" points. That is, if $f: R \rightarrow R$, the set that is being transformed is called the *domain* of the function, and the set that is at the head of the arrow is the *range* of the function. Then a function is continuous at a point in the domain, called x, if points close to x get sent to points close to the image or transformation of x, called $f(x)$. Thus, a diagram like that in Figure 2.4 does not represent a continuous function. Formally, continuity requires that for any distance $\epsilon > 0$ around $f(x)$, there is a distance $\delta > 0$ around x, so that points within distance δ of x get sent to points within distance ϵ of $f(x)$, as in Figure 2.5.

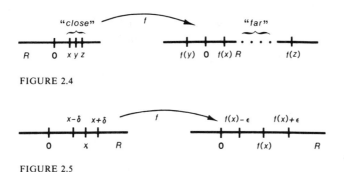

FIGURE 2.4

FIGURE 2.5

Speaking pictorially, a continuous function preserves some of the structure of the domain set as this domain set gets transformed into the range. The structure that is preserved is the "togetherness" of points; that is, a property of a subset of the domain that can be defined by behavior of nearby points is preserved under transformation by continuous functions. If, of course, a function preserves the "nearbyness" of points, it is reasonable that the property of "being a closed set" is preserved by a continuous function, because a closed set contains its limit points, and limit points are characterized by the "nearness" of an infinite number of points of a sequence. If the property of "closedness" of a set is preserved by a continuous function, all structures such as open sets, or compact sets, that are defined by the property of closedness are likewise preserved under the action of continuous functions. In brief, a continuous function from R to R preserves the topological structure of the sets it transforms.

EXAMPLE

If p is the price of a commodity and q is the amount of that commodity, a demand function, denoted D, can be written as $q = D(p)$. If $p \in [0, \infty) = S_1$ and $q \in [0, \infty) = S_2$, then $D: S_1 \rightarrow S_2$, where S_1 and S_2 are subsets of R. It is economically reasonable that a small change in the price of a good will not lead to a large change in the amount of that good that people will wish to purchase. Model this assumption by requiring that D be a continuous function. The constant-elasticity demand function $q = 3/p$ is not continuous at $p = 0$ (see Exercise 2.1). If demand functions must be continuous, it is possible to redefine S_1 to exclude the point $p = 0$. One way of doing this is to define $\bar{S}_1 = (0, \infty)$ and say that $D : \bar{S}_1 \to S_2$.

Linear functions

A second way to classify functions is to distinguish between those that preserve the algebraic structure of the real numbers and those that do not. A function $f : R \to R$ is *linear* if, for $a, b, \lambda \in R$,

(1) $f(a + b) = f(a) + f(b)$

and

(2) $f(\lambda a) = \lambda f(a)$.

The first condition says that the image of the real number $f(a + b)$ is identical (in the range) with the real number $f(a) + f(b)$. That is, the function preserves the additive structure of the real numbers, as in Figure 2.6. The second condition says that a stretching of an arrow from 0 to a by a factor λ is preserved under the action of a linear function, or linear transformation, as in Figure 2.7.

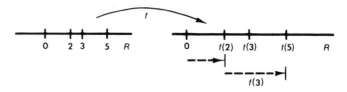

FIGURE 2.6

FIGURE 2.7

Because ordinary language suggests that "linear" pertains to lines, the preceding two conditions suggest that something about lines is implicit. This, of course, is true. Later sections will show that the graph of a linear function is a line, and Chapters 4 and 5 will demonstrate that linear functions preserve those geometric structures that are developed from straight lines.

EXAMPLES

1. Let q represent units of output flow and L represent a flow of input services. Define a production function of the form $q = AL^\alpha$, where A and α are constants. This function is linear if, and only if, $\alpha = 1$ (see Exercise 2.2).
2. The exponential function $f: R \to R$, defined by $f: x \to e^x$ (or $f(x) = e^x$) is not linear (see Exercise 2.3).

Graph of a function

The pictorial representation of a function given by Figures 2.2 and 2.3 is not the standard one familiar to economics students. Although it is the picture that generalizes most usefully to higher dimensions, another picture is more frequently used to see functions, especially functions from R to R. For a given function f with range R and domain R, take the range and the domain and place these number lines, with their origins coincident, at a right angle. The domain is a horizontal line, and the range is a vertical line, as in Figure 2.8. Now, for every point in the domain, say x, find the related point in the range, $f(x)$, and create the point in the plane $(x, f(x))$. The *graph* of a function $f: R \to R$ is the locus of all such points in the plane as x varies in the domain. As x varies, the graph of the function traces out a curve, as in Figure 2.9. The graph does represent a function, because any y

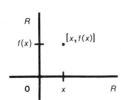

FIGURE 2.8

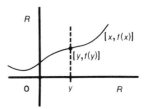

FIGURE 2.9

is sent to only one point on a vertical line drawn through y.

Continuity has the nice pictorial representation that the curve, the graph of the function, has no gaps. Looking at Figure 2.10, the function whose graph is the two horizontal line segments must be discontinuous at x, because a point y near x gets sent to $f(y)$, which is far from $f(x)$.

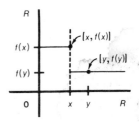

FIGURE 2.10

What does the graph of a linear function look like? Notice that because

$f(1-1)=f(1)-f(1)$ for a linear function, it must be true that $f(0)=0$; the graph of a linear function passes through the origin. Let $f(1)=a$. Then $f(2)=2a$, $f(3)=3a$, etc. This generates points on the graph of a linear function, as in Figure 2.11. Now fill in the gaps on the graph using the fact that $f(\lambda x)=\lambda f(x)$. For example, let $\lambda=\frac{2}{3}$. Then $f(\frac{2}{3})=f(\frac{2}{3}\cdot1)=\frac{2}{3}f(1)=\frac{2}{3}a$. Thus the graph is drawn as in Figure 2.12. Thus the graph of a linear function is a straight line, passing through the origin, with slope equal to $f(1)$.

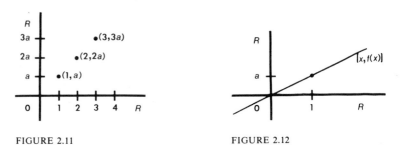

FIGURE 2.11   FIGURE 2.12

All linear functions from R to R are of the form

$$f(x) = ax \quad (\text{with } a = f(1)).$$

The geometry makes it obvious that all linear functions from R to R are continuous. This fact should be surprising, because linear functions were created to preserve arithmetic properties, whereas continuous functions were created to preserve topological (or geometric closeness) properties of the real numbers. Thus, linear functions are completely described by the number a. There are three possibilities: $a>0$, $a=0$, $a<0$. If $a>0$, the graph is a line with positive slope; if $a<0$, the line has negative slope; if $a=0$, the function transforms R into a point, the zero point of the range. This is a rather degenerate transformation, because $f(x)=0$ for all x entails that every point x in the domain gets transformed into the single point 0 in the range. All the structure of the domain set is lost as the set is collapsed, by the transformation f, to a single point. Information is lost.

Functions model arguments. Writing $f: x \rightarrow f(x)$ captures the idea that the rule or law or theory embodied in f takes a variable, denoted by x, and transforms it into another variable $f(x)$. Thus, $f(x)=0$ for all x models an argument such as "no matter what happens, nothing changes."

Even though functions from R to R model arguments of the form "changes in one variable are associated with changes in a second variable," such functions are the building blocks of more sophisticated arguments. Such functions, because of their simplicity, have played a major role in economic analysis.

EXAMPLES

1. Real consumption expenditures are a function of real disposable income: $C=f(Y_d)$.
2. The quantity of labor demanded is a function of the real
wage: $N^d=f(w/p)$.
3. Real investment expenditures are a function of the interest
rate: $I=f(r)$.
4. The inflation rate is a function of the rate of growth of the
money supply: $\dot{p}/p=f(\dot{m}/m)$.

None of these example functions are sensibly described as linear functions. Yet linear functions are especially nice to study because of the
simplicity of their structure. What about nonlinear functions? The differential calculus, when all is said and done, is the study of linear approximations to nonlinear functions. If any nonlinear function has an associated
linear function that approximates it closely, then analysis of nonlinear
functions is rather easy. To compare two nonlinear functions, compare
their linear approximations; that is, compare the two linear functions that
are associated with the given nonlinear functions. Thus, there are two questions to answer:

1. Under what conditions does a given function from _R_ to _R_ possess an
associated linear function?
2. Given that a linear approximation to, or function associated with,
$f: R \rightarrow R$ exists, how is it found?

Differentiable functions

Figures 2.13(a) and 2.13(b) suggest that it may be difficult to produce a general answer to question (1). Panel (a) presents a "wild" function,

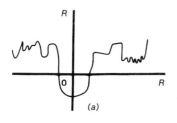

(a)

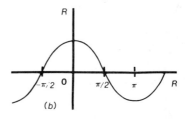

(b)

FIGURE 2.13

and panel (b) graphs $f(x) = \cos x$, which is nice and regular. In neither case does a linear function (one whose graph is a line through the origin with some arbitrary slope) appear to approximate the given function in any sensible fashion. Look at Figure 2.13(b) again. Restricting attention to the interval $[0, \pi]$, and shifting the origin of the horizontal axis to $\pi/2$, produce the diagram in Figure 2.14. In this case the dotted line represents (is the graph of) a linear function, $f(x) = (-1)x = -x$, that seems to approximate the cosine fairly well.

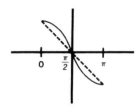

FIGURE 2.14

This observation is, in fact, central to the calculus. It is not possible to associate a linear function with an arbitrary function from R to R. It is sometimes possible, however, to carve up the domain of the function to perform a local approximation. Gaining the simplicity of linearity requires forsaking the global picture. If it is feasible to do a local approximation in all the chunks of the carved-up domain, it may be possible to patch together the local approximations into some coherent picture. Differential calculus is local analysis. Our preceding question (1) thus becomes question (1′):

1′. Under what conditions does a given function $f: R \rightarrow R$ possess an associated linear function locally?

This is equivalent to asking if there is a point $\bar{x}$ in the domain of f such that there is a linear function L that is a good approximation to f near $\bar{x}$. Consider an interval beginning at $\bar{x}$ as the realization of "near $\bar{x}$," and define it as $[\bar{x}, \bar{x} + h]$. Figure 2.15 may help to visualize the argument. The basic idea is that the slope of the chord joining $f(\bar{x})$ to $f(\bar{x} + h)$ is a "good" approximation to the slope of the function $f: R \rightarrow R$ near the point $(\bar{x}, f(\bar{x}))$, and this approximation gets better closer to $\bar{x}$ (i.e., the smaller is h).

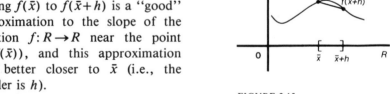

FIGURE 2.15

Notice that the interval $[\bar{x}, \bar{x} + h]$ is the interval $[0, h]$ when $\bar{x}$ is the origin. A linear mapping, or transformation, or function, on such an interval is certainly of the form $L(h) = ah$, for some $a = L(1)$, as shown earlier. Recognizing that h can be positive or negative, compare the slope of the chord

$$\frac{f(\bar{x} + h) - f(\bar{x})}{h}$$

with the slope of the linear mapping, a, as h gets small. Now h gets "small" from some initial value. This produces a sequence of numbers, the slopes of the associated chords. Is the limit point or limit of this sequence the number a? If it is, then the limit point of the sequence generates the slope of the appropriate linear mapping.

EXAMPLE

Find the linear mapping that best approximates the slope of the function $f(x) = 2x^2 + 1$ near $(\bar{x}, f(\bar{x}))$. The slope of the chord, for given h, is simply

$$\frac{[2(\bar{x} + h)^2 + 1] - [2\bar{x}^2 + 1]}{h}.$$

Compare this number with a as h gets small. To indicate the shrinking of h, write $\lim_{h \to 0}$. Thus, compare

$$\lim_{h \to 0} \frac{[2(\bar{x} + h)^2 + 1] - [2\bar{x}^2 + 1]}{h}$$

with a. A good approximation has the property that

$$\lim_{h \to 0} \frac{[2(\bar{x} + h)^2 + 1] - [2\bar{x}^2 + 1]}{h} = a$$

or

$$\lim_{h \to 0} \frac{[2(\bar{x} + h)^2 + 1] - [2\bar{x}^2 + 1] - ah}{h} = 0.$$

Performing the indicated algebraic operations yields

$$\lim_{h \to 0} \frac{[2\bar{x}^2 + 4\bar{x}h + 2h^2 + 1 - 2\bar{x}^2 - 1 - ah]}{h} = 0.$$

Thus,

$$\lim_{h \to 0} \frac{4\bar{x}h + 2h^2 - ah}{h} = 0,$$

so that

$$\lim_{h \to 0} 4\bar{x} + 2h - a = 0,$$

or

$4\bar{x} - a = 0,$

because $2h \to 0$ when $h \to 0$. Thus, $a = 4\bar{x}$ gives the linear function $L(x) = 4(\bar{x})x$ that is associated with $f(x) = 2x^2 + 1$ near $(\bar{x}, f(\bar{x}))$. If $\bar{x} = \frac{3}{2}$, then $L(x) = 6x$ approximates the slope of $f(x) = 2x^2 + 1$ nicely near $\bar{x} = \frac{3}{2}$.

In general, given an arbitrary function $f: R \to R$, suppose there exists a number a such that

$$\lim_{h \to 0} \frac{f(\bar{x} + h) - f(\bar{x}) - ah}{h} = 0.$$

This is read as "a is the derivative of f at $\bar{x}$." Write this as $a = f'(\bar{x})$ to indicate that the number a will in general depend on both f and $\bar{x}$. The number a also defines the slope of a line, namely the graph of the linear mapping or function that best approximates the slope of the arbitrary function f near $\bar{x}$. This mapping $L(h) = ah$ is called the differential of f at $\bar{x}$ and is written $df(\bar{x})$. Thus $df(\bar{x}): R \to R$ is a linear function that has the same slope as the arbitrary function $f: R \to R$ near the point $\bar{x}$.

Not every function has a derivative at every point in its domain. For example, a calculus theorem says that if a function is differentiable (i.e., possesses a derivative) at some point in its domain, then it is continuous at that point. Consequently, a function that is not continuous at some point cannot possibly be differentiable at that point.

Thus, not every function is differentiable, even locally. It would appear that the only way to determine if a derivative does exist at a point is to compute

$$\lim_{h \to 0} \frac{f(\bar{x} + h) - f(\bar{x})}{h}$$

for every $\bar{x}$ in the domain of f. Fortunately, however, elementary calculus provides rules to calculate the derivatives (that exist) of the elementary functions and further provides rules to break up complicated functions into simpler ones whose derivatives are easily calculated.

EXAMPLES

1. The derivative of a utility function has the interpretation of a marginal utility. In many growth-theory models, the utility, U, of a society is a function of real per capita consumption of that society, C. Suppose the function U is defined by $U(C) = \log C$.

What is the marginal utility of consumption at consumption level $\bar{C}$? The mechanical calculus technique immediately yields

$$U'(\bar{C}) = \frac{1}{\bar{C}}.$$

This is much simpler than trying to compute $U'(\bar{C})$ from the definition (but see Exercise 2.4).

2. For the production function $q=f(L)$, where $f(L)=AL^{\alpha}$, the familiar calculus rule computes

$$f'(L) = \alpha AL^{\alpha-1}.$$

Thus, if $\alpha=1$, $f'(L)$ (which represents the marginal product) is constant.

Linear approximation

The derivative of a function f at $\bar{x}$, when it exists, generates a linear function, called the differential. This differential has the property that its slope is an approximation to the slope of f near $\bar{x}$. How good an approximation is the differential to the function itself? Let us look at an example. Consider $f(x)=e^x$ on the domain $[-1,1]$. Certainly

$$f: -1 \rightarrow 1/e$$

$$f: 0 \rightarrow 1$$

$$f: \tfrac{1}{2} \rightarrow \sqrt{e}$$

$$f: 1 \rightarrow e,$$

where e is approximately 2.7183, $\sqrt{e}$ is approximately 1.6487, and $1/e$ is approximately 0.36788. Examine Figure 2.16. It appears that the action of f on the interval $[-1,1]$ is like a nonuniform stretching of the real-number line; an interval of length equal to two units is stretched onto an interval of

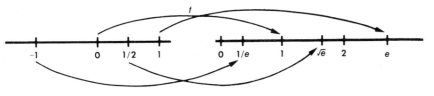

FIGURE 2.16

length roughly equal to $(e-1/e) \approx (2.7183-0.36788) = 2.35$ units. Now, any linear function from an interval in R to R is of the form $L(x)=ax$, which is a uniform stretching (or shrinking, if $a<0$). Approximating $f(x)=e^x$ on $[-1,1]$ by a linear function is geometrically equivalent to approximating a nonuniform stretching by a uniform stretching. Use the midpoint of $[-1,1]$, the point $x=0$, as the $\bar{x}$.

Computing the differential of f at $\bar{x}$ generates a linear map. Elementary calculus provides $f'(\bar{x})=e^{\bar{x}}$, and so $f'(0)=e^0=1$. Thus, $df(0)=1 \cdot x=x$; that is, the linear function $L(x)=x$ approximates the slope of $f(x)=e^x$ at $(0,f(0))$.

The linear function (the differential) called $L(x)$ or $df(x)$ is drawn in Figure 2.17 together with $f(x)$. $L(x)$ has the slope of $f(x)$ near $x=0$, but it is the dotted line, not the solid line, that approximates the function itself. Examination of the figure shows that, in fact, $L(x)$ is a linear function that approximates the function $[f(x)-f(0)]$ near $x=0$. [Alternatively, define an *affine* transformation as the sum of a constant plus a linear transformation; then $A(x) = f(0)+L(x)$ is an affine transformation that approximates the slope of $f(x)$ near $x=0$ and approximates $f(x)$ itself near $x=0$.] Thus, the interesting comparison is between $f(x)-f(0)$ and $L(x)$ in an interval around $x=0$. The "goodness" of the approximation is given in the following table:

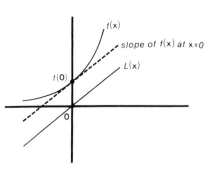

FIGURE 2.17

x	$f(x)$	$f(x)-f(0)$	$L(x)$
-1	0.36788	-0.63212	-1.0
0	1	0	0
$\frac{1}{2}$	1.6487	0.6487	0.50
1	2.7183	1.7183	1.0

As can be seen by comparing the third and fourth columns, the approximation is exact at $x=0$, but it gets worse farther away from $\bar{x}=0$.

To sum up this discussion, the linear function $df(\bar{x})=f'(\bar{x})\cdot x$ approximates the function $[f(x+\bar{x})-f(\bar{x})]$ near the point $\bar{x}$ when f is differentiable at $\bar{x}$. Thus, the function that approximates f itself can be written as the sum of two terms: $f(x+\bar{x})$ is approximated by $f(\bar{x})+f'(\bar{x})\cdot x$.

This chapter has presented two kinds of pictures used to think about functions from R to R: the graph of a function, and a transformation of the domain into the range. Each pictorial representation distinguishes how functions behave. Continuity, for example, can be seen either as an un-broken graph or as close images in the range for nearby pre-images in the domain. Differentiability of a function at a point may be pictured either as the existence of a well-defined tangent line to the graph or as the possibility of representing the action of the function near a point as a uniform stretch-ing (or shrinking). Both kinds of picture thinking are useful and ought to be exploited whenever possible.

FURTHER READING

The material on functions from _R_ to _R_ is absolutely standard, and any cal-culus book will be useful supplementary reading. The emphasis on linear-ity, and the differential as defining a linear transformation, is a bit less usual in math courses taken by economists. It does, however, provide the basic motivation for analyzing functions of several variables in later chap-ters. This idea that the derivative defines a linear mapping is exploited, with rigor and attention to detail, in Spivack's _Calculus on Manifolds_ and Dieudonné's _Foundations of Modern Analysis_.

The idea that functions are structure-preserving transformations repre-sents a point of view about mathematics that is associated with the group of mathematicians collectively known as Nicholas Bourbaki. The chapter on mathematics in Piaget's _Structuralism_ provides an introduction to this point of view. The mathematical subdiscipline called "category theory" is built on these notions (see Freyd's _Abelian Categories_).

EXERCISES

2.1 Show that $q = 3/p$ is not continuous at $p = 0$.

It is necessary to show that as p gets close to zero, q does not get close to any given number. Suppose, to the contrary, that q gets close to 300 as p gets close to zero. Because $q = 3/p$, when $p = 1/100$, q will equal 300. But if p gets closer to zero, say $p = 1/1,000$, then $q = 3,000$. Thus, no given number $\bar{q}$ can be the limit of $q = 3/p$ as p gets close to zero.

2.2 Show that $q = AL^\alpha$ is a linear function if, and only if, $\alpha = 1$.

To show that this is a linear function when $\alpha = 1$ is easy. In this case, $q = AL$, where A is a constant, and this is the form of a linear function. If α is not equal to 1, it must be the case that the second property of linear functions cannot hold. Thus, consider $q = A(\lambda L)^\alpha$ for any real λ, and show that this is not equal to λq when $\alpha \neq 1$. But $A(\lambda L)^\alpha =$

$A\lambda^{\alpha}L^{\alpha}=\lambda^{\alpha}AL^{\alpha}$. Thus, $q=A(\lambda L)^{\alpha}$ equals λq if, and only if, $\lambda=\lambda^{\alpha}$ for any choice of λ. This is, of course, impossible when $\alpha\neq1$.

2.3 Show that $f(x)=e^{x}$ is not linear.

If it were, then $f(1+1)=f(1)+f(1)$. But $f(1+1)=f(2)=e^{2}$, and $f(1)+f(1)=e+e=2e$. But if $e^{2}=2e$, then $e=2$, which is false.

2.4 Find the derivative of $f(x)=\log x$ from the definition of the derivative.

Compute

$$f'(x) = \lim_{h\to0} \frac{f(x+h) - f(x)}{h} = \lim_{h\to0} \frac{\log(x+h) - \log(x)}{h}.$$

Thus

$$f'(x) = \lim_{h\to0} \frac{1}{h}\log\left(\frac{x+h}{x}\right)$$

$$= \lim_{h\to0} \log\left(1 + \frac{h}{x}\right)^{1/h}.$$

Define $t=h/x$. Then, as $h\to0$, $t\to0$ also. Thus,

$$f'(x) = \frac{1}{x} \lim_{t\to0} \log[(1 + t)^{1/t}];$$

so

$$f'(x) = \frac{1}{x} \lim_{t\to0}\left[\frac{\log(1 + t) - \log(1)}{t}\right].$$

Hence, $f'(x)=f'(1)/x$, where $f(x)=\log x$. To evaluate $f'(1)$, it is necessary to evaluate $\lim_{t\to0}\log[(1+t)^{1/t}]$. This is not easy. [It is because of this fact that the function $f(x)=\log x$ usually is defined by $f(x)=\int_{1}^{x}dt/t$. The "fundamental theorem of calculus" is then used to compute the derivative of $\log x$.] It is a fact, however, that $\lim_{t\to0}(1+t)^{1/t}=e$. From this, $f'(1)=\log e=1$. Thus, $f'(x)=1/x$.

R^2 and R^n

Economic life is complicated. The number of variables that enter into a systematic explanation of an economic phenomenon is certainly larger than 1. Yet the previous chapter suggested that explanations have the form $y = f(x)$, where x and y are real numbers. In fact, most explanation statements take the form ''y depends on the variables $x_1, x_2, x_3, \ldots, x_n$.''

EXAMPLES

1. Output depends on the inputs of labor and capital services.
2. Gross investment depends on current sales, a structure of interest rates, the depreciation rate, the current capital stock, and expectations.

It is thus necessary to analyze the structure of collections of variables, or lists of variables, like $x_1, x_2, \ldots, x_n$, where $n > 1$, where each variable x_i is represented by a real number. Such a collection needs a name: A *vector* is an ordered n-tuple of real numbers, and the vector x is written as $x = (x_1, x_2, \ldots, x_n)$. This vector has n component parts; x_i is the ith component of the n-vector x. Each x_i is a real number; so x is a hypernumber, or a generalized real number, that includes real numbers as a special case when $n = 1$. If real numbers are important, vectors are doubly so, because they act as real numbers when $n = 1$, but they generalize the reals when $n > 1$.

Real numbers are now familiar. It is time to learn to use vectors. As a set, vectors can be endowed with the usual kinds of structure. They can have an algebraic structure, an order structure, and a topological structure. This chapter will develop, and analyze, these structures.

To engage the intuition, it is useful to picture or visualize vectors much as real numbers were pictured as points on a number line. The two dimensions of the printed page suggest that visualization will be simpler when $n = 2$, or when a vector is $x = (x_1, x_2)$.

Now, x_1 and x_2 are both real numbers. The idea is to represent x by using the two number lines for x_1 and x_2. Take two number lines and place their origins on top of each other, so that the line for x_1 goes horizontally and the line for x_2 goes vertically. The two lines intersect at a right angle at the origin, as in Figure 3.1. A vector $x = (x_1, x_2)$, such as $x = (2, 3)$, can be located as the point in the plane $(2, 3)$ with horizontal coordinate 2 and vertical coordinate 3, as in Figure 3.2. The x_i in the vector $x = (x_1, \ldots, x_n)$ is "the ith component of the vector x" when thinking algebraically and is "the ith coordinate of the vector x" when thinking geometrically. The set of all vectors $x = (x_1, x_2)$ is called R^2, or the plane or (real) 2-space. The set of all vectors $x = (x_1, \ldots, x_n)$ is called R^n, or (real) n-space.

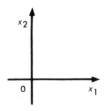

FIGURE 3.1

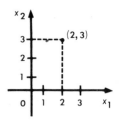

FIGURE 3.2

Algebraic structure

To add two vectors, they must live in the same space. It is possible to add $x = (2, 3)$ to $y = (1, 4)$. It is not possible to add $\alpha = (2, 3)$ to $\beta = (1, 3, -2)$. The idea is that $(2, 3)$ and $(2, 3, 0)$ are not the same vector, because $(2, 3)$ lives in R^2 and $(2, 3, 0)$ lives in R^3.

There is an obvious way to add $x = (2, 3)$ and $y = (1, 4)$: simply add the 2 and the 1, and the 3 and the 4, to get $(2 + 1, 3 + 4) = (3, 7)$. This is sensible because the result, the sum, lives in the same space, R^2, as do x and y. Formally, $(x_1, x_2, \ldots, x_n) + (y_1, y_2, \ldots, y_n) = (x_1 + y_1, x_2 + y_2, \ldots, x_n + y_n)$; vectors are added (and subtracted) component by component.

The geometric representation of vectors (Figure 3.3) clarifies this definition. Treating each number line separately, add the coordinates as in Chapter 1. Locate the point in the plane with these summed coordinates. This is the "sum" vector. Alternatively, connect x to the origin and y to the origin. Form a parallelogram with the two resulting lines as sides. The sum of the two points is the fourth corner of the parallelogram (Figure 3.4).

Subtraction is similar. Subtracting $y = (1, 4)$ from $x = (2, 3)$ yields

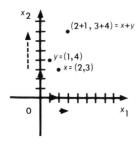

FIGURE 3.3

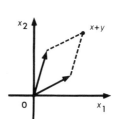

FIGURE 3.4

$(2-1, 3-4)$ or $(1, -1)$ (Figure 3.5). Alternatively, because $(x-y)+y=x$, the points $(x-y)$ and y sum to x. So if 0, x, and y are three points in a parallelogram, $x-y$ is the fourth (Figure 3.6). It should be easy to see that $x+y=y+x$, and $0+x=x+0=x$, and $x-x=0$.

Multiplication is a bit of a problem. Operating with each coordinate is unacceptable, because if $x=(0,2)$ and $y=(3,0)$, then $xy=(0,0)=0$; so

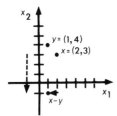

FIGURE 3.5

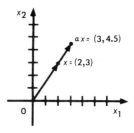

FIGURE 3.6

the product of two nonzero vectors would be zero, an unaesthetic result. (The idea is that in order to do division, the inverse operation to multiplication, $xy=1$ must solve to $x=1/y$ for reals. But if $x\neq0$ and $y\neq0$, but $xy=0$, then dividing by y entails that $x=0$, which is false.) Consequently, the product of two vectors will not be defined to yield a vector.

There is, however, a kind of multiplication of a vector by a number that produces another vector. It is called scalar multiplication. If α is a real number, and $x=(x_1, x_2, \ldots, x_n)$ is a vector, define $\alpha x=(\alpha x_1, \alpha x_2, \ldots, \alpha x_n)$. Thus, if $\alpha=\frac{3}{2}$ and $x=(2,3)$, then $\alpha x = (\frac{3}{2}\cdot 2, \frac{3}{2}\cdot 3) = (3, 4.5)$. Pictorially, scalar multiplication is a stretching of the line between 0 and x by a factor of α, as in Figure 3.7. This scalar multiplication imitates, or gen-

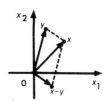

FIGURE 3.7

eralizes, the picture of multiplication developed in Chapter 1 for real numbers.

EXAMPLE

Define the vector $P = (x, y, z)$, where x is units of output, y is units of labor services input, and z is units of capital services input. The vector P thus represents a production plan. The set of all vectors $P = (x, y, z)$ that a firm could choose, all feasible production plans, is denoted $\hat{P}$ and can be called the production set. The problem for the firm is to choose that vector $P \in \hat{P}$ for which profits are a maximum. Sometimes it is useful to further characterize the production set $\hat{P}$. If, for example, whenever $P \in \hat{P}$, it is the case that $\alpha P \in \hat{P}$, then the production set, or available technology, is said to exhibit constant returns to scale. For if (x, y, z) is a feasible production plan, and $(\alpha x, \alpha y, \alpha z)$ is also, then any proportional scaling of inputs and outputs is feasible, and this proportional scaling defines the notion of constant returns to scale.

Given the set of all n-tuples, of real numbers, there is now an algebraic structure on this set. With this structure, the set is called a space, specifically a *vector space*. To use vectors as tools for economic explanation, vector spaces need topological structure and order structure, so that a comparison of two vectors represents or models a comparison between two descriptions of the reality of an economic problem.

Order structure of R^n

The basic topological properties of a vector space are related to the notion of "nearness" of points. The first step is to define the notion that one vector is larger than another vector. This is accomplished by defining the distance between two points in R^n. The standard idea is Euclidean distance. If $x = (x_1, x_2, \ldots, x_n)$ and $y = (y_1, y_2, \ldots, y_n)$ are two points in R^n, the distance between x and y is denoted $\|x - y\|$ and is given by

$$\|x - y\| = [(x_1 - y_1)^2 + (x_2 - y_2)^2 + \cdots + (x_n - y_n)^2]^{1/2}.$$

Thus the distance between two vectors is a nonnegative real number. Geometrically, this formula simply generalizes the Pythagorean theorem to R^n, as in Figure 3.8.

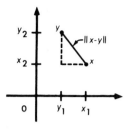

FIGURE 3.8

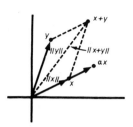

FIGURE 3.9

It is now easy to define a concept of size for a point or vector, x. The distance from x to the origin is $\|x - 0\|$. Define the length of *norm* of a vector $x = (x_1, x_2, \ldots, x_n)$ to be

$$\|x\| = [x_1^2 + x_2^2 + \cdots + x_n^2]^{1/2}.$$

From Figure 3.9 it can be seen that the following relationships make sense (are true): $\|x\| \geq 0$, $\|x + y\| \leq \|x\| + \|y\|$, and $\|\alpha x\| = |\alpha| \|x\|$, where α is a real number. (Here $|\alpha|$ is defined as $|\alpha| = \|\alpha\|$ when the real number α is thought of as a 1-vector.)

The notion that x is larger than y, when x and y are vectors in R^n, is clear: $x > y$ means $\|x\| > \|y\|$, and $x \geq y$ means $\|x\| \geq \|y\|$. [There are other ways to define $x > y$ when x and y are n-vectors. If $x = (x_1, x_2, \ldots, x_n)$ and $y = (y_1, y_2, \ldots, y_n)$, it makes sense to say that $x > y$ when $x_i > y_i$ for every component. Then $x \geq y$ if $x_i \geq y_i$ for all i, and $x \geq y$ if $x_i \geq y_i$ for all i and $x_j > y_j$ for some coordinate j. Alternatively, it is possible to define a lexographic order structure on R^n. If x and y are n-vectors, define $x > y$ if $x_1 > y_1$, or, if $x_1 = y_1$, if $x_2 > y_2$, or, if $x_1 = y_1$ and $x_2 = y_2$, if $x_3 > y_3$, etc. This notion imitates the notion of "word x appears after word y in the dictionary."]

Topological structure of R^n

Topological structures develop from closeness of points in a set. Considering the notion just developed, that two vectors x and y are close when $\|x - y\|$ is a small number, it is possible to create a topological structure on R^n. Let $\epsilon > 0$ be a small real number. Define the set

$$N_\epsilon(x) = \{y : [(x_1 - y_1)^2 + (x_2 - y_2)^2 + \cdots + (x_n - y_n)^2]^{1/2} \leq \epsilon\}.$$

Thus, $N_\epsilon(x)$ is the set of all points (or vectors) y lying a distance ϵ or less from x. In R^2, $N_\epsilon(x)$ defines a circle, centered at x, of radius ϵ (Figure

3.10). If $y \in N_\epsilon(x)$, y is in, or lives in, an ϵ-*neighborhood* of x. Intuitively, x and y should be considered "close" if x and y live in the same ϵ-neighborhood for some very small ϵ.

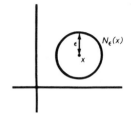

FIGURE 3.10

Take a sequence of points (vectors) in R^n. Identify points by superscripts, reserving subscripts for components; so x_i^j is the ith component or coordinate of the jth point. Let the sequence be $\{x^1, x^2, x^3, \ldots\}$ and denote this sequence by $\{x^j\}$. This sequence has a limit $\bar{x}$ if, by going far enough out in the sequence, the subsequent points in the sequence are close to $\bar{x}$. That is, given an $\epsilon > 0$, and the associated ϵ-neighborhood of $\bar{x}$, does there exist an integer, M, such that all points $x^{M+1}, x^{M+2}, \ldots$ live in an ϵ-neighborhood of $\bar{x}$? Clearly, the smaller is ϵ, the larger will be the required M if the sequence does have $\bar{x}$ as a limit. Look at Figure 3.11. In Figure 3.11(a), ϵ has been chosen, but $\bar{x}$ is not the limit of the sequence, because $x^5, x^6, \ldots$ are not in $N_\epsilon(\bar{x})$. In Figure 3.11(b), $\bar{x}$ is indeed the limit of the sequence $x^1, x^2, x^3, \ldots$, because for the given ϵ, if $M = 3$ all points $x^4, x^5, \ldots$ live in $N_\epsilon(\bar{x})$. If $\bar{x}$ is the limit of a sequence of points $\{x^j\}$ in R^n, $\bar{x}$ is a *limit point* of the sequence.

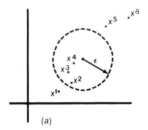

(a)

(b)

FIGURE 3.11

There is some important terminology that is used to describe and characterize sets of points in R^n. A set of points in R^n is a *closed set* if it contains all its limit points. That is, consider a set of vectors in R^n. Form all possible sequences using points in that set and find the limit points of all those sequences. If even one of those sequences has a limit point outside the set in question, that set cannot be closed. For example, look at Figure 3.12. Define the set

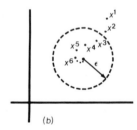

FIGURE 3.12

$$S = \{ y : [(\bar{x}_1 - y_1)^2 + (\bar{x}_2 - y_2)^2]^{1/2} < a \}.$$

This is the set of all points lying within a circle of radius a centered at $\bar{x} = (\bar{x}_1, \bar{x}_2)$. It is not closed. To see this, take as a test sequence the points represented by dots running along a radius from $\bar{x}$ to the outer rim. The limit point is certainly $\hat{x}$. But $\hat{x}$ does not live in S, because $\hat{x}$ is a distance a from $\bar{x}$, and S is made up of points that live at a distance less than a from $\bar{x}$.

EXAMPLE

If subscripts 1 and 2 identify two commodities, the set B is the set of bundles (of commodities) that the consumer considers "at least as desirable" as bundle $x = (x_1, x_2)$. B is usually called the better set of bundle x. Figure 3.13 shows the set B. In the theory of consumer choice, it is usually assumed that B is a closed set. Intuitively, any sequence of bundles such as y, drawn as dots in Figure 3.13, that consists of bundles worse than x and also bundles better than x must pass through the set I, the indifference class of x. Of course, the indifference curve itself can be defined by this construction. The *boundary* of a set X, denoted $\text{bd}\, X$, is a collection of points such that every one of those points contains a neighborhood in which can be found points of both X and X^C. Thus $\text{bd}\, B$ is just the indifference curve that passes through x. It is not difficult to show that boundaries of sets are closed; thus indifference curves are closed sets.

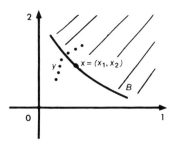

FIGURE 3.13

As noted in the example, if S is a set of vectors in R^n, then S^C is the complement of S in R^n; it consists of all vectors (points) in R^n not in S. A set S is open if S^C is closed.

EXAMPLE

Referring to the previous example, it is usually assumed in microeconomic theory that the set of bundles strictly preferred to a given bundle forms an open set.

EXAMPLE

If $p = (p_1, p_2, \ldots, p_n)$ refer to the prices of n goods, the set $P = \{p : p > 0\}$ is an open set.

A set, S, of vectors in R^n is *bounded* if there is some point $\bar{x}$, in R^n and some finite number a such that all the vectors in S live in an a-neighborhood of $\bar{x}$. That is, $S \subset N_a(\bar{x}) = \{x : \|x - \bar{x}\| \leq a\}$. A set of vectors (or points) in R^n is *compact* if that set is closed and bounded.

EXAMPLE

If p_1 is the price of commodity 1 and p_2 is the price of commodity 2, and an individual has income Y, the set of affordable bundles, or the consumer's feasible choice set, is defined by

$$S = \{x = (x_1, x_2) : x_1 \geq 0, x_2 \geq 0, p_1 x_1 + p_2 x_2 \leq Y\}.$$

This set is compact. It will be true in much of optimization theory (the theory of consumer behavior, the theory of the firm, etc.) that feasible sets are compact. This is extremely convenient because of some theorems in mathematics that state, intuitively, that optimizing choices made from compact sets lead to determinate outcomes.

There is another concept useful in categorizing general sets of points in R^n. A set S in R^n is *convex* if any two points in that set can be connected by a line segment that lies wholly within that set. In Figure 3.14, the set A is not convex, whereas the set B is convex. More formally, S is convex if for any x and y in S, all points in $Z = \{z = (z_1, \ldots, z_n) : \alpha x + (1 - \alpha) y = z$ for $\alpha \in [0, 1]\}$ are also in S.

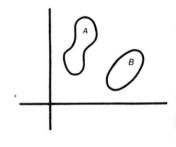

FIGURE 3.14

EXAMPLE

In the example described in Figure 3.13, it is true that the set of bundles at least as desirable as a given bundle x is usually assumed, in microeconomics, to be a convex set. Notice that if this is true, the indifference class of x (that is, the set of bundles

neither strictly better than nor strictly worse than x) does not
form a convex set. The worse set to bundle x, those bundles less
desirable than x, also forms a set that is not convex. Standard
microeconomics, the theory of the household, suggests that "the
better set of x is convex" is a precise formulation of "the law of
diminishing marginal rates of substitution."

EXAMPLE

In a multimarket equilibrium problem, the analyst usually has
the freedom to normalize prices by choice of a numeraire,
because only relative prices affect the market choices. A
standard normalization requires prices to be vectors in the set

$$P = \{(p_1, p_2, \ldots, p_n) = p : p_i \geq 0 \quad \text{and} \quad p_1 + p_2 + \cdots + p_n = 1\}.$$

It is not difficult to see that P is a convex and compact set.

The importance of convex sets in economics cannot be overemphasized.
It is convexity of the feasible choice set that allows an optimization problem to have a unique solution if it has any solution. Thus, if a feasible set is
compact and convex, an optimizing choice will exist (by compactness) and
will be unique (by convexity) (see Chapter 11).

Geometry in R^n

Because the most important sets of variables in economic analysis
usually are represented by, or are modeled on, subsets of R^n, the structure
of subsets of R^n is worth exploring. Going from assumptions about
economic variables to explanations of their behavior usually requires that
the variables be elements of a subset of R^n. The models of economic theory
make this identification explicit. The argument proceeds formally, in the
mathematical model, from assumptions to conclusions. The economist re-
interprets those conclusions in economic language. The logic of the argument depends on the mathematical structure. The more detailed the structure, the richer the interpretable conclusions of the analysis.

Combining ideas about the algebraic order and topological structure of
R^n informs the geometry of R^n. To do geometry, there must be some way
to phrase questions about relationships among points, lines, and angles.
The primary tool is the idea of the dot product, or scalar product, of two
vectors. If x and y are two vectors or points in R^n, the *dot product,* or
scalar product, of x and y is

$$x \cdot y = [x_1 y_1 + x_2 y_2 + \cdots + x_n y_n].$$

(It should be obvious that $x \cdot x = \|x\|^2$. Also, by construction, $x \cdot y$ is a real number or scalar; hence its name.)

A simple picture (Figure 3.15) should be of help in understanding the dot product.[1] Let θ be the angle between x and y. Dropping a perpendicular from x to the line from 0 to y yields an intersection with the line at ty, where t is a scalar. By the Pythagorean theorem,

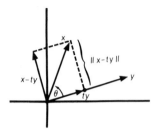

FIGURE 3.15

$$\|ty\|^2 + \|x - ty\|^2 = \|x\|^2.$$

But

$$\|ty\|^2 = t^2 \|y\|^2 = t^2 y \cdot y,$$

and

$$\|x - ty\|^2 = (x - ty) \cdot (x - ty) = x \cdot x - 2tx \cdot y + t^2 y \cdot y,$$

and

$$\|x\|^2 = x \cdot x.$$

Putting all this together yields

$$t^2 y \cdot y + x \cdot x - 2tx \cdot y + t^2 y \cdot y = x \cdot x.$$

So

$$2t^2 y \cdot y - 2tx \cdot y = 0,$$

and

$$ty \cdot y = x \cdot y,$$

or

$$t = \frac{x \cdot y}{y \cdot y}.$$

But now look at the angle θ. Certainly

$$\cos \theta = \frac{t \|y\|}{\|x\|},$$

---

[1] I am indebted to my colleague, Dan Graham, for this construction. A similar version appears in the Appendix to his book *Microeconomics: The Analysis of Choice* (Boston: D. C. Heath, 1980).

because the cosine of an angle is the ratio between the length of the side adjacent to the angle and the length of the hypotenuse of the induced right triangle. Thus,

$$\cos\theta = \frac{x \cdot y}{y \cdot y}\frac{\|y\|}{\|x\|};$$

So

$$\cos\theta = \frac{x \cdot y}{y \cdot y}\frac{(y \cdot y)^{1/2}}{(x \cdot x)^{1/2}} = \frac{x \cdot y}{(y \cdot y)^{1/2}(x \cdot x)^{1/2}},$$

and hence

$$\cos\theta = \frac{x \cdot y}{\|x\|\|y\|}.$$

This is an absolutely fundamental result that sustains geometry in R^n. It expresses the angle between two vectors x and y in terms of the dot product of those vectors and the length of those vectors.

Because the cosine of the angle between two lines (vectors) is zero when the lines are perpendicular, x and y are perpendicular vectors if and only if $x \cdot y = 0$. Further, if x and y form an acute angle (less than 90°), $x \cdot y > 0$. If $x \cdot y < 0$, the vectors x and y form an obtuse angle, an angle between 90° and 180°. This result will be important in what follows.

Suppose there is an n-vector of constants, $a = (a_1, a_2, \ldots, a_n)$. What does the equation $a \cdot x = 0$ mean? Because x is an n-vector, the left side is a dot product. A vector x that satisfies this equation, or solves it, is any vector that is perpendicular to the given vector, a.

EXAMPLE

Suppose there are n separate markets, and let x_i^s and x_i^D denote the ith supply and demand quantities, which both depend on prices. Let p_i be the price of the ith good. The usual way to represent the assertion that the value of purchases equals the value of sales, or Walras's law, is to write $p_1 x_1^D + \cdots + p_n x_n^D = p_1 x_1^s + \cdots + p_n x_n^s$. Walras's law becomes $p \cdot x^s = p \cdot x^D$. By the properties of the dot product, this is equivalent to $p \cdot (x^D - x^s) = 0$, or the value of excess demand is zero. Geometrically, the vector of prices lives in the nonnegative orthant so that $p_i \geq 0$. What must be true of the vector of excess demand quantities? Because this vector must be perpendicular to the price vector, it cannot live in the nonnegative orthant or in the nonpositive orthant. It must be the case that in at least one market there is excess demand whenever there is at least one market in which there is excess supply. This argument flavors the neoclassical synthesis of macroeconomics and microeconomics. For if all goods markets and money markets and asset markets are in equilibrium (so that $x_i^s = x_i^D$ for those markets), then assuming Walras's law to be true entails that the remaining labor market cannot be characterized by excess supply (unemployment).

A simple numerical illustration may be useful. If $a = (1, 2)$, a solution to $a \cdot x = 0$ is shown in Figure 3.16. Any point (vector) on the line L solves $a \cdot x = 0$, or $(1, 2) \cdot (x_1, x_2) = 0$, or $x_1 + 2x_2 = 0$. In general, this is how lines are defined; they are solutions to $a \cdot x = 0$ for a given vector of constants $a = (a_1, a_2)$.

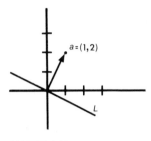

FIGURE 3.16

Hyperplanes

What about R^3? If $a = (1, 2, 1)$, $a \cdot x = 0$ is solved by finding the set of vectors $x = (x_1, x_2, x_3)$ in R^3 that are perpendicular to $(1, 2, 1)$. Consider Figure 3.17. It should be clear that vectors perpendicular to $(1, 2, 1)$ lie in a *plane*. The equation of that plane is $x_1 + 2x_2 + x_3 = 0$. In general, if $a = (a_1, a_2, \ldots, a_n)$, the equation $a \cdot x = 0$ defines what is called a *hyperplane*; this notion generalizes the geometrical idea of "line" in R^2 and "plane" in R^3 to an object in R^n. Hyperplanes are sets of points in R^n that depend only on a given vector a and the dot product value of zero.

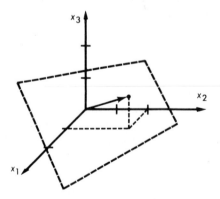

FIGURE 3.17

Geometrically, such hyperplanes are flat objects in n-space that pass through the origin. In 2-space they are lines such as $a_1 x_1 + a_2 x_2 = 0$. But an equation like $a_1 x_1 + a_2 x_2 = b$ also defines a line, one with vertical intercept b/a_2 and horizontal intercept b/a_1. Similarly, the equation

$$a_1 x_1 + a_2 x_2 + \cdots + a_n x_n = b$$

defines a hyperplane that does not pass through the origin. Thus, $a \cdot x = b$ also defines a unique hyperplane in R^n.

EXAMPLES

Many of the neoclassical constraints in choice problems are hyperplanes. If $p = (p_1, p_2, \ldots, p_n)$ is a vector of nonnegative prices and Y is income of a household, the constraint that a household must spend all its income on quantities of goods $x = (x_1, x_2, \ldots, x_n)$ is the statement that $p \cdot x = Y$; the bundles to be chosen lie on a hyperplane.

A neoclassical firm that is to hire inputs $x = (x_1, x_2, \ldots, x_n)$ at factor prices $w = (w_1, \ldots, w_n)$ for a given cost outlay c is constrained to make input choices satisfying $w \cdot x = c$. The inputs lie on a hyperplane.

Dimension

Another important geometric notion for R^n develops from the concepts of linear dependence and independence. A set of vectors $x^1, x^2, \ldots, x^m$ in R^n is *linearly dependent* if there is a nonzero vector of constants $a = (a_1, a_2, \ldots, a_m)$ such that $a_1 x^1 + a_2 x^2 + \cdots + a_m x^m = 0$. Because each vector $x^j = (x_1^j, x_2^j, \ldots, x_n^j)$, this relationship is actually the set of relationships

$$a_1(x_1^1, x_2^1, \ldots, x_n^1) + a_2(x_1^2, x_2^2, \ldots, x_n^2) + \cdots + a_m(x_1^m, x_2^m, \ldots, x_n^m)$$
$$= (0, \ldots, 0).$$

This is a system of n equations that can be written

$$a_1 x_1^1 + a_2 x_1^2 + \cdots + a_m x_1^m = 0$$
$$a_1 x_2^1 + a_2 x_2^2 + \cdots + a_m x_2^m = 0$$
$$\vdots \qquad \vdots \qquad \qquad \vdots$$
$$a_1 x_n^1 + a_2 x_n^2 + \cdots + a_m x_n^m = 0.$$

The first equation is

$$a \cdot (x_1^1, x_1^2, \ldots, x_1^m) = 0,$$

the second is

$$a \cdot (x_2^1, x_2^2, \ldots, x_2^m) = 0,$$

etc. Notice that these equations involve the dot product of a with the first components of all the vectors, with the second components of all the vectors, etc. Each of these equations defines a hyperplane through the origin. But because the vector a is common to all equations, all vectors in every hyperplane are perpendicular to this one vector. This is a demanding requirement. The question whether or not there is such a vector a for any set of vectors x is worth asking; the answer is likely to be affirmative only in special circumstances. Consequently, sets of linearly dependent vectors may have special characteristics.

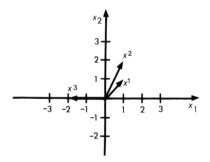

The set of m vectors living in R^n is linearly dependent if the n hyperplanes through the origin defined by the dot product relationships do exist. An example may help here. Consider the three vectors $x^1 = (1, 1)$, $x^2 = (1, 2)$, and $x^3 = (-2, 0)$ in R^2. Are they linearly dependent? Look at Figure 3.18. The answer depends on whether or not there exists a vector (a_1, a_2, a_3) such that the two hyperplanes

FIGURE 3.18

$$a \cdot (1, 1, -2) = 0$$

$$a \cdot (1, 2, \quad 0) = 0$$

exist. Treating the desired nonzero a's as though they were unknown x's means looking in R^3 for a vector x satisfying

$$x \cdot (1, 1, -2) = 0$$

$$x \cdot (1, 2, \quad 0) = 0.$$

Define two planes, and call them A and B. Plane A contains all vectors through the origin perpendicular to $(1, 1, -2)$, and plane B holds all vectors through the origin perpendicular to $(1, 2, 0)$. These two noncoincident planes intersect along a line L. Some point on L can be chosen away from the origin (a nonzero vector). This vector $\bar{a}$ simultaneously satisfies

$$\bar{a} \cdot (1, 1, -2) = 0$$

$$\bar{a} \cdot (1, 2, \quad 0) = 0.$$

Thus, x^1, x^2, x^3 are linearly dependent.

What can be said about the linear dependence of four vectors in R^2? This problem requires visualization, in four-dimensional space, of the intersection of two hyperplanes. If they intersect nontrivially (away from the origin), linear dependence can be established.

But suppose there were two vectors in R^2 that did not lie along the same line. In that case, linear dependence requires that there be two distinct two-dimensional hyperplanes (i.e., two lines) that pass through the origin and have a nonzero point of intersection. It is geometrically obvious that this cannot happen.

This argument generalizes. If a set of vectors in R^n are not linearly dependent, they are *linearly independent*. Thus, the last paragraph can be rephrased to conclude that two noncoincident vectors in R^2 are linearly independent. By analogy, three nonplanar vectors in R^3 are linearly independent. (Try to draw some pictures of this situation.) In general, m noncoincident vectors in R^n (i.e., m vectors not lying in the same hyperplane) are linearly dependent if $m > n$, and they are linearly independent if $m \leq n$.

EXAMPLE

Consider again the multimarket system where $x^D = (x_1^D, x_2^D, \ldots, x_n^D)$ represents demand in the n markets, $x^s = (x_1^s, x_2^s, \ldots, x_n^s)$ represents supply in those markets, and $p = (p_1, p_2, \ldots, p_n)$ are the market prices. If each and every market is in equilibrium, it must be the case that

$$x_1^D - x_1^s = 0$$
$$x_2^D - x_2^s = 0$$
$$\vdots \qquad \vdots$$
$$x_n^D - x_n^s = 0.$$

If Walras's law holds, then $p \cdot (x^D - x^s) = 0$ for all x^D and x^s. Thus the equilibria, defined by the equations, are not all independent. For $p \cdot (x^D - x^s) = 0$ entails that

$$p_1(x_1^D - x_1^s) + \cdots + p_n(x_n^D - x_n^s) = 0.$$

Thus, suppose the first $n-1$ markets are in equilibrium; so $x_1^D = x_1^s \ldots x_{n-1}^D = x_{n-1}^s$. Then Walras's law entails that $p_n(x_n^D - x_n^s) = 0$. So if $p_n \neq 0$, then $x_n^D - x_n^s = 0$, and so $x_n^D = x_n^s$. Thus, the nth market is also in equilibrium. The idea is that Walras's law produces the set of constants, actually prices, that act like the constants a in the previous paragraphs. Thus, Walras's law imposes a linear dependence on the vectors that define a solution to the multimarket problem.

Dimension and basis

It is possible to define the *dimension* of a space of vectors to be the largest number of nonplanar linearly independent vectors that can be selected in that space. This definition is convenient because the dimension of R^2 is two, R^3 is three, and R^n is n. R is one-dimensional. Further, a line embedded in R^2 has dimension one; a plane in R^3 has dimension two, and it still has dimension two even if it lives in R^4. Dimension is an "invariant" property.

This notion of an invariant property will play a significant role in subsequent chapters. To the degree that mathematical analysis is concerned with the investigation of mathematical structures, it is important to know whether or not particular structures, or properties of mathematical objects, maintain their characteristics when the underlying sets are transformed.

Plane geometry illustrates the concept of an invariant. The defining property of a plane figure called a triangle is three-sidedness. The figure retains this property when it is rotated, or when it is shifted from one position to another, or when the plane in which it is drawn is smoothly stretched. The property of a triangle called "having a side of length one inch" is preserved during a rotation of the plane, but not during stretching. Thus the properties of mathematical objects are studied in terms of the transformations that preserve those properties.

"Dimension" is an invariant in this sense. A set of vectors of dimension n continues to have dimension n when the space in which that set lives is transformed "nicely" into another space. As later chapters will show, the class of linear transformations consists of precisely those transformations of vector spaces that preserve the structures of those spaces. Any property (such as dimension) of sets of vectors that is preserved by linear transformations of the vector space in which those sets live can be called an invariant property. The fact that dimension is an invariant can be exploited to develop an extremely useful perspective on vectors.

Consider R^2. Look at the special two vectors $e^1=(1,0)$ and $e^2=(0,1)$. Take any other vector $x=(x_1,x_2)$. These vectors (e^1,e^2,x) form a set of three noncoincident (i.e., nonplanar) vectors in R^2. Thus, they are linearly dependent. There is then a nonzero vector of constants (a_1,a_2,a_3) such that $a_1e^1+a_2e^2+a_3x=0$. Hence,

$$x=\left(-\frac{a_1}{a_3}\right)e^1+\left(-\frac{a_2}{a_3}\right)e^2=\bar{a}_1e^1+\bar{a}_2e^2.$$

Thus, an arbitrary vector x is a linear combination of the two vectors e^1 and e^2. If $x=(3,4)$,

$$(3,4)=\bar{a}_1(1,0)+\bar{a}_2(0,1),$$

so that $\bar{a}_1 = 3$ and $\bar{a}_2 = 4$. The numbers 3 and 4 are the coefficients of the two vectors on which x depends.

A *basis* of a vector space of dimension n (or a basis of R^n, or a set of basic vectors in R^n) is any set of n linearly independent vectors in R^n. There are many potential sets of basis vectors in R^n. Any collection of n noncoincident vectors in R^n could serve as a basis for R^n. Each set chosen ought to have some special properties that justify its choice for a particular problem. However, one set of n vectors in R^n is chosen more frequently than others.

By convention, the *standard basis* of R^n is the set of n vectors denoted

$$e_1 = (1, 0, 0, \ldots, 0)$$
$$e_2 = (0, 1, 0, \ldots, 0)$$
$$\vdots$$
$$e_n = (0, 0, 0, \ldots, 1).$$

This set is used frequently because it has some nice properties. For example, all these vectors are pairwise perpendicular, and each has unit length (norm).

The practical usefulness of having a set of basis vectors should not be underestimated. Because any vector in R^n can be expressed as a linear combination of the n basic vectors, frequently it is unnecessary to examine all vectors in R^n to see whether or not they have a particular property. Often it will suffice to examine only the basic vectors instead. This idea will be the key to subsequent chapters that define functions whose domains are R^n. Any such function takes a vector in R^n and does something to it. It would be a tedious job to describe what the function does to every vector in R^n. But using the idea of a basic set of vectors in R^n, an arbitrary vector in R^n can be expressed simply in terms of the basis vectors. There are just n of these. Thus, to describe what a function does to any vector in R^n, it suffices to describe what it does to the n basis vectors. Because n is less than infinity, the task is greatly simplified.

FURTHER READING

One of the clearest expositions of vectors in R^n can be found in Halmos's *Finite Dimensional Vector Spaces*. Most algebra and analysis texts do not, in fact, linger over R^n; instead, they define abstract vector spaces that lead to the same concepts of independence, basis, and dimension. It is then shown that an (abstract) vector space of dimension n is isomorphic to R^n. That is, one really cannot distinguish between the abstract n-dimensional vector space and R^n. Economists do not require such generality for an understanding of vectors.

EXERCISES

3.1 If x and y are nonzero vectors in R^2, show that

$$\|x + y\| \le \|x\| + \|y\|.$$

If this is false, then $\|x+y\| > \|x\| + \|y\|$. This means that

(1) $\|x+y\|^2 > \|x\|^2 + \|y\|^2 + 2\|x\|\|y\|.$

But

$$\|x + y\|^2 = (x_1 + y_1)^2 + (x_2 + y_2)^2$$
$$= (x_1^2 + x_2^2) + (y_1^2 + y_2^2) + 2x_1 y_1 + 2x_2 y_2.$$

However,

$$\|x\|^2 = x_1^2 + x_2^2$$
$$\|y\|^2 = y_1^2 + y_2^2,$$

and

$$2\|x\|\|y\| = 2(x_1^2 + x_2^2)^{1/2}(y_1^2 + y_2^2)^{1/2}.$$

Thus (1) holds whenever

(2) $(x_1 y_1 + x_2 y_2) > (x_1^2 + x_2^2)^{1/2}(y_1^2 + y_2^2)^{1/2}.$

Squaring (2) yields

$$(x_1^2 y_1^2 + x_2^2 y_2^2 + 2x_1 x_2 y_1 y_2) > x_1^2 y_1^2 + x_2^2 y_2^2 + x_1^2 y_2^2 + x_2^2 y_1^2,$$

or

(3) $2x_1 x_2 y_1 y_2 > x_1^2 y_2^2 + x_2^2 y_1^2.$

If $x_1 < 0$ and x_2, y_1, and y_2 are positive, statement (3) is false. Because this possibility may occur, (1) cannot be true, and the proposition follows.

3.2 Demonstrate that the interior of the unit circle is convex.

The interior of the unit circle in R^2 is defined by

$$\{(x_1, x_2) = x_1^2 + x_2^2 < 1\}.$$

Consider any two points in the circle, such as x and y. Then certainly $x_1^2 + x_2^2 < 1$ and $y_1^2 + y_2^2 < 1$. Take any point, z, on the line connecting x and y. Is it in the circle? Certainly $z = \alpha x + (1-\alpha)y$ for some real number $\alpha \in [0, 1]$.

Rewrite the circle as $\{(x_1, x_2) : \|x\| < 1\}$. Then z is in the circle if $\|z\| < 1$. But

$$\|z\| = \|\alpha x + (1 - \alpha)y\|.$$

So

$$\|z\| \leq \|\alpha x\| + \|(1 - \alpha)y\|$$

by Exercise 3.1. Thus,

$$\|z\| \leq |\alpha|\,\|x\| + |(1 - \alpha)|\,\|y\|.$$

Because $\|x\| < 1$ and $\|y\| < 1$, certainly

$$\|z\| < |\alpha| \cdot 1 + |1 - \alpha| \cdot 1.$$

Because α and $1 - \alpha$ are both nonnegative real numbers, $|\alpha| = \alpha$ and $|1 - \alpha| = 1 - \alpha$. Thus,

$$\|z\| < \alpha + 1 - \alpha = 1.$$

3.3 Show that $x^1 = (1, 2)$, $x^2 = (3, 1)$, and $x^3 = (-1, -1)$ are linearly dependent vectors in R^2.

To show this, there must be three nonzero numbers a, b, and c such that

$$a(1, 2) + b(3, 1) + c(-1, -1) = (0, 0).$$

This yields the two equations

$$a + 3b - c = 0$$

$$2a + b - c = 0.$$

If $c = 1$, then $a = 2/5$ and $b = 1/5$; so the vector $(2/5, 1/5, 1)$ demonstrates the linear dependence among the vectors x^1, x^2, and x^3.

3.4 Show that the standard basis vectors in R^n are pairwise perpendicular.

Consider

$$e_i = (0, 0, \ldots, \overset{i\text{th}}{1}, 0, \ldots, 0)$$

$$e_j = (0, 0, \ldots, \overset{j\text{th}}{1}, 0, \ldots, 0).$$

These vectors are perpendicular, or orthogonal, if $e_i \cdot e_j = 0$. But

$$e_i \cdot e_j = 0 \cdot 0 + \cdots + \overset{i\text{th}}{1 \cdot 0} + \cdots + \overset{j\text{th}}{0 \cdot 1} + \cdots + 0 \cdot 0 = 0.$$

CHAPTER 4

Functions from R^n to R

E Pluribus Unum
Anon. (1776)

The previous chapter presented some basic information about subsets of
R^n. The natural next step is to use such subsets as the domains of functions. This chapter examines functions, defined on subsets of R^n, whose
range is R. Such functions assign a real number to a vector. Many of the
functions that economists use take this form.

EXAMPLES

1. If $x_1, x_2, \ldots, x_n$ are amounts of commodities, assume that
$x_i \geq 0$; that is to say, the vector $x = (x_1, x_2, \ldots, x_n)$ lives in the
nonnegative orthant of R^n (the generalized first quadrant). A
utility function is a function that assigns, to each such vector (or
bundle) x, a real number that measures utility. The utility function, or utility indicator, has some other properties to be dis-
cussed later.
2. If $x_1, x_2, \ldots, x_n$ are amounts of input services, and $x_i \geq 0$,
then a production function assigns to each such vector $x =$
$(x_1, x_2, \ldots, x_n)$ a real number that is the maximum output that a
known technology can produce from the inputs.
3. If $p_1, p_2, \ldots, p_n$ are prices of n goods in a multimarket system, and Y is total income, a demand function for the ith good
assigns a quantity, x_i, to the vector $(p_1, p_2, \ldots, p_n; Y)$.
4. If C_t is current real consumption, C_{t-1} is last period's real
consumption, Y_d is real disposable income, and W_{t-1} is last
period's real wealth, then $C_t = f(Y_d, C_{t-1}, W_{t-1})$ is a consumption function whose domain is R^3 and whose range is R.

There are two ways to visualize functions from R^n to R. Each
representation is itself useful; together they sharpen intuitions about the
analytical relationship. The first approach defines the graph of the func-

tion. If $f: R^n \to R$, then $y = f(x)$, where $x = (x_1, \ldots, x_n) \in R^n$ and $y \in R$. The graph of the function is the collection of points in R^{n+1} of the form $(x_1, x_2, \ldots, x_n; f(x))$. (When $f: R \to R$, the graph is in R^2.) To make matters concrete, look at the following functions from R^2 to R:

(1) $f(x_1, x_2) = x_1 + x_2$

(2) $f(x_1, x_2) = a + bx_1 + cx_2; \quad a \geq 0$

(3) $f(x_1, x_2) = x_1 x_2; \quad x_i \geq 0$

(4) $f(x_1, x_2) = e^{x_1 + x_2}.$

The graph as a set of points in R^{n+1} has the property that a line through any domain point in R^n intersects the graph in only one point; otherwise a point in R^n would not be mapped to a unique point in R. The graph is "thin" as an object in R^{n+1}. In R^3, the graph is a surface, an object of dimension two embedded in the space of dimension three.

Consider the function $f(x_1, x_2) = x_1 + x_2$ graphed in Figure 4.1. When $x_1 = 0$, $y = x_2$, and when $x_2 = 0$, $y = x_1$. Thus the graph rises, above the x_1 or x_2 axis, as a 45° line. When $x_1 = 0$ and $x_2 = 0$, then $y = 0$; so the graph contains the origin as well. A bit of thought shows that the graph is one plane. When $f(x_1, x_2) = a + bx_1 + cx_2$, the graph is again a plane. It goes up or down or sideways depending on the signs of b and c, but it does not go through the origin.

The function $f(x_1, x_2) = x_1 x_2$ is graphed in Figure 4.2. This graph looks like a bandshell or a cornucopia, with vertex at the origin, tied down on the x_1 and x_2 axes. It gets wider and higher in the direction of the arrow.

The second picture of functions from R^n to R depicts their transforming properties. That is, f takes certain sets in R^n and sends them to subsets of R.

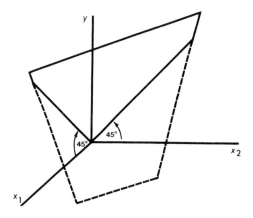

FIGURE 4.1

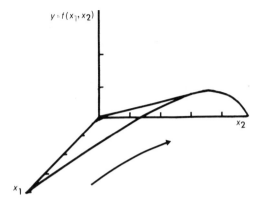

FIGURE 4.2

Consider $f(x_1, x_2) = x_1 + x_2$. This maps the plane to the real line, as in Figure 4.3. One way to visualize the behavior of this function is to study "what goes where." For example, what points in R^2 get sent to the origin in R? Answer: the points such that $x_1 + x_2 = 0$. This is a line in R^2, slope equal to -1, vertical intercept equal to 0. What points go to the point $1 \in R$? Answer: all points in R^2 such that $x_1 + x_2 = 1$ (i.e., the line with slope equal to -1 and vertical intercept equal to 1). Thus, draw the family of lines in R^2 with slope equal to -1 in Figure 4.4. It should be clear that f sends the entire line designated (0) to the origin, the entire line designated (1) to 1, etc. The function f maps lines to points in an orderly way; every point in the plane lives on exactly one such line, and that entire line goes to a point. [The obvious connection between Figures 4.4 and 4.1 is similar to the connection between Figures 2.8 and 2.3. If the number line in Figure 4.4 is placed at a right angle to the (x_1, x_2) plane (out of the page) and the origins are made to coincide, then above each point in the (x_1, x_2) plane there is a number that represents the height of the graph over the plane.]

For $f(x_1, x_2) = a + bx_1 + cx_2$, again it is true that lines in R^2 go to points in R. What about $f(x_1, x_2) = x_1 x_2$? All points in R^2 with either $x_1 = 0$ or

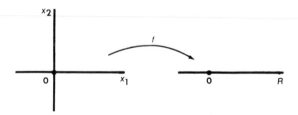

FIGURE 4.3

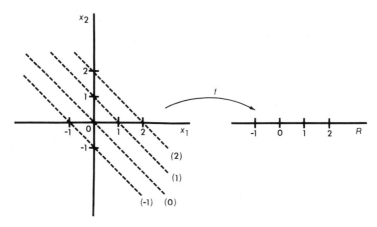

FIGURE 4.4

FIGURE 4.4

$x_2 = 0$ (i.e., the axes) go to $x = 0$. What points go to $x = 1$? Answer: those points such that $x_1 x_2 = 1$ or $x_1 = 1/x_2$. This is a pair of rectangular hyperbolas in R^2 denoted (1) in Figure 4.5. What set in R^2 goes to $x = -1$? Answer: the pair of rectangular hyperbolas denoted (-1). The function $f(x_1, x_2) = x_1 x_2$ transforms rectangular hyperbolas into points in an orderly fashion. What sets in R^2 go to 0, to 1, to 2, etc., under the transformation $f(x_1, x_2) = \exp(x_1 + x_2)$? See Exercise 4.1.

The two methods of visualizing the behavior of a function, the graph of the function, and the transformation of space will be used over and over again in subsequent pages.

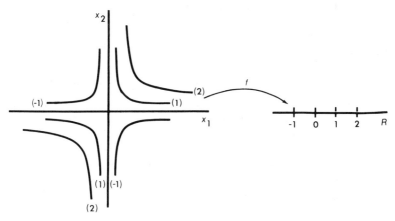

FIGURE 4.5

Linear functions

Functions from R^n to R change sets in R^n into sets in R. But R^n is a vector space with both algebraic structure and topological structure. What happens to these structures under a transformation of R^n into R? Consider the question of algebraic structure first. In R^n there are two algebraic operations: vector addition and scalar multiplication. Because R is also a space of vectors, a one-dimensional space, R^n and R have similar algebraic structures. It is possible to perform the same algebraic operations in each space. But what happens to the algebraic structure of R^n when it is transformed into R using a function f? Can functions be compared, or categorized, by what they do to the algebraic structure? The first item of business is to identify or classify all those functions from R^n to R that preserve the algebraic structure. Such functions allow performing the algebraic operations in either R^n or R.

In other words, if x and y are points in R^n, then $z=x+y$ is also a point in R^n. If f sends x, y, and z to $f(x), f(y)$, and $f(z)$, is it true or false in R that $f(x)+f(y)=f(z)$? If α is a real number and x is in R^n, $\alpha x=z$ is a point in R^n. If f sends x to $f(x)$ and f sends z to $f(z)$, is it true or false in R that $\alpha f(x)=f(z)$?

A function $f: R^n \to R$ is a *linear function* (or a *linear transformation*) if for x and y in R^n and α a scalar (a real number),

(1) $f(x + y) = f(x) + f(y)$

and

(2) $f(\alpha x) = \alpha f(x).$

Linear functions from R^n to R are exactly the functions that preserve algebraic structure. What do they look like? How can they be represented? The machinery developed in the last chapter helps to answer these questions.

If $x \in R^n$, the vectors $e^1, e^2, \ldots, e^n$ are a basis for R^n. Recall that this standard basis has the form $e^1 = (1, 0, \ldots, 0), \ldots, e^n = (0, 0, \ldots, 1)$. Because the $\{e^i\}$ form a basis, it is true for some set of real numbers $\{a_1, a_2, \ldots, a_n\}$ that $x = a_1 e^1 + a_2 e^2 + \cdots + a_n e^n$. If f is a linear function, then $f(x) = f(a_1 e^1 + \cdots + a_n e^n) = a_1 f(e^1) + a_2 f(e^2) + \cdots + a_n f(e^n)$. Hence, the action of a linear function on a point is entirely determined by its action on (what it does to) the basis vectors.

For the standard basis in R^2, if $x = (3, 4)$, then $x = 3(1, 0) + 4(0, 1)$. The numbers a_i are just the coordinates of x with respect to the standard basis. Consequently, $a_1 = x_1$, $a_2 = x_2$, etc. Thus, $x = x_1 e^1 + x_2 e^2 + \cdots + x_n e^n$. Denote the images in R of the standard basis vectors by $f(e^i)$. These are certainly real numbers. Defining $b_1 = f(e^1)$, $b_2 = f(e^2)$, etc., and using the fact that $a_i = x_i$ yields

$$f(x) = b_1 x_1 + b_2 x_2 + \cdots + b_n x_n,$$

where $b_1, b_2, \ldots, b_n$ are real numbers (or scalars or constants) determined by the action of f on the basis vectors. To restate this point, *the action of a linear transformation on a point in* R^n *is entirely determined by its action on the basis vectors, and its action on the basis vectors is completely characterized by a set of* n *numbers* (which in this case are $b_1, b_2, \ldots, b_n$).

What does f look like? Its graph looks much like Figure 4.1. The graph of a linear function is a hyperplane. As a transformation, a linear transformation acts like the function shown in Figure 4.4. The set of points in R^n sent to a real number is a hyperplane.

Suppose a nonstandard basis is chosen for R^n. Consider, for example, the n linearly independent vectors $h^1 = (2, 0, \ldots, 0)$, $h^2 = (0, 2, \ldots, 0), \ldots,$ $h^n = (0, 0, \ldots, 2)$ as the basis; $f(h^1)$ is still a real number, just like b_1. Call it b_1'. The graph of the function still looks like a hyperplane. Thus, the set of all linear functions from R^n to R is identical with the set of all functions from R^n to R that have graphs that are hyperplanes. What could be simpler?

EXAMPLE

Suppose an economist wishes to predict real consumption expenditures in period t. This real number can be denoted C_t. Standard economic theory suggests that C_t will depend on, or be a function of, several other economic variables. Demand theory suggests that real disposable income in period t, denoted Y_t^d, is one such variable. W_{t-1}, last period's real wealth, is also an explanatory variable that affects C_t by the permanent income hypothesis. The value of last period's consumption expenditure, or lagged consumption, is denoted C_{t-1}. This term, too, can be justified as an explanatory variable for current consumption by the permanent income hypothesis. This information may be gathered in

$$C_t = f(Y_t^d, W_{t-1}, C_{t-1}).$$

At this stage in the argument, regression analysis is brought into play. Assume that f is a linear function. Then

$$C_t = aY_t^d + bW_{t-1} + cC_{t-1} + d$$

defines a hyperplane in R^4, the graph of $f: R^3 \rightarrow R$. Standard statistical techniques, such as ordinary least squares, produce estimates of a, b, c, and d. These estimates, real numbers, are the constants that characterize the hyperplane.

Continuous functions

There is another structure associated with R^n besides the algebraic structure. Topological properties of sets in R^n, such as openness, compactness, boundedness, and closedness, may or may not be preserved by a function that transforms R^n to R.

Without getting too formal in this analysis, is it possible to find or to characterize those functions from R^n to R that preserve the topological structure? Note that compactness and openness of sets in R^n are defined in terms of the closedness of sets. A set is closed if it contains all its limit points. Any function that preserves the property of limits ought to be a candidate for a topological-structure-preserving function. What does this mean?

Consider Figure 4.6, representing a function $f: R^n \to R$. As the picture is drawn, there is a sequence of points $\{x^1, x^2, x^3, \ldots\}$ in R^2 converging on (having a limit point of) y. The function f sends all the points of the same sequence, as well as y, to points in R. To assert that the property of convergence is preserved by the function f is to say that if $x^1, x^2, \ldots, x^n, \ldots$ converge on y as a sequence in R^n, then $f(x^1), f(x^2), f(x^3), \ldots$ converge on $f(y)$ as a sequence in R. Convergence means that going out far enough in the sequence, past the index N, all points x^n will be very close to y. Formally, given a number $\delta > 0$, *convergence* means that there is an integer N such that for $n > N$, $\|x^n - y\| < \delta$. In the space R, convergence means that for some $\epsilon > 0$ there is some integer M such that for $m > M$, $\|f(x^m) - f(y)\| < \epsilon$.

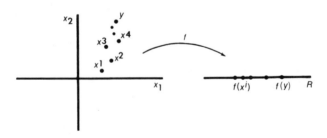

FIGURE 4.6

Now consider the larger of the two integers N and M. Take $T = \max(N, M)$. Then it is certainly true that $\|x^n - y\| < \delta$ and $\|f(x^n) - f(y)\| < \epsilon$ for $n > T$. By definition, a function $f: R^n \to R$ is *continuous at a point* $y \in R^n$ if for any $\epsilon > 0$ there exists a $\delta > 0$ such that $\|x - y\| < \delta$ implies $\|f(x) - f(y)\| < \epsilon$.

It would take some work to make matters precise, but it is intuitively plausible that this definition of continuity is the definition that transforms a convergent sequence in R^n to a convergent sequence in R. And if continuous functions preserve convergence and limits, they preserve the other topological structures as well.

With this definition of continuity, it is possible to determine whether or not functions are continuous by examining their graphs. The idea is that nearby points in the domain give rise to nearby points on the graph. Consider, for example, $f(x_1, x_2) = x_1 + x_2$. This graph is a hyperplane passing through the origin in R^3. Take any two points such as x and y that are close to each other in R^2. Forming $f(x) = x_1 + x_2$ and $f(y) = y_1 + y_2$, locate the points $(x_1, x_2, f(x))$ and $(y_1, y_2, f(y))$ on the graph of f in R^3. This hyperplane rises smoothly, with no holes or crevices, as a surface. Thus, if x and y are close, so are $(x_1, x_2, f(x))$ and $(y_1, y_2, f(y))$. Intuition about smoothness of planes suggests that f is a continuous function.

A function may fail to be continuous when its graph, as a surface, has the property that a point moving along the surface suddenly falls off. Consider $f(x_1, x_2) = 1/(x_1 - x_2)$, whose graph is a surface in R^3. Along the line $x_1 = x_2$ in the domain set R^2, this function is not defined, because division by zero is not allowed. A little below this line, at, say, $x_2 = x_1 + \delta$ (where δ is a small number), the point on the graph $(x_1, x_1 + \delta, f(x))$ is actually $(x_1, x_1 + \delta, -1/\delta)$. As δ gets small (i.e., as x_1 and x_2 get close in R^2), the height of the graph falls precipitously into the abyss of $-\infty$. This suggests that the function is not continuous at the domain points where $x_1 = x_2$. It would, however, appear to be continuous at the domain point $x_1 = 3$, $x_2 = 17$.

This discussion of continuity, and the example of $f(x_1, x_2) = x_1 + x_2$, gives rise to an obervation of singular importance: *Linear functions are continuous.* Thus, any function of $R^n \to R$ that preserves the algebraic structure also preserves the topological structure.

EXAMPLE

The domain of a utility function is the set of vectors of commodities $x = (x_1, x_2, \ldots, x_n)$, where x_i is the amount of commodity i. The function itself, denoted U, assigns a utility number to each vector. A commonly used utility indicator is the log-linear function. This has the form

$$U(x) = \sum_{i=1}^{n} a_i \log x_i,$$

where the real numbers a_i are nonnegative weights. So $\sum_{i=1}^{n} a_i = 1$; $\log x_i$ is the natural logarithm of the number x_i.

U is not a linear function, although it is a linear function of the natural logarithms of the x_i. Is U a continuous function from R^n to R? Certainly the ith term in the sum is a continuous function if $\log x_i$ is a continuous function from R to R. Looking at the graph of $\log x_i$ suggests that as long as x_i is not zero, $\log x_i$ is continuous. Hence, U is a continuous function on the domain set S, where

$$S = \{x \in R^n : x_1 > 0, x_2 > 0, \dots, x_n > 0\}.$$

Using this utility function restricts the economic analysis to goods bundles that contain positive amounts of all goods. This function cannot produce a utility indicator of preferences between the two bundles x (three apples, two oranges, one lemon) and y (two apples, three oranges, no lemons).

Differentiability

Linearity and continuity are two useful characteristics of functions from R^n to R. However, an arbitrary function does not have to be either linear or continuous. Functions can be rather ugly: Suppose $f(x_1, x_2) = 0$ if either x_1 or x_2 is a rational number, and $f(x_1, x_2) = 1$ if both x_1 and x_2 are irrational numbers. This function is not continuous, and thus it cannot be linear. Such functions cannot be ignored. But how can they be treated? The answer is to identify functions that, at least locally, *act like* linear functions. Such functions are *differentiable functions*. Most all economic models will require the associated functions to be differentiable. Their "almost" linear form, or locally linear structure, permits visualization almost like linear functions, which are continuous. (This point is worth a side comment. If functions model explanations, so that a vector of events $x \in R^n$ is associated with a further event $y \in R$, a horribly discontinuous function would suggest an explanation that is extremely sensitive to changes in the "event vector." In other words, discontinuity suggests that small changes in the variables $x_1, \dots, x_n$ induce large changes in the variable y. Thus, the use of continuous functions to model economic relationships is an expression of faith by economists. It represents a belief that small changes in some economic variables do not induce huge changes in other variables. To the extent that such a method appears restrictive, there is some current interest in what is called catastrophe theory, a branch of dynamic analysis in mathematics that can model apparently discontinuous phenomena.[1])

Returning to the main theme of this chapter, a linear function from R^n

---

[1] See, for example, E. R. Weintraub, "Catastrophe Theory and Intertemporal Equilibrium." *Economie Appliquée* 32:303–15, 1980.

to R can be pictured, as before, in two ways. As a transformation, it maps parallel hyperplanes to points. As a surface in R^{n+1} (i.e., the graph), a linear function is a hyperplane. Thus, a differentiable function should have the property that near any point in its domain, hyperplanes get mapped to points or, alternatively, that above any point in the domain, the graph looks locally like a hyperplane. This idea is not difficult to formalize. An arbitrary function $f: R^n \rightarrow R$ is differentiable at the point $\bar{x} = (\bar{x}_1, \ldots, \bar{x}_n)$ if, when x is near $\bar{x}$, $f(x)$ near $\bar{x}$ is well approximated by a linear function $L(x)$.

Now any linear function $L: R^n \rightarrow R$ can be written as

$$L(x) = a_1 x_1 + \cdots + a_n x_n = a \cdot x,$$

where a is an n-vector of constants. This function sends $0 \rightarrow 0$. But f might not. Thus, f needs to be "translated," as it were, by setting the origin of the graph space R^{n+1} at the point $\bar{x}$. Consequently, the question is how well does L approximate $f(\bar{x}+h) - f(\bar{x})$ near $\bar{x}$? How good is the approximation as h gets small? Of course, h is a vector of small positive length based at $\bar{x}$. The formalization reads that f is differentiable at $\bar{x}$ if there exists an n-vector a, depending on $\bar{x}$, such that

$$\lim_{\|h\| \to 0} \frac{\|(f(\bar{x}+h) - f(\bar{x})) - a \cdot h\|}{\|h\|} = 0.$$

Some additional terminology will be useful. If such a vector a exists, it is called the *derivative* (or *gradient*) of f at $\bar{x}$, and it is written $f_x(\bar{x})$ or $\operatorname{grad} f(\bar{x})$. As a vector, it is written out as

$$\left(\frac{\partial f}{\partial x_1}, \frac{\partial f}{\partial x_2}, \ldots, \frac{\partial f}{\partial x_n} \right)_{\bar{x}} \quad \text{or} \quad \left(\frac{\partial f(\bar{x})}{\partial x_1}, \frac{\partial f(\bar{x})}{\partial x_2}, \ldots, \frac{\partial f(\bar{x})}{\partial x_n} \right).$$

The linear mapping $a \cdot h$ is called the *differential* of f at $\bar{x}$, and it is written $df(\bar{x})$, or $f_x(\bar{x}) \cdot h$, or $\operatorname{grad} f(\bar{x}) \cdot h$. The components of the derivative vector are called *partial derivatives*.

Chapter 2 showed how to calculate derivatives of functions from R to R. To calculate derivatives of functions from R^n to R, simply treat the function first as a function of x_1 with all other variables held constant. It is then a function from R to R whose derivative is the partial derivative $a_1 = \partial f(\bar{x})/\partial x_1$. Continue variable by variable to build up the gradient vector.

EXAMPLE

Suppose $f(x_1, x_2, x_3) = x_1 x_2 + x_2 x_3$. What is the derivative at $\bar{x} = (1, 2, 3)$? What is the derivative at the arbitrary point $\bar{x} =$

(x_1, x_2, x_3)? To compute $\partial f / \partial x_1$, simply treat x_2 and x_3 as constants in $f(x_1, x_2, x_3)$ and compute the derivative of f with respect to the single variable x_1. This yields

$$\frac{\partial f}{\partial x_1} = x_2.$$

Similarly,

$$\frac{\partial f}{\partial x_2} = x_1 + x_3$$

and

$$\frac{\partial f}{\partial x_3} = x_2.$$

Evaluating these partial derivatives at $\bar{x} = (1, 2, 3)$ gives the gradient

$$f_x(\bar{x}) = \left(\frac{\partial f}{\partial x_1}, \frac{\partial f}{\partial x_2}, \frac{\partial f}{\partial x_3} \right)_{\bar{x}} = (2, 4, 2).$$

At the point $\bar{x} = (x_1, x_2, x_3)$ the gradient is

$$f_x(\bar{x}) = \left(\frac{\partial f}{\partial x_1}, \frac{\partial f}{\partial x_2}, \frac{\partial f}{\partial x_3} \right)_{\bar{x}} = (x_2, x_1 + x_3, x_2).$$

Thus, the derivative generates a linear mapping, the differential, that is associated with the function f locally. That is, near the point $\bar{x}$ at which the derivative is computed, the function $f(\bar{x} + h) - f(\bar{x}) : R^n \to R$ "looks like" the linear function $f_x(\bar{x}) \cdot h : R^n \to R$.

Because a function is called differentiable if it is differentiable at every point in its domain, a differentiable function is locally represented by a linear map. Thus, it has a representation as a linear mapping at every point in its domain (although these linear mappings may be different at different points). In any event, because a differentiable function is locally linear, and linear functions are continuous, it follows that if f is differentiable at $\bar{x}$ it is continuous at $\bar{x}$.

EXAMPLE

To continue the previous example, what is the linear mapping that is associated with the function $f(x_1, x_2, x_3) = x_1 x_2 + x_2 x_3$ near $\bar{x} = (1, 2, 3)$? The differential of f at $\bar{x} = (1, 2, 3)$ is the linear mapping

$f_x(\bar{x}) \cdot h = (2,4,2) \cdot (h_1, h_2, h_3) = 2h_1 + 4h_2 + 2h_3.$

Thus, if $\approx$ denotes "approximately equal to,"

$f(\bar{x} + h) - f(\bar{x}) \approx f_x(\bar{x}) \cdot h,$

so that

$f((1,2,3) + (h_1, h_2, h_3)) - f(1,2,3) \approx 2h_1 + 4h_2 + 2h_3.$

But

$$[f(h_1 + 1, h_2 + 2, h_3 + 3)] - [f(1,2,3)]$$
$$= [(h_1 + 1)(h_2 + 2) + (h_2 + 2)(h_3 + 3)] - [1 \cdot 2 + 2 \cdot 3]$$
$$= h_1 h_2 + 2h_1 + h_2 + 2 + h_2 h_3 + 2h_3 + 3h_2 + 6 - 2 - 6.$$

Thus,

$h_1 h_2 + h_2 h_3 + 2h_1 + 4h_2 + 2h_3 \approx 2h_1 + 4h_2 + 2h_3.$

Certainly the right side is an exact approximation of the left side at $h = (h_1, h_2, h_3) = (0,0,0)$, and the approximation gets worse the larger is $\|h\|$, or the farther away from $\bar{x} = (1,2,3)$ one checks.

Now because h is an arbitrary name for a variable, relabel h as x to re-write the approximation result. Thus, if f is differentiable at $\bar{x}$, for points x near $\bar{x}$, it is true that

$f(x + \bar{x}) \approx f(\bar{x}) + f_x(\bar{x}) \cdot x.$

It is possible to indicate just how good this approximation is. Let $\mu(x)$ be the error made approximating $f(x + \bar{x})$ by $f(\bar{x}) + f_x(\bar{x}) \cdot x$. Then, if the function f is differentiable at $\bar{x}$,

$f(x + \bar{x}) = f(\bar{x}) + f_x(\bar{x}) \cdot x + \mu(x)$

exactly, where $\mu(x)$ is the error of the approximation and where $\mu(x)$ is small relative to $\|x\|$. Thus, $\mu(x)$ represents all the nonlinear terms that might drive a wedge between $[f(x + \bar{x}) - f(\bar{x})]$ and $df(\bar{x})$.

The expression $f(\bar{x}) + f_x(\bar{x}) \cdot x$ is the sum of a constant and a linear mapping. As in Chapter 2, such a form is called an *affine* transformation, or affine function. Because its domain is R^n and its range is R, this function has a graph in R^{n+1}. The graph is a plane that does not go through the origin unless $f(\bar{x}) = 0$. As Figure 4.7 indicates, this affine transformation $f(\bar{x}) + f_x(\bar{x}) \cdot x = A(x)$ represents the tangent plane to the graph of f over the domain point $\bar{x}$.

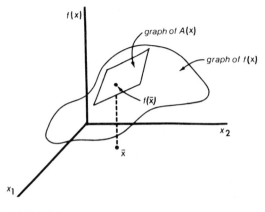

FIGURE 4.7

Is it possible to determine if a function f is differentiable at a point? Consider the graph of f, a surface in R^{n+1}. If the function is not continuous at a point, it cannot be differentiable at that point. Further, the graph must look approximately like a hyperplane if it is examined under a strong enough microscope. Figure 4.8 shows two blowups of small sections of surfaces (on graphs) in R^3 (from unspecified functions $f: R^n \to R$). The surface in Figure 4.8(a) is like a rubber sheet with an amoeba under it. In Figure 4.8(b) it is like a small pyramid's outer shell. In the former case, looking at a small enough section of R^2, and the portion of the surface over it, the surface seems smooth enough to be approximated there by a (hyper)plane. In Figure 4.8(b), at the point in R^2 that generates the vertex of the pyramid, no matter how close a look is taken at the vertex it cannot be flattened out with a plane – there really is a sharp point there. Some other points on the pyramid's shell may admit approximation by planes,

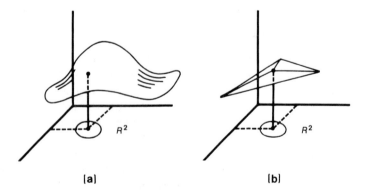

[a]   [b]

FIGURE 4.8

but not the vertex. The function that gives rise to Figure 4.8(b) is not differentiable, at that point at least.

EXAMPLE

Consider the Cobb–Douglas production function $Q = f(K, L) = AK^\alpha L^\beta$; $A, \alpha, \beta \geq 0$. This function is differentiable, and the partial derivatives are $\partial f/\partial K = \alpha AK^{\alpha-1}L^\beta$ and $\partial f/\partial L = \beta AK^\alpha L^{\beta-1}$. Near the point $(K, L) = (1, 1)$,

$$Q \approx A + \left(\frac{\partial f}{\partial K}, \frac{\partial f}{\partial L} \right)_{(1,1)} \cdot (K, L),$$

or

$$Q \approx A + (\alpha A, \beta A) \cdot (K, L),$$

and so

$$Q \approx A + \alpha AK + \beta AL = A(1 + \alpha K + \beta L).$$

The partial derivatives, of course, are marginal products of capital and labor. The ratio of the marginal products at the point (K, L) is equal to the marginal rate of substitution, the MRS, at (K, L). This equals $(\alpha/\beta)(L/K)$. Hence, the MRS depends only on the ratio of labor to capital, not on the amounts.

Contours and level sets

Another approach to "seeing" functions from R^n to R involves projecting the graph of the function onto the domain space. Because R^n for $n \geq 4$ is difficult to visualize, this technique is restricted to functions whose graphs are surfaces in R^3. Thus, it is useful only in the case of functions from R^2 to R (although the language that formally describes the process seems to allow consideration of functions defined on higher-dimensional domains).

A *level set* of a function $f: R^n \to R$ is a subset of the domain of f such that all points in that subset get sent to the same point in the range. In other words, the level sets of a function are the pre-images of points in R under the mapping f. The level set of the point $x = 1$ for the function $f(x_1, x_2) = x_1 + x_2$ is the set denoted (1) in Figure 4.4. The level set of the point $x = 2$ for the function $f(x_1, x_2) = x_1 x_2$ is the set denoted (2) in Figure 4.5. The collection of level sets forms what is called a *contour map* of the function.

Using the alternative picture of a function, consider the graph of a function from R^2 to R. This is a surface in R^3. Suppose there is a plane, parallel to the (x_1, x_2) plane, at a height of $x_3 = a$ above the plane. This plane will slice the surface. The intersection of the surface and the plane generates a curve in R^3 that actually lies in the plane used to do the cutting. Let that curve "drop" onto the (x_1, x_2) plane. This is the level set of the function for the point a. It is pictured in Figure 4.9.

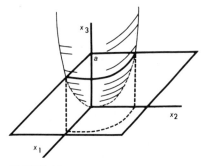

It is really the idea of a level set that is intrinsic, not the business of projections of planes intersecting with surfaces. Recall the discussion of $f(x_1, x_2) = x_1 + x_2$. There are the two usual geometric representations of

FIGURE 4.9

this function. The first, as a mapping, is determined by the sets in R^2 that get sent to points. Figure 4.4 shows the sets to be lines. The other representation is the graph of f, a plane in R^3. Certainly the two representations are related; they have similar geometric properties.

For economists, the most important use of this relationship is in a discussion of concave and convex functions. Doing the job right, however, will require matrix algebra and quadratic forms. Level sets and contour maps will reappear in Chapter 10, which examines convex functions in appropriate detail.

FURTHER READING

Apostol's *Mathematical Analysis* is a standard reference on differentiation of real-valued functions of several variables. For economists, Frisch's *Maxima and Minima* is worth examining. See also Lang's *Calculus of Several Variables*.

EXERCISES

4.1 (a) Graph $y = f(x_1, x_2) = \exp(x_1 + x_2)$.
   (b) Sketch the contour map of this function.
4.2 Show that the utility function $U(x) = \sum_{i=1}^{n} a_i \log x_i$, $0 < a_i < 1$ and $\sum_{i=1}^{n} a_i = 1$, is not linear.
4.3 Show that a linear function $f: R^n \to R$ is continuous at $\bar{x} = 0$ by using the definition of continuity.

4.4 (a) Find the gradient of $f(x_1, x_2) = x_1^2 + x_2^2$ at $\bar{x} = (1, 1)$ using the definition of the derivative.

 (b) What is the error in the affine approximation to this function at $x = (0, 0)$?

4.5 Find the gradient, using calculus techniques, of the function

$$f(x) = \sum_{i=1}^{n} \frac{c_i}{1 + \exp(-x_i)}.$$

CHAPTER 5

Functions from R^m to R^n: the linear case

It was said of Jordan's writings that if he had four things on the same footing (as a, b, c, d) they would appear as a, M_3', ϵ_2, $\pi_{1,2}''$.

J. E. Littlewood (1953)

The previous chapters have all pointed toward this chapter (and the next). The fully general case allows both the domain and range of a function to be spaces of any dimension. Functions from R^m to R^n model arguments such as "a set of m variables is related to a set of n variables." Many economic problems take this form.

1. Consider individual demand (or excess-demand) functions. Suppose there are m people and n goods. Individual j has an excess demand, such as $x_i^j = f_i^j(p_i, p_2, \ldots, p_n)$. In words, j's demand for good i is a function of the prices of all the n goods. Thus, the total demand for good i is the sum of all individuals' demand functions. Writing $x_i = \sum_j x_i^j$ and $f_i = \sum_j f_i^j$, then $x_i = f_i(p_1, \ldots, p_n)$. This function expresses the relationship between the quantity of good i demanded in the market and the n prices of all market goods. Because there are n goods, the market excess-demand functions are

$$x_1 = f_1(p_1, p_2, \ldots, p_n)$$
$$x_2 = f_2(p_1, p_2, \ldots, p_n)$$
$$\vdots$$
$$x_n = f_n(p_1, p_2, \ldots, p_n).$$

This is a system of excess-demand functions. Given an n-vector of prices, this system provides an n-vector of excess-demand quantities. The system defines a relationship whose domain is R^n and whose range is R^n. It is possible to write the system as $f = R^n \to R^n$, noting that

$$f(p_1, p_2, \ldots, p_n) \equiv (f_1(p_1, \ldots, p_n), \ldots, f_n(p_1, \ldots, p_n)).$$

2. Market demand is actually a function of income as well as prices. If the individual demand functions of the preceding example are properly specified, they will appear as $x_i = f_i(p_1, p_2, \ldots, p_n; y)$, where y is income. In this case, the demand system becomes

$$x_1 = f_1(p_1, p_2, \ldots, p_n; y)$$
$$x_2 = f_2(p_1, p_2, \ldots, p_n; y)$$
$$\vdots$$
$$x_n = f_n(p_1, p_2, \ldots, p_n; y).$$

The system becomes $f: R^{n+1} \rightarrow R^n$.

3. The demand function $x_i = a_i \bar{x}_i / p_i$ in an n-good world arises from a log-linear utility function in an exchange system. The a_i represent a "taste" parameter, and $\bar{x}_i$ is society's initial holding of good i. If the a_i are constant but $\bar{x}_i$ is a variable, the demand functions become $x_i = f_i(p_i; \bar{x}_i)$ or $f = R^{2n} \rightarrow R^n$, because it takes n p's and n $\bar{x}_i$'s to specify the demand structure.

4. A "small" demand-type macroeconomic model will include the identity $Y_t = C_t + I_t$, a consumption function $C_t = c_0 + c_1 Y_t^d + c_2 C_{t-1}$, a disposable-income relationship $Y_t^d = d_0 + d_1 Y_t$, and an investment function such as $I_t = a_0 + a_1 Y_t + aK_{t-1} + a_3 i_t$, where the symbols have their usual meanings. There are four endogenous variables (C_t, I_t, Y_t, Y_t^d), one exogenous variable (i_t), two predetermined variables (C_{t-1}, K_{t-1}), and nine parameters $(a_0, a_1, a_2, a_3, c_0, c_1, c_2, d_0, d_1)$. Fixing the parameters, these equations determine a system in which the exogenous and predetermined variables jointly determine the values of the endogenous variables as $(C_{t-1}, K_{t-1}, i_t) \xrightarrow{f} (C_t, I_t, Y_t, Y_t^d)$. Thus, the model is a system like $f: R^3 \rightarrow R^4$.

Systems of interrelationships in economics lead to the study of functions or transformations like $f: R^m \rightarrow R^n$. Picturing such functions is difficult. The graph of the function is of little help, because the graph is a construction in R^{m+n}. If $m + n > 3$, visualization is problematic. The other kind of picture, the transformation picture, is more useful, because it can be employed as long as $m \leq 3$ and $n \leq 3$.

Consider an example function $f: R^3 \rightarrow R^3$ defined by $f(x_1, x_2, x_3) = (x_2, x_1, x_3)$. This is a shorthand way of writing the system

$$f_1(x_1, x_2, x_3) = x_2$$

$$f_2(x_1, x_2, x_3) = x_1$$

$$f_3(x_1, x_2, x_3) = x_3,$$

where $f(x) = (f_1(x), f_2(x), f_3(x))$ for $x \in R^3$. (Each $f_i: R^3 \to R$.) Figure 5.1 shows that the action of f interchanges the x_1 and x_2 axes, or rotates the (x_1, x_2) plane $180°$ around the plane $x_1 = x_2$. There is a useful technique for drawing functions from R^3 to R^3: Pick an axis in the domain space and see where it is sent in the range space.

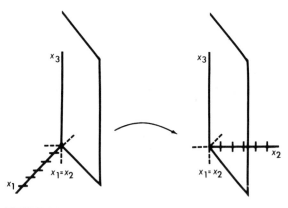

FIGURE 5.1

This dimensionality problem means that pictures will play less of a role in the general case. But geometry still guides the exposition. This paradox is resolved by recognizing that the previous chapters have used "algebraized" geometry. Lines, planes, hyperplanes, length, angle, and perpendicularity have representations in terms of dot products and norms. As the tale unfolds in this and future chapters, hyperplanes, for example, will play significant roles, but they will rarely be drawn. Instead, there will be an equation nearby, such as $a \cdot x = b$. Although the algebra dominates the exposition, the geometry suggests the organization and directs the flow of the arguments.

The first step to reduce complications is to search for those functions from R^m to R^n that preserve the algebraic structure of the spaces. Limiting the discussion as in the preceding chapter, what are the characteristics of the class of functions that send the vectors $x + y$ and αx in R^m to the vectors $f(x) + f(y)$ and $\alpha f(x)$ in R^n? A linear function L from R^m to R^n is defined as a function such that if x and y are in R^m and α is a scalar (i.e., $\alpha \in R$),

$$L(x + y) = L(x) + L(y) \quad \text{and} \quad L(\alpha x) = \alpha L(x).$$

The ideas of Chapter 3 simplify the task of identifying such functions. Suppose that x is any vector in the domain of L. Then x can be represented in terms of m basis vectors, because any vector in R^m is a linear combination of the basis vectors. If $e^1, \ldots, e^m$ is a basis, then $x = x_1 e^1 + \cdots + x_m e^m$. Thus, if L is a linear function, it is true that $L(x) = x_1 L(e^1) + \cdots + x_m L(e^m)$. The action of L on x is completely known by its action on $e^1, e^2, \ldots, e^m$. But how does L act on e^i, say?

From this point on, by convention, all vectors will be written as column vectors. That is, $x \in R^n$ will not be written $x = (x_1, x_2, \ldots, x_n)$. Instead, x will be expressed as

$$x = \begin{bmatrix} x_1 \\ x_2 \\ \vdots \\ x_n \end{bmatrix}.$$

This convention will greatly simplify the notation.

Certainly, L sends e^i into R^n. Suppose $L(e^i) = a^i$, where a^i is a point (column vector) in R^n. Any point in R^n can be written as a linear combination of the basis vectors in R^n. If those basis (column) vectors are denoted $\bar{e}^1, \bar{e}^2, \ldots, \bar{e}^n$, then

$$a^i = a_1^i \bar{e}^1 + a_2^i \bar{e}^2 + \cdots + a_n^i \bar{e}^n.$$

To get used to the convention, it is worthwhile writing this expression out completely. Because a^i is an n-vector,

$$a^i = \begin{bmatrix} a_1^i \\ a_2^i \\ \vdots \\ a_n^i \end{bmatrix}.$$

Similarly, because $\bar{e}^j$ is a standard basis vector in R^n, it can be written

$$\bar{e}^j = \begin{bmatrix} 0 \\ 0 \\ \vdots \\ 1 \\ 0 \\ \vdots \\ 0 \end{bmatrix} j\text{th place} \quad .$$

Thus,

$$\begin{bmatrix} a_1^i \\ a_2^i \\ \vdots \\ a_n^i \end{bmatrix} = a_1^i \begin{bmatrix} 1 \\ 0 \\ \vdots \\ 0 \end{bmatrix} + a_2^i \begin{bmatrix} 0 \\ 1 \\ 0 \\ \vdots \\ 0 \end{bmatrix} + \cdots + a_n^i \begin{bmatrix} 0 \\ 0 \\ \vdots \\ 1 \end{bmatrix}.$$

Thus, given the standard bases in R^m and R^n, it is easy to see where the basis vectors of R^m get sent in R^n:

$$L(e^1) = a_1^1 \bar{e}^1 + \cdots + a_n^1 \bar{e}^n$$
$$L(e^2) = a_1^2 \bar{e}^1 + \cdots + a_n^2 \bar{e}^n$$
$$\vdots$$
$$L(e^m) = a_1^m \bar{e}^1 + \cdots + a_n^m \bar{e}^n.$$

To avoid writing both subscripts and superscripts, it is useful to establish the additional convention that $a_{ij} = a_i^j$ is the ith coordinate of the image of the jth basis vector in R^m. Thus, the previous set of equations becomes

$$L(e^1) = a_{11} \bar{e}^1 + \cdots + a_{n1} \bar{e}^n$$
$$L(e^2) = a_{12} \bar{e}^1 + \cdots + a_{n2} \bar{e}^n$$
$$\vdots$$
$$L(e^m) = a_{1m} \bar{e}^1 + \cdots + a_{nm} \bar{e}^n.$$

Where does the point $x \in R^m$ go under the action of L? Because $x = x_1 e^1 + x_2 e^2 + \cdots + x_m e^m$,

$$L(x) = L(x_1 e^1 + x_2 e^2 + \cdots + x_m e^m)$$
$$= x_1 L(e^1) + x_2 L(e^2) + \cdots + x_m L(e^m),$$

by linearity of the transformation L. Thus,
$$L(x) = x_1(a_{11}\bar{e}^1 + \cdots + a_{n1}\bar{e}^n) + \cdots + x_m(a_{1m}\bar{e}^1 + \cdots + a_{nm}\bar{e}^n).$$

EXAMPLE

Suppose $f: R^2 \rightarrow R^3$ is defined by $f(x_1, x_2) = (x_1 + x_2, x_1 - x_2, 0)$. It is easy to check that this function is a linear transformation. Hence, denote f by L. Where does the point $\begin{bmatrix} 2 \\ 1 \end{bmatrix}$ in R^2 get sent in R^3? Although the answer, $\begin{bmatrix} 3 \\ 1 \\ 0 \end{bmatrix}$, is obvious, the preceding formalism gives the same answer. For

$$x = \begin{bmatrix} 2 \\ 1 \end{bmatrix} = 2\begin{bmatrix} 1 \\ 0 \end{bmatrix} + 1\begin{bmatrix} 0 \\ 1 \end{bmatrix}.$$

Where does $e^1 = \begin{bmatrix} 1 \\ 0 \end{bmatrix}$ get sent in R^3? And $e^2 = \begin{bmatrix} 0 \\ 1 \end{bmatrix}$?

$$L\begin{bmatrix} 1 \\ 0 \end{bmatrix} = a_{11}\begin{bmatrix} 1 \\ 0 \\ 0 \end{bmatrix} + a_{21}\begin{bmatrix} 0 \\ 1 \\ 0 \end{bmatrix} + a_{31}\begin{bmatrix} 0 \\ 0 \\ 1 \end{bmatrix},$$

and

$$L\begin{bmatrix} 0 \\ 1 \end{bmatrix} = a_{12}\begin{bmatrix} 1 \\ 0 \\ 0 \end{bmatrix} + a_{22}\begin{bmatrix} 0 \\ 1 \\ 0 \end{bmatrix} + a_{32}\begin{bmatrix} 0 \\ 0 \\ 1 \end{bmatrix}.$$

Because

$$L\begin{bmatrix} 1 \\ 0 \end{bmatrix} = \begin{bmatrix} 1 \\ 1 \\ 0 \end{bmatrix} \quad \text{and} \quad L\begin{bmatrix} 0 \\ 1 \end{bmatrix} = \begin{bmatrix} 1 \\ -1 \\ 0 \end{bmatrix},$$

it is immediate that $a_{11}=1$, $a_{21}=1$, $a_{31}=0$, whereas $a_{12}=1$, $a_{22}=-1$, and $a_{32}=0$. Thus,

$$L\begin{bmatrix} 2 \\ 1 \end{bmatrix} = 2\left[1\begin{bmatrix} 1 \\ 0 \\ 0 \end{bmatrix} + 1\begin{bmatrix} 0 \\ 1 \\ 0 \end{bmatrix} + 0\begin{bmatrix} 0 \\ 0 \\ 1 \end{bmatrix} \right]$$

$$+ 1\left[1\begin{bmatrix} 1 \\ 0 \\ 0 \end{bmatrix} - 1\begin{bmatrix} 0 \\ 1 \\ 0 \end{bmatrix} + 0\begin{bmatrix} 0 \\ 0 \\ 1 \end{bmatrix} \right].$$

Thus

$$L\begin{bmatrix} 2 \\ 1 \end{bmatrix} = 2\begin{bmatrix} 1 \\ 1 \\ 0 \end{bmatrix} + 1\begin{bmatrix} 1 \\ -1 \\ 0 \end{bmatrix} = \begin{bmatrix} 3 \\ 1 \\ 0 \end{bmatrix}.$$

Matrices

Consider the array of real numbers, with n rows and m columns, defined by

$$A = \begin{bmatrix} a_{11}\,a_{12} \cdots a_{1m} \\ a_{21}\,a_{22} \cdots a_{2m} \\ \vdots \\ a_{n1}\,a_{n2} \cdots a_{nm} \end{bmatrix}.$$

Here, a_{ij} is the ith coordinate of the image in R^n of the jth basis vector in R^m. Think of A as a list of m column vectors of length n. Let the ith column be denoted by the vector

$$a^i = \begin{bmatrix} a_{1i} \\ a_{2i} \\ \vdots \\ a_{ni} \end{bmatrix}.$$

Then A, which is called an $n \times m$ ("n by m") *matrix*, is simply an array of mn real numbers that has, as its ith column, the coordinates of the image of the ith basis vector of R^m.

This is a fundamental observation. *Any linear transformation of* R^m *to* R^n *generates an* $n \times m$ *matrix for given bases of* R^m *and* R^n. Further, given any $n \times m$ matrix, there is a choice of bases of R^m and R^n, so that the matrix is the matrix associated with the given linear transformation. (Simply define the ith coordinate of the image in R^n of the jth basis vector in R^m to be a_{ij}.)

How do these matrices, as representatives of linear transformations, help to characterize linear transformations? Define the object Ax as follows: If A is $n \times m$ and x is a column m-vector (an $m \times 1$ array of numbers), define

$$Ax = \begin{bmatrix} a_{11} & \cdots & a_{1m} \\ \vdots & & \vdots \\ a_{n1} & \cdots & a_{nm} \end{bmatrix} \begin{bmatrix} x_1 \\ \vdots \\ x_m \end{bmatrix} = \begin{bmatrix} a_{11}x_1 + \cdots + a_{1m}x_m \\ \vdots \\ a_{n1}x_1 + \cdots + a_{nm}x_m \end{bmatrix}.$$

Equivalently, if a_i is the ith row of A, define

$$Ax = \begin{bmatrix} a_1 \cdot x \\ a_2 \cdot x \\ \vdots \\ a_n \cdot x \end{bmatrix}.$$

Now, if $\bar{e}^1, \bar{e}^2, \ldots, \bar{e}^n$ is the standard basis of R^n, it is true that

$$L(x) = x_1(a_{11}\bar{e}^1 + \cdots + a_{n1}\bar{e}^n) + \cdots + x_m(a_{1m}\bar{e}^1 + \cdots + a_{nm}\bar{e}^n).$$

Thus,

$$L(x) = x_1 \left[a_{11} \begin{bmatrix} 1 \\ 0 \\ \vdots \\ 0 \end{bmatrix} + \cdots + a_{n1} \begin{bmatrix} 0 \\ 0 \\ \vdots \\ 1 \end{bmatrix} \right] + \cdots$$

$$+ x_m \left[a_{1m} \begin{bmatrix} 1 \\ 0 \\ \vdots \\ 0 \end{bmatrix} + \cdots + a_{nm} \begin{bmatrix} 0 \\ 0 \\ \vdots \\ 1 \end{bmatrix} \right].$$

So

$$
L(x) = x_1 \left[\begin{bmatrix} a_{11} \\ 0 \\ \vdots \\ 0 \end{bmatrix} + \cdots + \begin{bmatrix} 0 \\ 0 \\ \vdots \\ a_{n1} \end{bmatrix} \right] + \cdots
$$

$$
+ x_m \left[\begin{bmatrix} a_{1m} \\ 0 \\ \vdots \\ 0 \end{bmatrix} + \cdots + \begin{bmatrix} 0 \\ 0 \\ \vdots \\ a_{nm} \end{bmatrix} \right] ,
$$

and thus

$$
L(x) = x_1 \begin{bmatrix} a_{11} \\ a_{21} \\ \vdots \\ a_{n1} \end{bmatrix} + \cdots + x_m \begin{bmatrix} a_{1m} \\ a_{2m} \\ \vdots \\ a_{nm} \end{bmatrix} .
$$

Hence,

$$
L(x) = \begin{bmatrix} a_{11}x_1 \\ a_{21}x_1 \\ \vdots \\ a_{n1}x_1 \end{bmatrix} + \cdots + \begin{bmatrix} a_{1m}x_m \\ a_{2m}x_m \\ \vdots \\ a_{nm}x_m \end{bmatrix} .
$$

So

$$
L(x) = \begin{bmatrix} a_{11}x_1 + \cdots + a_{1m}x_m \\ a_{21}x_1 + \cdots + a_{2m}x_m \\ \vdots \qquad\qquad \vdots \\ a_{n1}x_1 + \cdots + a_{nm}x_m \end{bmatrix} ,
$$

and thus

$$
L(x) = \begin{bmatrix} a_1 \cdot x \\ a_2 \cdot x \\ \vdots \\ a_n \cdot x \end{bmatrix} .
$$

But this is just the definition of Ax. Thus,

(1) $L(x) = Ax$.

This result establishes the value of the notation. The left side of equation (1) says that L, an operator, acts on x written to its right. The right side of equation (1) says that A, which represents L given bases for R^m and R^n, is an operator that acts on x written to its right.

To repeat the major point, *given bases for* R^m *and* R^n, *there is a one-to-one correspondence between linear transformations from* R^m *to* R^n *and* $n \times m$ *matrices.* This correspondence between linear transformations and matrices suggests a strategy for characterizing linear transformations. If matrices, which are arrays of real numbers, can be characterized easily and their properties can be identified, then the related transformations may share the same properties. It is this insight that will guide the analysis.

Matrix algebra: a beginning

Suppose there are two $n \times m$ matrices A and B. They must come from two linear transformations, L and $\hat{L}$, of R^m to R^n with given bases. Take a vector $x \in R^m$. Define $(L + \hat{L})(x)$ to be the point in R^n given by $L(x) + \hat{L}(x)$. In this case, $(L + \hat{L})$ itself is a linear transformation. What is its matrix? A little work (see Exercise 5.1) shows that it is the $n \times m$ matrix whose entries are $a_{ij} + b_{ij}$. Thus, if $A + B$ is the matrix obtained from A and B by adding entries in corresponding positions, it is possible to preserve the correspondence between linear transformations of R^m to R^n and $n \times m$ matrices.

If α is a scalar, define $(\alpha L)(x)$ as $\alpha L(x)$. This definition ensures that the object (αL) is indeed a linear transformation from R^m to R^n whenever L is. The $n \times m$ matrix associated with αL is actually (see Exercise 5.1) αA, whose entries are αa_{ij}, which motivates the multiplication of matrices by scalars.

Now suppose $L: R^m \rightarrow R^n$ and $\hat{L}: R^p \rightarrow R^m$. Let A be associated with L and $\hat{A}$ be associated with $\hat{L}$. Certainly A is $n \times m$ and $\hat{A}$ is $m \times p$. Pick an $x \in R^p$. Look at Figure 5.2. $\hat{L}$ sends x to $\hat{L}(x)$. But $\hat{L}(x) \in R^m$, and L sends

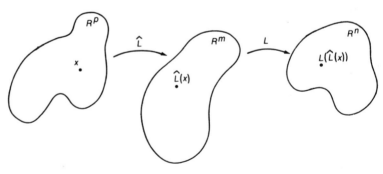

FIGURE 5.2

something in R^m to a point in R^n. Thus, $L(\hat{L}(x))$ lives in R^n. Looking at R^p and R^n, it is clear that x gets sent to $L(\hat{L}(x))$; so $(L(\hat{L}))$ or $(L\hat{L})$ is itself a transformation (verify that it is a linear transformation) of R^p to R^n. What is the matrix associated with $(L\hat{L})$? It turns out (the computations are simple, straightforward, but messy; see Exercise 5.2) that the answer is $A\hat{A}$, where the i,jth entry in $A\hat{A}$ is the dot product of the ith row of A with the jth column of $\hat{A}$. This is the usual multiplication of two matrices. If A is $n \times m$ and $\hat{A}$ is $m \times p$, then $(A\hat{A})$ is $n \times p$; it comes from a linear transformation of R^p to R^n, specifically the transformation $(L\hat{L})$.

EXAMPLE

A production function for a firm can be described as a transformation of inputs into output. If x is an m-vector of inputs, and y is output, then the function $f: R^m \to R$. Suppose that x and $\hat{x}$ are input vectors. If the output associated with input vector $x+\hat{x}$ is equal to the sum of the outputs associated with x and $\hat{x}$, then $f(x+\hat{x}) = f(x) + f(\hat{x})$. If, further, α is a real number, αx is an input vector. If $f(\alpha x)$ is the output associated with αx, then $f(\alpha x) = \alpha f(x)$. These economic assumptions of linearity and constant returns to scale suffice to characterize the production function as a linear transformation.

EXAMPLE

If there are n firms in the economy producing distinct outputs, and all firms use the same kinds of inputs, the production function for the economy is $f: R^m \to R^n$, where $f = (f_1, f_2, \ldots, f_n)$ and f_i is the production function for the ith firm. Suppose all f_i are linear transformations. Then the economy is described by $L: R^m \to R^n$. Choosing units in which to measure inputs and outputs is equivalent to choosing standard basis vectors for R^m and R^n.

With these bases, the production of the economy is described by an $n \times m$ matrix A, where a_{ij} represents the ith coordinate of the image in R^n of the jth basis vector in R^m. Suppose the jth basis vector in R^m refers to the input "steel," and the ith basis vector in R^n refers the the output "automobiles," the former measured in tons, the latter in "standard" car units. Then a_{ij} represents the amount of steel input used to produce one standard automobile. Economists call the numbers a_{ij} input-output coefficients. They arise from fixed-coefficient linear production functions. If A represents the technology, then $Ax = y$ describes the production relationships.

It is now possible to develop a nonelementary observation in matrix algebra via the correspondence between $n \times m$ matrices and linear transformations from R^m to R^n, given bases for R^m and R^n. Suppose $L: R^m \to R^n$. Consider a different basis for R^m. Certainly any other basis for R^m is linearly related to the original basis. Thus, a change of basis in R^m can be represented by a linear transformation $U: R^m \to R^m$ that sends nonzero vectors to nonzero vectors. This transformation U has an $m \times m$ matrix associated with it; call it B. Analogously, any change of basis in R^n can be represented by the linear transformation $T: R^n \to R^n$, which has the matrix representation (for those two bases) C. L, of course, has the $n \times m$ matrix A, given the original bases in R^m and R^n.

Consider the linear transformation (TLU). Certainly, $(TLU)(x)$ picks the point $x \in R^m$ expressed in the original basis of R^m and then acts on it. First, $(TL)(U(x))$; so U takes x and expresses it in the new basis of R^m. Then $L(U(x))$ scoots the relabeled x over to R^n, where it is expressed in the original basis for R^n. Finally, T takes $L(U(x))$, which is a point (vector) in R^n, and expresses it in terms of the new basis in R^n. Consequently, TLU is a linear transformation of R^m to R^n that sends a given point in R^m to a point in R^n, and the given points are the same points in R^m and R^n that L had as domain and image. They are the same points, but they have different coordinates in different bases. Thus, a change in basis is a change in the coordinate labels of the points in the space, which themselves can be pictured as fixed. The matrix associated with TLU is simply CAB, and so, with the usual matrix multiplication,

$$(TLU)(x) = CABx.$$

Here C is $n \times n$, A is $n \times m$, B is $m \times m$, and x is $m \times 1$. Of course, the result of the operations produces an n-vector.

As actual transformations of spaces, the transformations TLU and L act similarly. Further, if the different bases of R^m and R^n had been present from the beginning, it would have been the matrix CAB, not A, that would have corresponded to the linear transformation L.

To repeat, given bases of R^m and R^n, there was an $n \times m$ matrix corresponding to the linear transformation L. It was denoted A. With the new bases, the corresponding $n \times m$ matrix is CAB. For any other change of basis in R^m or R^n or both, there will be a different $n \times m$ matrix to represent the transformation L. In short, any linear transformation L from R^m to R^n has an infinite number of $n \times m$ matrices associated with it, corresponding to all alternative bases of R^m and R^n. Despite this fact, however, all these matrices have something in common: They are associated with the same transformation. All $n \times m$ matrices coming from the same linear transformation are said to be members of the same *similarity class*. Any two matrices coming from L are said to be similar. When are two $n \times m$

matrices A and $\hat{A}$ similar? The answer is easy. If there are two other non-degenerate (i.e., nonzero) matrices, B and C, where B is $m \times m$ and C is $n \times n$, such that $\hat{A} = CAB$, then $\hat{A}$ and A are similar. If such a representation of $\hat{A}$ is not possible, then A and $\hat{A}$ are each associated with different linear transformations of R^m to R^n.

EXAMPLE

A standard linear model that arises in econometric work is of the form

$$y = x\beta + u,$$

where x is a $J \times K$ matrix of observations, β is a $K \times 1$ vector of parameters to be estimated, y is a $J \times 1$ vector of variables, and u ia a J-vector of disturbances. A standard approach to handling this model is to multiply it through on the left by the diagonal matrix $H = \text{diag}(h_j)$, where $h_j = [\text{Var}(U_j)]^{1/2}$, to correct for heteroskedasticity. This yields

$$Hy = Hx\beta + Hu.$$

Define $Hy = y^*$, $Hx = x^*$, and $Hu = u^*$. Then

$$y^* = x^*\beta + u^*.$$

Because the ordinary least-squares estimator of β is $\hat{\beta} = (x^T x)^{-1} x^T y$, and the properties[1] of $(x^T x)^{-1}$ are sometimes difficult to develop, econometricians frequently introduce the matrix C, which solves $C^T x^{*T} x^* C = I_k$ in the following manner:

$$y^* = x^* CC^{-1}\beta + u^*.$$

So

$$y^* = x^* C(C^{-1}\beta) + u^*.$$

Thus, $y^* = x^* C\tilde{\beta} + u^*$, where $\tilde{\beta} = C^{-1}\beta$, and so, finally,

$$y^* = [HxC]\tilde{\beta} + u^*.$$

Because H is a nonsingular $J \times J$ matrix and C is a nonsingular $K \times K$ matrix, HxC is a $J \times K$ matrix similar to x, and it shares with x the essential information that the data provide. This "similarity transformation" of x is useful because x and HxC can be thought of as coming from the same underlying linear mapping.

---

[1] T is the transpose operator (see Chapter 6).

Rank

There is a subtle but fruitful line of inquiry that is appropriate here. Consider a linear transformation L from R^m to R^n. It may be the case that the dimension of the set $L(R^m)$ is not equal to n (see Exercise 5.3). If $L: R^2 \to R^3$ by $L(x_1, x_2) = (x_1, x_2, 0)$, the image of R^2 has dimension 2 in R^3 (i.e., the image is a plane). Denote the image of the domain of L by $\text{Im } L$. It is a subset in R^n. If $\hat{L}: R^3 \to R^2$ by $\hat{L}(x_1, x_2, x_3) = (x_1, x_2)$, the dimension of the image of R^3 under $\hat{L}$ is 2. In this case, $\hat{L}$ "loses" one dimension as it changes R^3 into R^2. The *kernel* of a linear transformation from R^m to R^n is that set in the domain that has zero as its image. Thus, if $L(S) = 0$ for $S \subset R^m$, S is the kernel of the map L. For $\hat{L}$, the set in R^3 defined by $S = \{(x_1, x_2, x_3): x_1 = 0, x_2 = 0\}$ is the kernel, $\text{Ker } \hat{L}$. The kernel of $\hat{L}$ is thus the x_3 axis, a one-dimensional object. The image of R^3 under $\hat{L}$ is $\{(x_1, x_2): x_1 \text{ and } x_2 \text{ are not both zero}\}$. $\text{Im } \hat{L}$ is a two-dimensional object.

There is a general result here. Given $L: R^m \to R^n$, dimension$(\text{Ker } L)$ + dimension$(\text{Im } L) = m$. Now, what does it mean for the dimension of the kernel of L to be zero? In this case, the image of R^m under L has dimension m, and so there is a "copy" of R^m within R^n, the range space. Thus, any vector in the image can be expressed as a linear combination of exactly m linearly independent vectors. With given bases for R^m and R^n, $L(x) = Ax$ for some $m \times n$ matrix A. If the kernel of L has dimension zero, it cannot be the case that $L(x) = 0$ for a nonzero vector x. Thus $Ax \neq 0$.

Recall that the columns of A are vectors that live in R^n and represent the images of the basis vectors of R^m. Consider cases. If $m < n$, then a smaller-dimensional space is being sent, under L, into a larger-dimensional space. If dim$(\text{Ker } L) = 0$, then because A has m columns, as vectors these columns must be linearly independent, for if not, then $Ax = 0$. If dim$(\text{Ker } L) = 1$, then dim$(\text{Im } L) = m - 1$; so exactly $m - 1$ of the column vectors of A are linearly independent, etc. If $m > n$, then L sends a larger-dimensional space into a smaller-dimensional space. But dim$(\text{Im } L) \leq n$. If dim$(\text{Im } L) = n$, then dim$(\text{Ker } L) = m - n$, and so exactly n of the column vectors of A can be linearly independent.

Define the *rank* of an $n \times m$ matrix A to be the maximum number of linearly independent column vectors of A. Thus, if A is the $n \times m$ matrix associated with $L: R^m \to R^n$ given bases for R^m and R^n, rank $A = $ dim$(\text{Im } L)$. Because the dimension of the image of L is independent of the choice of bases for R^m and R^n, all matrices similar to A (all those "coming from" the same linear transformation $L: R^m \to R^n$) have the same rank. A property of a matrix A that is true for all matrices in the similarity class of A is an *invariant property* of the matrix – all matrices coming from a specific linear transformation have that property. Thus, rank is an invariant.

EXAMPLE

Many economic problems are modeled by systems of simultaneous linear equations. Suppose there are n excess-demand functions, one for each market. The equilibrium of supply and demand forces all excess demands to be zero. If the excess-demand functions are linear, then there is a set of n linear homogeneous equations in the n "unknown" prices:

$$a_{11}p_1 + a_{12}p_2 + \cdots + a_{1n}p_n = 0$$
$$a_{21}p_1 + a_{22}p_2 + \cdots + a_{2n}p_n = 0$$
$$\vdots$$
$$a_{n1}p_1 + a_{n2}p_2 + \cdots + a_{nn}p_n = 0.$$

The notation thus generates $Ap = 0$. A comes from a linear mapping $L: R^n \to R^n$. It is important to describe the kernel of L, because this is the set of p's (prices) that satisfies the equations. What is $\dim(\mathrm{Ker}\, L)$? Because $\dim(\mathrm{Ker}\, L) + \dim(\mathrm{Im}\, L) = n$ and $\mathrm{rank}\, A = \dim(\mathrm{Im}\, L)$, what is the rank of A? From Walras's law, if $n - 1$ markets are in equilibrium, the nth is also. Thus, one of the equations is redundant. There are only $n - 1$ linearly independent rows of A. Thus, there are $n - 1$ linearly independent columns of A as well; so $\mathrm{rank}\, A = n - 1$. Hence, $\dim(\mathrm{Ker}\, L) = 1$, which means that any price vector in the solution is a scalar multiple of any other solution vector; that is, if p and $\hat{p}$ are equilibrium price vectors, $\hat{p} = \alpha p$ for some scalar α. Consequently, the equilibrium prices for the multiple-market problem are unique only up to a scalar multiple. Equivalently, the system has a solution in relative (not absolute) prices.

FURTHER READING

To readers of books in the "math for economists" genre, my treatment of matrices and linear mappings may appear surprising. It is geometry, not modernity, that recommends it.

Mills's *Introduction to Linear Algebra for Social Scientists* has an extensive review of basic properties of matrices. Chapter 3 of Hirsch and Smale's *Differential Equations, Dynamical Systems, and Linear Algebra* presents the material on matrices and transformations more completely than I have done. I have followed the spirit of their presentation and that of Lang's *Second Course in Calculus*.

5.1 Suppose $L: R^m \to R^n$ is a linear function, with matrix (a_{ij}) for given bases, and $\hat{L}: R^m \to R^n$ is linear, with matrix (b_{ij}) for those same bases. Let α be a real number. Define the transformations $(L + \hat{L})$ and (αL) by $(L + \hat{L})(x) = L(x) + \hat{L}(x)$ and $(\alpha L)(x) = \alpha L(x)$. Show that $(L + \hat{L})$ and (αL) are linear transformations from $R^m \to R^n$. What are the matrices associated with these transformations?

5.2 Choose bases for R^p, R^m, and R^n. Let $\hat{L}: R^p \to R^m$ and $L: R^n \to R^n$ be linear mappings with associated matrices $\hat{A}$ and A. Define $(L\hat{L})$ as a function from R^p to R^n by the rule $(L\hat{L})(x) = L(\hat{L}(x))$.

   (a) Show that $(L\hat{L})$ is a linear transformation.
   (b) Show that the matrix associated with $(L\hat{L})$ is $(a_i \cdot a^j)$, where a_i is the ith row of A and a^j is the jth column of $\hat{A}$.
   (c) Let $p = m = n = 2$. Suppose $L(x_1, x_2) = (x_2, x_1)$ and $\hat{L}(x_1, x_2) = (x_1 + x_2, x_1 - x_2)$. Using the standard bases for R^2, find A, $\hat{A}$, $(L\hat{L})$, and the matrix associated with $(L\hat{L})$.

5.3 If $L: R^m \to R^n$ is a linear transformation, show that $\text{Ker} L$ and $\text{Im} L$ are vector spaces. (Hint: Show that x and y in these sets entails $x + y$ in the sets. Also, if $\alpha \in R$, αx is in the set when x is.) Thus, it makes sense to speak of the dimension of the kernel and image sets.

CHAPTER 6

Differentiable functions from R^m to R^n

All the notions by aid of which we describe and measure change are geometrical, *and thus are not real perceptual limits.*

Karl Pearson (1911)

Not all functions from R^m to R^n are linear. Yet the strategy developed in Chapters 2 and 4 suggests using the derivative to approximate nonlinear functions by linear functions. The derivative of a function $f: R^m \to R^n$ is defined in language that by now is familiar. The function $f: R^m \to R^n$ is differentiable at $\bar{x} \in R^m$ if there is a linear mapping $L: R^m \to R^n$ such that, for small $h \in R^m$,

$$\lim_{\|h\| \to 0} \frac{\|f(\bar{x}+h) - f(\bar{x}) - L(h)\|}{\|h\|} = 0.$$

With standard bases chosen in R^m and R^n, $L(h) = Ah$, where A is an $n \times m$ matrix and h is, by convention, a column m-vector. If f is differentiable, the linear map L or the matrix A exists. The linear mapping is called the derivative of f at $\bar{x}$ and is written $Df(\bar{x})$. Because L is represented by the matrix A, the derivative can be written as A. But what are the entries in the A matrix?

For $f: R^m \to R^n$, $f(h)$ is actually equal to the column[1] n-vector $(f_1(h), f_2(h), \ldots, f_n(h))^T$, where each f_i maps $R^m \to R$. Because $Df(\bar{x})$ is linear, the derivative is actually $(Df_1(\bar{x}), \ldots, Df_n(\bar{x}))^T$. Each component is a gradient. Consequently, $Df(\bar{x})h$ can be represented as

$$\begin{bmatrix} \dfrac{\partial f_1}{\partial x_1}(\bar{x}) & \dfrac{\partial f_1}{\partial x_2}(\bar{x}) & \cdots & \dfrac{\partial f_1}{\partial x_m}(\bar{x}) \\[2ex] \dfrac{\partial f_2}{\partial x_1}(\bar{x}) & & & \vdots \\[2ex] \vdots & & & \\[2ex] \dfrac{\partial f_n}{\partial x_1}(\bar{x}) & \cdots & & \dfrac{\partial f_n}{\partial x_m}(\bar{x}) \end{bmatrix} \begin{bmatrix} h_1 \\[2ex] h_2 \\[2ex] \vdots \\[2ex] h_m \end{bmatrix}$$

---

[1] I maintain the convention that all vectors are column vectors. When for typographical convenience I must write them as row vectors, I shall use the T to indicate the transpose operator. A row vector x, transposed as x^T, is thus a column vector.

The $n \times m$ matrix

$$\left(\frac{\partial f_i}{\partial x_j}(\bar{x})\right)_{\substack{i=1,2,\ldots,n \\ j=1,2,\ldots,m}}$$

is called the *Jacobian matrix* of f at $\bar{x}$. In Chapter 4, where $n=1$, this matrix was the row vector called the gradient. If $m=n=1$, as in Chapter 2, it was the real number called the derivative. It is easy to calculate the entries of this matrix. The first row is just the gradient (the vector of partial derivatives) of the first component function of f, etc.

EXAMPLE

Consider a utility function $u(x_1,x_2,\ldots,x_n)$ and a budget constraint $p_1x_1 + \cdots + p_nx_n = y$ for an individual. For given income y and prices $p=(p_1,p_2,\ldots,p_n)^T$ it is true in equilibrium that the marginal utility of good i is proportional to the price of good i for all goods $i=1,2,\ldots,n$. In equilibrium, it is also true that the budget constraint is binding.

These equilibrium conditions frequently are called first-order conditions. The marginal utility of good i at equilibrium $\bar{x}= (\bar{x}_1,\ldots,\bar{x}_n)^T$ is simply $(\partial u/\partial x_i)(\bar{x})$. In equilibrium, it must be true that

$$\frac{\partial u}{\partial x_1}(x) - \lambda p_1 = 0$$

$$\frac{\partial u}{\partial x_2}(x) - \lambda p_2 = 0$$

$$\vdots$$

$$\frac{\partial u}{\partial x_n}(x) - \lambda p_n = 0$$

$$p_1x_1 + \cdots + p_nx_n - y = 0,$$

when λ is the constant of proportionality. For any choice of p and y, these equations might define an equilibrium $\bar{x}$. From another perspective, each equation defines a function that must take on the value of zero in equilibrium. Thus,

$$\phi^1(x_1,x_2,\ldots,x_n; p_1,\ldots,p_n; \lambda,y) = 0$$

is an alternative way of writing $(\partial u/\partial x_1)(x) - \lambda p_1 = 0$. Thus,

$$\phi^1(x;p;y;\lambda) = 0$$
$$\phi^2(x;p;y;\lambda) = 0$$
$$\vdots \qquad\qquad \vdots$$
$$\phi^{n+1}(x;p;y;\lambda) = 0,$$

If $\phi = (\phi^1, \phi^2, \ldots, \phi^{n+1})^T$, then $\phi: R^{2n+2} \to R^{n+1}$. The mapping ϕ is extremely important. It relates prices, income, and equilibrium purchases. Many results in the "theory of the household" are related to this mapping.

To study this mapping's properties, approximate it by a linear mapping from R^{2n+2} to R^{n+1} near an equilibrium. This is accomplished by computing the derivative. The Jacobian of ϕ is an $(n+1) \times (2n+2)$ matrix of the following form:

$$\begin{bmatrix} \dfrac{\partial \phi^1}{\partial x_1} & \cdots & \dfrac{\partial \phi^1}{\partial x_n} & \dfrac{\partial \phi^1}{\partial p_1} & \cdots & \dfrac{\partial \phi^1}{\partial p_n} & \dfrac{\partial \phi^1}{\partial y} & \dfrac{\partial \phi^1}{\partial \lambda} \\ \vdots & & & & & & & \\ \dfrac{\partial \phi^{n+1}}{\partial x_1} & & \dfrac{\partial \phi^{n+1}}{\partial x_n} & \dfrac{\partial \phi^{n+1}}{\partial p_1} & \cdots & \dfrac{\partial \phi^{n+1}}{\partial p_n} & \dfrac{\partial \phi^{n+1}}{\partial y} & \dfrac{\partial \phi^{n+1}}{\partial \lambda} \end{bmatrix}.$$

Because ϕ^i is $\partial u/\partial x_i - \lambda p_i$ for $i = 1, 2, \ldots, n$ and ϕ^{n+1} is $p \cdot x - y$, the Jacobian becomes

$$\begin{bmatrix} \dfrac{\partial^2 u}{\partial x_1^2} & \cdots & \dfrac{\partial^2 u}{\partial x_n \partial x_1} & -\lambda & \cdots & 0 & 0 & -p_1 \\ \dfrac{\partial^2 u}{\partial x_1 \partial x_n} & \cdots & \dfrac{\partial^2 u}{\partial x_n^2} & 0 & \cdots & -\lambda & 0 & -p_n \\ p_1 & \cdots & p_n & x_1 & \cdots & x_n & -1 & 0 \end{bmatrix}.$$

This Jacobian matrix has several parts, including a submatrix of second-order partial derivatives (partial derivatives of partial derivatives) and vectors of relevant variables. The structure of the theory of the household is summarized in this Jacobian matrix. It will be a source of many examples later.

The important point is that the derivative of $f: R^m \to R^n$ is a linear mapping, and any linear mapping from R^m to R^n can be represented as an $n \times m$ matrix; with the standard bases chosen for R^m and R^n, this matrix representation is called the Jacobian matrix of f. The properties of the

Jacobian matrix help to describe the behavior of the differentiable function f.

Higher-order derivatives

Given a differentiable function f from R^m to R^n for any positive integers m and n, the derivative is a linear function from R^m to R^n. The derivative, as a function of the variable $\bar{x}$, may itself be differentiable. To compute the derivative of the derivative, it suffices to calculate the Jacobian of the derivative mapping or to calculate partial derivatives of partial derivatives.

As a function of $\bar{x} \in R^m$, $Df(\bar{x})$ maps R^m to R^n; so the second-order Jacobian is itself a linear mapping. This linear mapping is not, however, a mapping from R^m to R^n. To see this, suppose $f: R^n \rightarrow R$, and assume that f is differentiable. Then

$$Df(\bar{x}) = \left(\frac{\partial f}{\partial x_1}(\bar{x}), \ldots, \frac{\partial f}{\partial x_n}(\bar{x}) \right)^T = (f_1(\bar{x}), \ldots, f_n(\bar{x}))^T.$$

The derivative of this linear map involves operating with $\partial/\partial x_i$ on each of the $f_j(\bar{x})$'s. The result is the $n \times n$ matrix

$$\begin{bmatrix} \dfrac{\partial}{\partial x_1}\left(\dfrac{\partial f}{\partial x_1} \right) & \dfrac{\partial}{\partial x_1}\left(\dfrac{\partial f}{\partial x_2} \right) & \cdots & \dfrac{\partial}{\partial x_1}\left(\dfrac{\partial f}{\partial x_n} \right) \\ \vdots & & & \\ \dfrac{\partial}{\partial x_n}\left(\dfrac{\partial f}{\partial x_1} \right) & \dfrac{\partial}{\partial x_n}\left(\dfrac{\partial f}{\partial x_2} \right) & \cdots & \dfrac{\partial}{\partial x_n}\left(\dfrac{\partial f}{\partial x_n} \right) \end{bmatrix}.$$

In standard calculus notation, this matrix of second-order partial derivatives, called the *Hessian matrix*, is written

$$Hf(\bar{x}) = \begin{bmatrix} \dfrac{\partial^2 f}{\partial x_1^2}(\bar{x}) & \cdots & \dfrac{\partial^2 f}{\partial x_1 \partial x_n}(\bar{x}) \\ \vdots & & \\ \dfrac{\partial^2 f}{\partial x_n \partial x_1}(\bar{x}) & \cdots & \dfrac{\partial^2 f}{\partial x_n^2}(\bar{x}) \end{bmatrix}.$$

The Hessian of $f: R^n \rightarrow R$ is thus an $n \times n$ matrix. Now return to

$$f: R^m \rightarrow R^n.$$

Each element of $Df(\bar{x})$ is a partial derivative, some term like $\partial f_i/\partial x_j$, $i=1, 2, \ldots, n$ and $j=1, 2, \ldots, m$, in the Jacobian. To take the derivative of a term like this, it is necessary to operate on it by each of the symbols

$\partial/\partial x_1, \partial/\partial x_2, \ldots, \partial/\partial x_m$. Thus, three indices identify the second-order partial derivative, one index running as $1, 2, \ldots, n$ and two separate indices running as $1, 2, \ldots, m$. Intuitively, this produces a three-dimensional (!) matrix, with n rows, m columns, and m stacks.

In actual practice in economics, however, there are no applications of this. Either the function is $f\colon R \to R$, in which case the second derivative is a number (a $1 \times 1 \times 1$ matrix), or else $f\colon R^n \to R$, in which case the Hessian is an $n \times n$ ($\times 1$) matrix.

Implicit functions

Suppose $f\colon R^m \to R^n$, with $m > n$. In this case, f maps a subset of a higher-dimensional space to a set in a lower-dimensional space. Hence, f acts as follows:

$$f(x_1, x_2, \ldots, x_n, x_{n+1}, \ldots, x_m) = (y_1, y_2, \ldots, y_n)^T.$$

Thus, f defines the system of n equations in m unknowns:

$$f^1(x_1, \ldots, x_n, \ldots, x_m) = y_1$$
$$f^2(x_1, \ldots, x_n, \ldots, x_m) = y_2$$
$$\vdots \qquad\qquad\qquad \vdots$$
$$f^n(x_1, \ldots, x_n, \ldots, x_m) = y_n.$$

If f were a linear function, the system would appear as

$$a_{11}x_1 + \cdots + a_{1m}x_m = y_1$$
$$a_{21}x_1 + \cdots + a_{2m}x_m = y_2$$
$$\vdots \qquad\qquad \vdots$$
$$a_{nm}x_1 + \cdots + a_{nm}x_m = y_n,$$

or $Ax = y$, where A is $n \times m$, x is $m \times 1$, and y is $n \times 1$.

Using the result of the preceding chapter, $\dim \mathrm{Ker}(f) + \dim \mathrm{Im}(f) = m$. If the rank of the matrix A is n, then $m - n$ dimensions are "lost" as f transforms R^m to R^n. Equivalently, n dimensions are "preserved" by f, and thus f linearly transforms an n-dimensional subset of R^m into R^n.

If the $y_1, \ldots, y_n$ are given numbers, it is possible to solve for precisely n of the unknown x's. The remaining $m - n$ of the x's are left out of the solution. Consequently, the solution is defined by functions θ^i such that

$$x_1 = \theta^1(y_1, \ldots, y_n; x_{n+1}, \ldots, x_m)$$
$$x_2 = \theta^2(y_1, \ldots, y_n; x_{n+1}, \ldots, x_m)$$
$$\vdots$$
$$x_n = \theta^n(y_1, \ldots, y_n; x_{n+1}, \ldots, x_m).$$

The functions $\theta^1, \ldots, \theta^n$ are *implicit functions* of the $x_{n+1}, \ldots, x_m$.

In the general case, when $f: R^m \to R^n$ is defined by $f(x) = y$ and $m > n$, frequently it is important to be able to solve the n equations for x in terms of y. Can this be done? That is, do there exist functions θ^i such that

$$x_1 = \theta^1(y_1, \ldots, y_n)$$
$$x_2 = \theta^2(y_1, \ldots, y_n)$$
$$\vdots$$
$$x_m = \theta^m(y_1, \ldots, y_n)?$$

The preceding paragraphs show that when $m > n$, the x's cannot be represented as functions of the y's alone, even in the case where f is a linear transformation. The best result possible would be a solution for exactly n of the x's in terms of the n y's and the remaining $m - n$ x's, where n is the rank of the matrix A representing the linear mapping f.

This result has an analogue in the case where f is not a linear transformation. If f is differentiable at $\bar{x}$, represent f near $\bar{x}$ by the linear mapping defined by the Jacobian. Suppose, near $\bar{x}$, the Jacobian has rank n. Then exactly n of the x's can be found as functions of the n y's and the remaining $m - n$ x's. Thus, for $m > n$, if $f: R^m \to R^n$ is differentiable at $\bar{x}$ and the Jacobian of f has rank n, then near $\bar{x}$ it is possible to find n differentiable functions $\theta^1, \ldots, \theta^n$ such that

$$x_1 = \theta^1(x_{n+1}, \ldots, x_m; y_1, \ldots, y_n)$$
$$x_2 = \theta^2(x_{n+1}, \ldots, x_m; y_1, \ldots, y_n)$$
$$\vdots$$
$$x_n = \theta^n(x_{n+1}, \ldots, x_m; y_1, \ldots, y_n).$$

This result is called the *Implicit Function Theorem*. It is an important tool in economic analysis.

EXAMPLE

The utility function and budget constraint of the preceding example generated equilibrium conditions

$$\phi^i(x_1, \ldots, x_n; p_1, \ldots, p_n; y, \lambda) = 0 \quad i = 1, 2, \ldots, n+1.$$

Treating $p_1, \ldots, p_n$ and y as constants, the Jacobian of $\phi = (\phi^1, \ldots, \phi^{n+1})^T$ has the form

$$
J\phi =
\begin{bmatrix}
\dfrac{\partial \phi^1}{\partial x_1} & \cdots & \dfrac{\partial \phi^1}{\partial x_n} & \dfrac{\partial \phi^1}{\partial \lambda} \\[2ex]
\vdots & & & \\[1ex]
\dfrac{\partial \phi^n}{\partial x_1} & \cdots & \dfrac{\partial \phi^n}{\partial x_n} & \dfrac{\partial \phi^n}{\partial \lambda} \\[2ex]
\dfrac{\partial \phi^{n+1}}{\partial x_1} & \cdots & \dfrac{\partial \phi^{n+1}}{\partial x_n} & \dfrac{\partial \phi^{n+1}}{\partial \lambda}
\end{bmatrix} .
$$

The Jacobian, evaluated at equilibrium, is thus an $(n+1) \times (n+1)$ matrix. What is its rank? The rank certainly depends on whether or not a particular column (or row) is linearly dependent on the remaining columns. A little reflection suggests that this depends on assumptions about the utility function. As will be shown later, if the utility function expresses a property such as "the law of diminishing marginal utility," then this Jacobian does in fact have rank $= (n+1)$.

The Implicit Function Theorem immediately yields the result that the $n+1$ variables $(x_1, \ldots, x_n; \lambda)$ can be expressed as differentiable functions of the p's and y as

$$
x^i = \theta^i(p_1, \ldots, p_n; y) \quad i = 1, 2, \ldots, n
$$
$$
\lambda = \theta^{n+1}(p_1, \ldots, p_n; y).
$$

It is apparent, from the definition of the variables, that each relationship such as

$$
x^i = \theta^i(p_1, \ldots, p_n; y)
$$

defines a demand function for commodity i. The relationship states, in words, that the quantity demanded of good i is a funcion of prices of all goods, and income.

Inverse functions

When $m = n$, the Implicit Function Theorem becomes especially interesting. Consider the differentiable function $f: R^n \to R^n$ defined by

$$
f^1(x_1, x_2, \ldots, x_n) = y_1
$$
$$
f^2(x_1, x_2, \ldots, x_n) = y_2
$$
$$
\vdots \qquad\qquad\qquad \vdots
$$
$$
f^n(x_1, x_2, \ldots, x_n) = y_n.
$$

Is it possible to solve this system for the x's in terms of the y's? If it is, then there is a function $g: R^n \to R^n$ such that

$$g^1(y_1, \ldots, y_n) = x_1$$
$$g^2(y_1, \ldots, y_n) = x_2$$
$$\vdots \qquad\qquad \vdots$$
$$g^n(y_1, \ldots, y_n) = x_n.$$

The original system is described by $f(x) = y$. The problem is to find a function g such that $g(y) = x$. The situation is pictured in Figure 6.1. Notice that because $y = f(x)$, $g(y) = g(f(x))$; so $g(f(x)) = x$. The composition of the functions g and f sends x to itself, because f sends x to y and g sends y back to x. Thus, the composite function $g(f)$ sends every point in R^n to itself. The function $g(f)$ is called the *identity function* and the function g is called the *inverse function* of f.

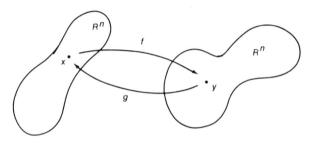

FIGURE 6.1

In the linear case, f is a linear transformation. For standard bases in R^n, f is the matrix $A = (a_{ij})$. Suppose f sends the n-vector x to the n-vector of constants b, as

$$a_{11}x_1 + a_{12}x_2 + \cdots + a_{1n}x_n = b_1$$
$$a_{21}x_1 + a_{22}x_2 + \cdots + a_{2n}x_n = b_2$$
$$\vdots \qquad\qquad\qquad\qquad \vdots$$
$$a_{n1}x_1 + a_{n2}x_2 + \cdots + a_{nn}x_n = b_n.$$

Thus, $Ax = b$, where A is $(n \times n)$ and x and b are $(n \times 1)$. If an inverse (linear) function to f exists, it must be true that $g(f(x)) = x$.

Let the $n \times n$ matrix associated with g be identified by the symbol A^{-1}. Because matrix multiplication is the analogue of the composition of linear mappings, $A^{-1}Ax = x$. Equivalently, $A^{-1}A$ acts like the linear transformation that sends x to itself. Define the $n \times n$ *identity matrix* as

$$I_n = \begin{bmatrix} 1 & & & & \\ & 1 & & 0 & \\ & & 1 & & \\ & 0 & & \ddots & \\ & & & & 1 \end{bmatrix}_{n \times n}.$$

Then, if x is $n \times 1$, $I_n x = x$. Thus, $A^{-1}A = I_n$, as matrices or representations of linear mappings.

This discussion makes sense only if an inverse linear function exists. Provided that the rank of A is equal to n, it is clear that dim Im$f = n$. The Implicit Function Theorem then guarantees the existence of the function g, an inverse linear function whose matrix is A^{-1}.

What happens, though, when f is nonlinear? Answer: linearize f using the Jacobian matrix. This generates a linear mapping that represents f at or near a point $\bar{x}$ where f is differentiable.

Determining whether or not $f: R^n \to R^n$ has an inverse function g at $\bar{x} \in R^n$ requires computing the Jacobian of f at $\bar{x}$. Suppose this Jacobian, J, has rank n. The linearity of the J map guarantees the existence of a matrix J^{-1}. J^{-1}, as a matrix, itself defines a linear map. Let J^{-1} be the Jacobian of a function g at $\bar{x}$. It is not difficult to see that near $\bar{x}$, g and f are inverse functions. If $f: R \to R$, this result is especially nice. The Jacobian of f at x is the real number (1×1 matrix) $f'(\bar{x})$. The inverse Jacobian is that number (1×1 matrix) J^{-1} whose *product* with $f'(\bar{x})$ equals $I_1 = 1$. Thus,

$$J^{-1} f'(\bar{x}) = 1.$$

So

$$J^{-1} = \frac{1}{f'(\bar{x})}.$$

The function that is the inverse function to f at $\bar{x}$ is the function g that has a derivative equal to $1/f'(\bar{x})$ at $\bar{x}$.

EXAMPLE

The usual demand and supply functions for a good are written as

$$q^D = D(p) \quad \text{and} \quad q^S = S(p).$$

If $q^S = q^D = \bar{q}$, then the market is "in equilibrium," when p is the price of the good, q^D is the quantity demanded, and q^S is the quantity supplied. The Walrasian adjustment process states that if the quantity demanded exceeds (is less than) the quantity supplied, the price increases (falls). If $\bar{p}$ is the equilibrium price, the Walrasian stability condition (this will be shown in Chapter 8) is that $D'(\bar{p}) < S'(\bar{p})$. In other words, if the derivative of the demand curve at $\bar{p}$ is less than the derivative of the supply curve at $\bar{p}$, then any nonequilibrium price is forced back to equilibrium by the "market pressure."

The alternative Marshallian adjustment process says that if the price at which individuals wish to buy exceeds (is less than) the price at which individuals wish to sell, then output quantity increases (decreases). This gives rise to the Marshallian stability condition that the derivative of the demand–price curve at equilibrium $\bar{q}$ be less than the derivative of the supply–price curve at $\bar{q}$.

What is the relationship between these Walrasian and Marshallian stability conditions? Notice that if $q^D = D(p^D)$ relates demand quantity to demand price, the inverse function D^{-1} relates demand price to demand quantity as $p^D = D^{-1}(q^D)$. Similarly, $p^S = S^{-1}(q^S)$. Because, in equilibrium, $q^D = q^S = \bar{q}$ and $p^S = p^D = \bar{p}$, the Marshallian condition can be written $(D^{-1})'(\bar{q}) < (S^{-1})'(\bar{q})$. But $(D^{-1})'(\bar{q}) = 1/D'(\bar{p})$, and $(S^{-1})'(\bar{q}) = 1/S'(\bar{p})$. Thus, the Walrasian condition is $D'(\bar{p}) < S'(\bar{p})$, whereas the Marshallian condition is $1/D'(\bar{p}) < 1/S'(\bar{p})$. Of course, if the demand curve is downward-sloping and the supply curve is upward-sloping, both conditions are satisfied, because both left sides are negative numbers and both right sides are positive numbers. It is not difficult, however, to construct backward-bending supply curves that satisfy one or the other set (but not both sets) of stability conditions. Some economists have made much of this distinction between the two sets of stability conditions without realizing that, given the results about inverse functions, either condition is formally derivable from the other. However, the economic meaning of these inverse functions is a more delicate and confusing subject.

FURTHER READING

Chapter 2 of Spivack's *Calculus on Manifolds* is the best single source to consult, and study, in conjunction with this chapter. See especially Spivack's section on "Notation," which ought to be required reading for purveyors of partial derivatives.

EXERCISES

6.1 If $f: R^3 \to R^2$ by $f(x, y, z) = (\sin z, \cos xy)$, find the Jacobian of f at $(0, 0, 0)$.

6.2 Show that if $f: R^m \to R^n$ is differentiable at $\bar{x}$, then f is continuous at $\bar{x}$.

6.3 Suppose a demand function for a single market is defined by $q = D(p)$. Show that if demand is perfectly inelastic, no inverse demand function exists.

CHAPTER 7

Square matrices

*Our propensity to 'geometrize' our
analysis may only be evidence that we
have not yet grown up.*
James R. Newman (1956)

God bless the child....
Billie Holiday

The last chapter examined functions $f: R^n \to R^n$ that had, at $\bar{x} \in R^n$, a Jacobian of rank n. For such functions, the local existence of an inverse function generated a local copy of the domain set in the range set. For linear functions from R^n to R^n, represented by a square matrix A for the standard basis of R^n, even stronger results obtain. This chapter concerns $n \times n$ matrices. Its point of view is that any $n \times n$ matrix represents a linear transformation from R^n to R^n given some choice of basis in R^n. A square matrix represents a transformation of R^n into itself. Consider the $n \times n$ matrix A:

$$\begin{bmatrix} a_{11} & a_{12} & \cdots & a_{1n} \\ a_{21} & a_{22} & \cdots & a_{2n} \\ \vdots & & & \\ a_{n1} & a_{n2} & \cdots & a_{nn} \end{bmatrix}.$$

As a transformation, A sends column n-vectors to column n-vectors. What does A do to the standard basis vectors of R^n? Recall that the standard basis vectors are

$$e^1 = \begin{bmatrix} 1 \\ 0 \\ \vdots \\ 0 \end{bmatrix}, e^2 = \begin{bmatrix} 0 \\ 1 \\ 0 \\ \vdots \\ 0 \end{bmatrix}, \ldots, e^n = \begin{bmatrix} 0 \\ 0 \\ \vdots \\ 1 \end{bmatrix}.$$

To see what A does to e^1, form Ae^1, or

$$\begin{bmatrix} a_{11} & a_{12} & \cdots & a_{1n} \\ a_{21} & a_{22} & \cdots & a_{2n} \\ \vdots & & & \\ a_{n1} & a_{n2} & \cdots & a_{nn} \end{bmatrix} \cdot \begin{bmatrix} 1 \\ 0 \\ \vdots \\ 0 \end{bmatrix}.$$

Certainly,

$$Ae^1 = \begin{bmatrix} a_{11} \\ a_{21} \\ a_{31} \\ \vdots \\ a_{n1} \end{bmatrix}.$$

Similarly,

$$Ae^i = \begin{bmatrix} a_{1i} \\ a_{2i} \\ \vdots \\ a_{ni} \end{bmatrix}.$$

Thus, the ith column of A is the image of the ith standard basis vector in R^n under the transformation A. For example, in R^2, if $A = \begin{bmatrix} 1 & 3 \\ 2 & 4 \end{bmatrix}$, then $(1,0)^T \xrightarrow{A} (1,2)^T$ and $(0,1)^T \xrightarrow{A} (3,4)^T$, as in Figure 7.1. This information determines the action of the transformation A. It certainly sends 0 to 0. Any vector in the first quadrant of R^2 gets sent to region I. Effectively, A takes the plane and "squeezes" it from the west and south.

If $A = \begin{bmatrix} 1 & 2 \\ 2 & 1 \end{bmatrix}$, Figure 7.2 shows that A first rotates the plane around the origin $180°$ and then squeezes it from the west and south until Ae^1 and Ae^2 lie, as shown, in the first quadrant. If $A = \begin{bmatrix} 0 & 1 \\ 1 & 0 \end{bmatrix}$, then $(1,0)^T \xrightarrow{A} (0,1)^T$

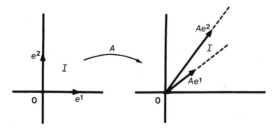

FIGURE 7.1

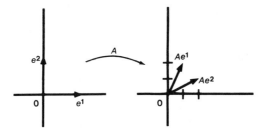

FIGURE 7.2

and $(0, 1)^T \xrightarrow{A} (1, 0)^T$. A acts on the plane by rotating the plane and then pushing the negative x_2 axis from the east until it settles as the positive x_2 axis. Alternatively, A rotates the plane, out of the plane, around $x_1 = x_2$. The point is clear. A square matrix deforms R^n by rotating and/or compressing the (standard) coordinate axes or basis vectors.

Change of basis

An $n \times n$ matrix A represents a linear transformation $L : R^n \to R^n$ given a basis of R^n. Each choice of a basis in R^n generates an $n \times n$ matrix. Each matrix equally well represents the same linear transformation L. Recall that properties common to this entire class of matrices were called invariants of the matrix. Rank was one such invariant. Are there others? Answering this question involves examining the matrices associated with L as the bases change in R^n.

Consider, for simplicity, R^2. Linear maps are associated with 2×2 matrices. Begin with the standard basis e^1 and e^2, and consider a different basis, say b^1 and b^2, where

$$b^1 = \begin{bmatrix} b_1^1 \\ b_2^1 \end{bmatrix} \quad \text{and} \quad b^2 = \begin{bmatrix} b_1^2 \\ b_2^2 \end{bmatrix}.$$

Define the matrix B by

$$B = \begin{bmatrix} b_1^1 & b_1^2 \\ b_2^1 & b_2^2 \end{bmatrix}.$$

If b^1 and b^2 are noncoincident vectors, they are linearly independent; so the rank of B is 2. Thus, there exists an inverse matrix, B^{-1}, such that $BB^{-1} = I_2$. Because $e^1 \xrightarrow{B} b^1$ and $e^2 \xrightarrow{B} b^2$, certainly $b^1 \xrightarrow{B^{-1}} e^1$ and $b^2 \xrightarrow{B^{-1}} e^2$. Thus, the matrix B^{-1} represents the change of basis in R^2 from the set

$\{e^1, e^2\}$ to the set $\{b^1, b^2\}$. Alternatively, the matrix B represents the change of basis[1] from the set $\{b^1, b^2\}$ to the set $\{e^1, e^2\}$.

EXAMPLE

Let $b^1 = (1, 1)^T$ and $b^2 = (0, 2)^T$. These vectors form a basis of R^2. Consider the vector $x = (3, 4)^T$, where the coordinates are taken with respect to the standard basis. Thus, $x = 3(1, 0)^T + 4(0, 1)^T$. What are the coordinates of x in the basis $\{b^1, b^2\}$?

Define $B = \begin{bmatrix} 1 & 0 \\ 1 & 2 \end{bmatrix}$. Then

$$B^{-1} = \begin{bmatrix} 1 & 0 \\ -\frac{1}{2} & \frac{1}{2} \end{bmatrix},$$

because $BB^{-1} = I_2$. $B^{-1}x$ gives the coordinates of the point x in the $\{b^1, b^2\}$ basis.

$$B^{-1}x = \begin{bmatrix} 1 & 0 \\ -\frac{1}{2} & \frac{1}{2} \end{bmatrix} \begin{bmatrix} 3 \\ 4 \end{bmatrix} = \begin{bmatrix} 3 \\ \frac{1}{2} \end{bmatrix}.$$

Thus, the coordinates of the point x in the $\{b^1, b^2\}$ basis are $(3, \frac{1}{2})$. This is verified easily, because

$$3\begin{bmatrix} 1 \\ 1 \end{bmatrix} + \frac{1}{2}\begin{bmatrix} 0 \\ 2 \end{bmatrix} = \begin{bmatrix} 3 \\ 4 \end{bmatrix}.$$

Thus, any 2×2 matrix of rank 2 represents a change of basis in R^2.

---

[1] It is easy to remember which matrix to use in changing bases by using the idea that although the location of a given point (vector) remains the same, the "mileposts" or nominal address may change. Thus, the point $(x_1, \ldots, x_n)$ in standard basis may be alternatively stated:

$$\begin{bmatrix} 1 & 0 \cdots 0 \\ 0 & 1 \cdots 0 \\ \vdots \\ 0 & \cdots 1 \end{bmatrix} \begin{bmatrix} x_1 \\ \vdots \\ x_n \end{bmatrix} = \begin{bmatrix} B_{11} & \cdots & B_{1m} \\ \vdots \\ B_{m1} & \cdots & B_{mn} \end{bmatrix} \begin{bmatrix} b_1 \\ \vdots \\ b_n \end{bmatrix} = \begin{bmatrix} C_{11} & \cdots & C_{1n} \\ \vdots \\ C_{m1} & \cdots & C_{mn} \end{bmatrix} \begin{bmatrix} c_1 \\ \vdots \\ c_n \end{bmatrix}$$

Standard   B basis   C basis

The columns of B (or C) are, of course, the B (or C) basis vectors written in the standard basis, and b (or c) is the point written in the B (or C) basis. It becomes clear that because $I \cdot x = B \cdot b = C \cdot c$, $B^{-1} \cdot I \cdot x = b$, $C^{-1} \cdot B \cdot b = c$, $x = B \cdot b$, etc.

Now take the linear transformation $L: R^2 \to R^2$ that is represented by the 2×2 matrix A with the choice of the standard basis $\{e^1, e^2\}$ for R^2. What 2×2 matrix represents L with the different basis $\{b^1, b^2\}$? It should be obvious that the matrix that represents L in the basis $\{b^1, b^2\}$ is $B^{-1}AB$. This 2×2 matrix takes the vector x, written in the basis $\{b^1, b^2\}$, rewrites in the standard basis via B, transforms it via A, then transforms it back to the $\{b^1, b^2\}$ basis via B^{-1}.

This procedure generalizes to R^n. The problem is to find all matrices similar to a given matrix A. Put another way, is it possible to find all matrices that represent a given linear transformation from R^n to R^n? The answer is clear. Take a linear transformation $L: R^n \to R^n$. Given some basis, L is represented by the $n \times n$ matrix A, of rank $k \leq n$. Take any $n \times n$ matrix B of rank n. It represents a change of basis. It also has an inverse matrix B^{-1}. Thus, $B^{-1}AB$ is an $n \times n$ matrix of rank k, similar to A. Finding all such matrices B generates a family of $n \times n$ rank-k matrices $B^{-1}AB$. Any one of these matrices represents the transformation $L: R^n \to R^n$ for some basis of R^n.

There is some standard terminology associated with $n \times n$ matrices. If an $n \times n$ matrix has rank n, then the matrix is called *nonsingular*. The inverse function theorem yields the result that nonsingular $n \times n$ matrices can be inverted. That is, for any nonsingular $n \times n$ matrix A there exists a nonsingular $n \times n$ matrix A^{-1} such that $AA^{-1} = I_n$.

Given an $n \times n$ matrix A, define the *transpose* of A, written A^T, to be the $n \times n$ matrix whose rows are the columns of A and whose columns are the rows of A. If

$$A = \begin{bmatrix} a_{11} & a_{12} \\ a_{21} & a_{22} \end{bmatrix},$$

then

$$A^T = \begin{bmatrix} a_{11} & a_{21} \\ a_{12} & a_{22} \end{bmatrix}.$$

A matrix is *symmetric* if it equals its transpose; if A is 2×2, this means $a_{12} = a_{21}$. For any matrix A, it is easy to see that $(A + A^T)/2$ is a symmetric matrix (which equals A itself when A is symmetric).

Trace and determinant

The discussion in the preceding pages facilitates the study of invariants. Specifically, what properties of an $n \times n$ matrix, besides its rank, are shared by all members of its similarity class? What properties of an $n \times n$ matrix arise from the linear transformation of $R^n \to R^n$ that it represents?

What properties are accidents, incidental on a choice of a specific basis for R^n?

Consider an example for $n = 2$. Let there be given a linear transformation $L: R^2 \rightarrow R^2$, with a matrix representation A in some basis for R^2. Suppose that A is symmetric, as

$$A = \begin{bmatrix} 1 & 1 \\ 1 & 2 \end{bmatrix}.$$

Let $B = \begin{bmatrix} 1 & 3 \\ 2 & 4 \end{bmatrix}$. Thus B is nonsingular and represents a change of basis in R^2. A little computation shows that

$$B^{-1} = \begin{bmatrix} -2 & \frac{3}{2} \\ 1 & -\frac{1}{2} \end{bmatrix}.$$

Now compute $B^{-1}AB$:

$$B^{-1}AB = \begin{bmatrix} \frac{3}{2} & \frac{5}{2} \\ \frac{1}{2} & \frac{3}{2} \end{bmatrix}.$$

What properties of A are also true of $B^{-1}AB$? Look at the main diagonal of A. The sum of the elements on the main diagonal of A is $1 + 2 = 3$; the sum of the elements on the main diagonal of $B^{-1}AB$ is $\frac{3}{2} + \frac{3}{2} = 3$. Define the *trace* of an $n \times n$ matrix to be the algebraic sum of the elements on the main diagonal. It is plausible that the trace is an invariant. Similar matrices have the same trace.

Now multiply the elements on the main diagonal and subtract the product of the elements on the off diagonal. Thus, $1 \cdot 2 - 1 \cdot 1 = 1$ for A and $(\frac{3}{2})(\frac{3}{2}) - (\frac{1}{2})(\frac{5}{2}) = 1$ for $B^{-1}AB$. This number is called the *determinant* of the 2×2 matrix. It is plausible that the determinant is an invariant. Similar matrices have the same determinant. The result that the determinant of an $n \times n$ matrix is an invariant is not difficult to demonstrate. However, it requires familiarity with the definition and properties of the determinant.

To avoid tedious exposition,[2] it will be assumed (1) that any reader can calculate the determinant of an $n \times n$ matrix, (2) that the determinant of (AB), written $\det(AB)$, where A and B are $n \times n$ matrices, equals $(\det A)(\det B)$, (3) that $\det(I_n) = 1$, (4) that if A is $n \times n$, $\det A \neq 0$ if and only if A is nonsingular (i.e., if and only if A is invertible). Assuming these properties of the determinant facilitates the demonstration that the determinant is an invariant. Certainly, if B is invertible,

$$B^{-1}B = I_n.$$

---

[2] For a quick review of determinants, see pages 39–41 and Appendix I in Hirsch and Smale's *Differential Equations*. For a fuller treatment, see Lang's *Second Course in Calculus*.

Thus, $\det(B^{-1})(\det B) = 1$, and so

$$\det B^{-1} = \frac{1}{\det B}.$$

Let A be any $n \times n$ matrix that represents $L: R^n \to R^n$. Then any other matrix representation of L, call it C, has the form

$$C = B^{-1}AB$$

for some nonsingular $n \times n$ matrix B. Thus,

$$\det C = \det(B^{-1}AB).$$

So

$$\det C = (\det B^{-1})(\det A)(\det B),$$

and thus

$$\det C = \det A.$$

EXAMPLE

Suppose there are two commodities that a household can buy. Let the household income be y and the prices of the goods be p_1 and p_2. Suppose the preferences of the household are described by the log-linear utility function U, where $U(x_1, x_2) = a_1 \log x_1 + a_2 \log x_2$. Assume $a_1 > 0$, $a_2 > 0$, and $a_1 + a_2 = 1$. The equilibrium purchases x_1 and x_2 must satisfy the first-order conditions

$$\frac{\partial u}{\partial x_1} - \lambda p_1 = 0$$

$$\frac{\partial u}{\partial x_2} - \lambda p_2 = 0$$

$$p_1 x_1 + p_2 x_2 - y = 0,$$

where λ is a constant. For the given utility function, these equations define the system

$$\phi^1(x_1, x_2, \lambda) = 0$$
$$\phi^2(x_1, x_2, \lambda) = 0$$
$$\phi^3(x_1, x_2, \lambda) = 0$$

by

$$\frac{a_1}{x_1} - \lambda p_1 = 0$$

$$\frac{a_2}{x_2} - \lambda p_2 = 0$$

$$p_1 x_1 + p_2 x_2 - y = 0.$$

Demand functions for x_1 and x_2 can be obtained, using the Implicit Function Theorem, if the Jacobian of $\phi = (\phi^1, \phi^2, \phi^3)^T$ is nonsingular. This will be the case provided the determinant of the Jacobian of ϕ is nonzero. The problem reduces to computing $\det J(\phi)$.

$$J(\phi) = \begin{bmatrix} \dfrac{-a_1}{x_1^2} & 0 & -p_1 \\ 0 & \dfrac{-a_2}{x_2^2} & -p_2 \\ p_1 & p_2 & 0 \end{bmatrix}.$$

The familiar rules for calculating determinants of 3×3 matrices yield

$$\det[J(\phi)] = -\left(\frac{p_1^2 a_2}{x_2^2} + \frac{p_2^2 a_1}{x_1^2} \right).$$

The Jacobian, of course, is evaluated at the equilibrium values of x_1 and x_2. It is easy to verify, by substitution in the first-order conditions, that the equilibrium quantities are given by

$$\bar{x}_1 = \frac{a_1 y}{p_1} \quad \text{and} \quad \bar{x}_2 = \frac{a_2 y}{p_2}.$$

Thus, the determinant of $J(\phi)$, at the equilibrium, is

$$\det[J(\phi(x))] = -\frac{p_1^2 p_2^2}{y^2}\left(\frac{1}{a_1} + \frac{1}{a_2} \right).$$

Consequently, the determinant is not zero, in a neighborhood of equilibrium, as long as $p_1 > 0$, $p_2 > 0$, and y is bounded. These restrictions on prices and income guarantee the existence of demand functions

$$x_1 = D_1(p_1, p_2, y) \quad \text{and} \quad x_2 = D_2(p_1, p_2, y).$$

Eigenvalues and eigenvectors

Linear transformations of R^n to R^n are represented by $n \times n$ matrices. Given such a transformation, the use of all different bases for R^n gives a class, a similarity class, of matrices. Is there one matrix in that class that can be taken as a canonical representation of the transformation? Structurally, the simplest $n \times n$ matrix has the form

$$D = \begin{bmatrix} \lambda_1 & & \\ & \lambda_2 & 0 \\ & & \ddots \\ & 0 & & \lambda_n \end{bmatrix},$$

where the n numbers $\lambda_1, \ldots, \lambda_n$ are arrayed down the diagonal, and zeros appear everywhere else. D is called a *diagonal matrix*.

As a transformation, the first standard basis vector $(1, 0, \ldots, 0)^T$ gets sent, by D, to $(\lambda_1, 0, \ldots, 0)^T$, and so on. Thus, the action of D on $x \in R^n$ is particularly nice: All standard basis vectors in R^n, say e^i, get stretched by a factor λ_i, but they do not change their angular positions. Alternatively, if $\lambda_i \neq 0$, A represents a change of basis in R^n that does not rotate the standard basis vectors. The usual axes are preserved.

Can complicated matrices be represented by such simple ones? Given a linear transformation $L: R^n \to R^n$ that, in some basis, has the $n \times n$ matrix representation

$$A = \begin{bmatrix} a_{11} & a_{12} & \cdots & a_{1n} \\ a_{21} & a_{22} & \cdots & a_{2n} \\ \vdots & & & \vdots \\ a_{n1} & a_{n2} & \cdots & a_{nn} \end{bmatrix},$$

is there some other basis, with basis vectors $(b^1, b^2, \ldots, b^n)$, in which L has the diagonal matrix representation

$$D = \begin{bmatrix} \lambda_1 & & \\ & \lambda_2 & 0 \\ & & \ddots \\ & 0 & & \lambda_n \end{bmatrix} ?$$

Alternatively, does there exist a nonsingular $n \times n$ matrix B such that

$$B^{-1}AB = D,$$

where D is a diagonal matrix?

Consider the case $L: R^2 \to R^2$ and a given matrix

$$A = \begin{bmatrix} 4 & 2 \\ -5 & -3 \end{bmatrix}.$$

The trace and the determinant are invariants, and trace $A = 1$ and determinant $A = -2$. Is there a diagonal matrix D with $\lambda_1 + \lambda_2 = 1$ and $\lambda_1 \lambda_2 = -2$? Certainly, $\lambda_2 = -2/\lambda_1$, so that $\lambda_1 + (-2/\lambda_1) = 1$ or $\lambda_1^2 - \lambda_1 - 2 = 0$. Hence,

$\lambda_1 = 2$ or $\lambda_1 = -1$. But the symmetry of λ_1 and λ_2 yields $\lambda_1 = 2$ and $\lambda_2 = -1$, or $\lambda_1 = -1$ and $\lambda_2 = 2$. Thus,

$$D = \begin{bmatrix} 2 & 0 \\ 0 & -1 \end{bmatrix}$$

represents the same linear transformation that A does.

In what basis of R^2 does L have the representation D? It is necessary to find the matrix B such that

$$B^{-1} \begin{bmatrix} 4 & 2 \\ -5 & -3 \end{bmatrix} B = \begin{bmatrix} 2 & 0 \\ 0 & -1 \end{bmatrix}.$$

If

$$B = \begin{bmatrix} b_1 & b_2 \\ b_3 & b_4 \end{bmatrix},$$

then

$$B^{-1} = \frac{1}{b_1 b_4 - b_2 b_3} \begin{bmatrix} +b_4 & -b_2 \\ -b_3 & +b_1 \end{bmatrix}.$$

Thus,

$$\begin{bmatrix} b_4 & -b_2 \\ -b_3 & b_1 \end{bmatrix} \begin{bmatrix} 4 & 2 \\ -5 & -3 \end{bmatrix} \begin{bmatrix} b_1 & b_2 \\ b_3 & b_4 \end{bmatrix} = [b_1 b_4 - b_2 b_3] \begin{bmatrix} 2 & 0 \\ 0 & -1 \end{bmatrix}.$$

This yields

$$\begin{bmatrix} 4b_4 + 5b_2 & 2b_4 + 3b_2 \\ -4b_3 - 5b_1 & -2b_3 - 3b_1 \end{bmatrix} \begin{bmatrix} b_1 & b_2 \\ b_3 & b_4 \end{bmatrix} = \begin{bmatrix} 2b_1 b_4 - 2b_2 b_3 & 0 \\ 0 & b_2 b_3 - b_1 b_4 \end{bmatrix}.$$

Continuing the multiplication produces

$$\begin{bmatrix} 4b_4 b_1 + 5b_2 b_1 + 2b_4 b_3 + 3b_2 b_3 & 4b_4 b_2 + 5b_2 b_2 + 2b_4 b_4 + 3b_2 b_4 \\ -4b_3 b_1 - 5b_1 b_1 - 2b_3 b_3 - 3b_1 b_3 & -4b_3 b_2 - 5b_1 b_2 - 2b_3 b_4 - 3b_1 b_4 \end{bmatrix}$$

$$= \begin{bmatrix} 2b_1 b_4 - 2b_2 b_3 & 0 \\ 0 & b_2 b_3 - b_1 b_4 \end{bmatrix}.$$

The equality of these two matrices entails that their entries are equal. This produces four equations in the unknowns b_1, b_2, b_3, b_4:

$$4b_4 b_1 + 5b_2 b_1 + 2b_4 b_3 + 3b_2 b_3 = 2b_1 b_4 - 2b_2 b_3$$
$$-4b_3 b_1 - 5b_1 b_1 - 2b_3 b_3 - 3b_1 b_3 = 0$$
$$4b_4 b_2 + 5b_2 b_2 + 2b_4 b_4 + 3b_2 b_4 = 0$$
$$-4b_3 b_2 - 5b_1 b_2 - 2b_3 b_4 - 3b_1 b_4 = b_2 b_3 - b_1 b_4.$$

Routine computations show that, when b_1 is set equal to 1, then $\det B \neq 0$ entails

$$B = \begin{bmatrix} 1 & -\frac{2}{5} \\ -1 & 1 \end{bmatrix} \quad \text{and} \quad B^{-1} = \frac{5}{3}\begin{bmatrix} 1 & \frac{2}{5} \\ 1 & 1 \end{bmatrix}.$$

The basis $\{b^1, b^2\}$, in which A has the diagonal form D, is

$$b^1 = \begin{bmatrix} 1 \\ -1 \end{bmatrix} \quad \text{and} \quad b^2 = \begin{bmatrix} -\frac{2}{5} \\ 1 \end{bmatrix}.$$

Put another way, the vectors b^1 and b^2 have the property that if they are the basis for R^2, then $L(x) = \lambda x$, where λ_1 or λ_2 can be taken as λ. Alternatively,

(1) $Ax = \lambda x$

has the solution $x = b^1$ or b^2 when $\lambda = \lambda_1$ or $\lambda = \lambda_2$.

Some terminology will be useful. The number λ in equation (1) is an *eigenvalue* of the matrix A. The vector that is associated with the ith eigenvalue, the vector that solves equation (1) given $\lambda = \lambda_i$, is the *eigenvector* associated with the eigenvalue λ_i. The procedure just outlined generalizes from $n = 2$ to arbitrary square matrices.

Given an $n \times n$ matrix A, what are its eigenvalues? Suppose that for some change of basis, A has a diagonal representation. Thus, A is similar to the matrix λI_n if λ is an eigenvalue, and

$$I_n = \begin{bmatrix} 1 & & & \\ & 1 & & 0 \\ & & \ddots & \\ & 0 & & 1 \end{bmatrix},$$

the $n \times n$ identity matrix.

Consider the matrix $A - \lambda I_n$. Because A and λI_n are similar, if A sends x to y, then so does λI_n. Thus $A - \lambda I_n$ sends x to the zero vector for any vector x. That is, if λ is an eigenvalue of A, and x is any n-vector,

$$(A - \lambda I_n)x = 0.$$

Hence, the kernel of $(A - \lambda I_n)$ has dimension at least equal to 1, and thus rank $(A - \lambda I_n) < n$, if λ is an eigenvalue of A. Equivalently, $A - \lambda I_n$ is singular, and thus

$$\det(A - \lambda I_n) = 0.$$

Because A and I_n are known matrices, the solution for this equation, for the variable λ, determines the eigenvalues of A.

Consider again the 2×2 matrix $A = \begin{bmatrix} 4 & 2 \\ -5 & -3 \end{bmatrix}$. Then

$$\det(A - \lambda I_n) = \det\left[\begin{bmatrix} 4 & 2 \\ -5 & -3 \end{bmatrix} - \lambda\begin{bmatrix} 1 & 0 \\ 0 & 1 \end{bmatrix}\right]$$

$$= \det\begin{bmatrix} 4-\lambda & 2 \\ -5 & -3-\lambda \end{bmatrix}.$$

Thus, $\det(A - \lambda I_n) = (4-\lambda)(-3-\lambda) - (2)(-5) = \lambda^2 - \lambda - 2$. When $\lambda = 2$ or $\lambda = -1$, then $\det(A - \lambda I_n) = 0$. The roots, λ, of the polynomial equation $\det(A - \lambda I_n) = 0$ are the eigenvalues of A. This polynomial is called the *characteristic polynomial* of A.

In general, if A is an $n \times n$ matrix, the equation $\det(A - \lambda I_n) = 0$ is a polynomial of degree n in λ. The "fundamental theorem of algebra"[3] ensures that such a polynomial has exactly n roots. Thus, an $n \times n$ matrix A has exactly n eigenvalues.

There is one major difficulty. Some of the roots of a polynomial of degree n may not turn out to be real numbers. For example, if $A = \begin{bmatrix} 2 & 1 \\ -5 & -2 \end{bmatrix}$, then $\det(A - \lambda I_2) = \det\begin{bmatrix} 2-\lambda & 1 \\ -5 & -2-\lambda \end{bmatrix} = \lambda^2 + 1$. The roots of $\lambda^2 + 1 = 0$ are the imaginary numbers i and $-i$, where $i = \sqrt{-1}$. In this case, the matrix $D = \begin{bmatrix} i & 0 \\ 0 & -i \end{bmatrix}$ represents L. This diagonalization of $\begin{bmatrix} 2 & 1 \\ -5 & -2 \end{bmatrix}$ is rather strange, because A has only real numbers for entries, whereas its diagonalization has imaginary numbers as entries.

What kinds of matrices are guaranteed to have only real eigenvalues? It turns out that *symmetric matrices have real eigenvalues*, although some nonsymmetric matrices, recall $A = \begin{bmatrix} 4 & 2 \\ -5 & -3 \end{bmatrix}$, have real eigenvalues also. In any event, it is frequently the case that matrices used in economic analysis are symmetric. Those matrices have real eigenvalues. The meaning and use of complex or imaginary eigenvalues will be explored later.

EXAMPLE

Consider a utility function $U: R^n \to R$. Certain economic optimization problems involve the gradient of U, which is a linear mapping from R^n to R. The kind of optimum (maximum or minimum) found will depend on whether or not the second

---

[3] It is often noted that this theorem is neither fundamental nor a theorem of algebra. See Appendix II of Hirsch and Smale's *Differential Equations*.

derivative, the Hessian, has certain properties. The Hessian is an $n \times n$ matrix of second-order partial derivatives given by

$$H(U) = \begin{bmatrix} \dfrac{\partial^2 u}{\partial x_1^2} & \dfrac{\partial^2 u}{\partial x_1 \partial x_2} & \cdots & \dfrac{\partial^2 u}{\partial x_1 \partial x_n} \\ \vdots & & & \\ \dfrac{\partial^2 u}{\partial x_n \partial x_1} & & \cdots & \dfrac{\partial^2 u}{\partial x_n^2} \end{bmatrix}.$$

The Hessian is symmetric, because $\partial^2 u / \partial x_i \partial x_j = \partial^2 u / \partial x_j \partial x_i$. This is a general result for $f: R^n \to R$. Thus, the fact that f is twice continuously differentiable allows computing second partial derivatives in any order.

EXAMPLE

Consider the system of demand functions

$$q^1 = D^1(p_1, \ldots, p_n)$$
$$q^2 = D^2(p_1, \ldots, p_n)$$
$$\vdots$$
$$q^n = D^n(p_1, \ldots, p_n).$$

The Jacobian of this system is the matrix

$$\begin{bmatrix} \dfrac{\partial q_1}{\partial p_1} & \dfrac{\partial q_1}{\partial p_2} & \cdots & \dfrac{\partial q_1}{\partial p_n} \\ \vdots & & & \\ \dfrac{\partial q_n}{\partial p_1} & \dfrac{\partial q_n}{\partial p_2} & \cdots & \dfrac{\partial q_n}{\partial p_n} \end{bmatrix}.$$

It is well known from the Slutsky equation that each term such as $\partial q_i / \partial p_j$ is actually the sum of a substitution effect (i.e., a change in quantity demanded along an indifference curve) and an income effect (i.e., a change in quantity measured along parallel indifference curves). Separating out the substitution terms yields

$$\begin{bmatrix} \dfrac{\partial q_1}{\partial p_1}\bigg|_{u=\text{const}} & \cdots & \dfrac{\partial q_1}{\partial p_n}\bigg|_{u=\text{const}} \\ \vdots & & \\ \dfrac{\partial q_n}{\partial p_1}\bigg|_{u=\text{const}} & \cdots & \dfrac{\partial q_n}{\partial p_n}\bigg|_{u=\text{const}} \end{bmatrix}$$

when the partial derivatives are evaluated along a given indifference curve. One of the major results in neoclassical demand theory is that this matrix of substitution effects is symmetric.

Eigenvalues are important. The use of eigenvalues to investigate linear transformations is based on the fact that the eigenvalues of an $n \times n$ matrix A are invariants. That is, similar matrices have the same eigenvalues. To see this, suppose A and $\hat{A}$ are similar matrices. Now consider the diagonalization of A. If A is diagonalizable, there exists a nonsingular B such that

$$B^{-1}AB = D.$$

Because D is diagonal, let the entries on the main diagonal of D be denoted λ_i. Then

$$\begin{bmatrix} \lambda_1 & & \\ & \ddots & 0 \\ 0 & & \lambda_n \end{bmatrix} - \lambda \begin{bmatrix} 1 & & \\ & 1 & 0 \\ 0 & & \ddots \\ & & & 1 \end{bmatrix}$$

is the matrix

$$D - \lambda I_n.$$

When $\lambda = \lambda_i$, $D - \lambda I_n$ is singular; so the entries of a diagonal matrix D are exactly the eigenvalues of the matrix D. But similar matrices, if diagonalizable, have the same diagonalization. To see this, suppose A and $\hat{A}$ are similar. Then there is a nonsingular $n \times n$ matrix C such that

$$C^{-1}\hat{A}C = A.$$

Multiplying this equation on the left by B^{-1} and on the right by B yields

$$B^{-1}C^{-1}\hat{A}CB = B^{-1}AB.$$

Because $B^{-1}C^{-1} = (CB)^{-1}$, and CB is just a nonsingular $n \times n$ matrix,

$$(CB)^{-1}\hat{A}(CB) = D.$$

Thus, $\hat{A}$ has the same diagonalization as A. Because the diagonalization of A exhibits the eigenvalues of A, the similar matrices $\hat{A}$ and A have the same eigenvalues.

Visualizing eigenvectors

It was shown earlier that the matrix $A = \begin{bmatrix} 4 & 2 \\ -5 & -3 \end{bmatrix}$ had the eigenvalues 2 and -1 and the diagonal form $\begin{bmatrix} 2 & 0 \\ 0 & -1 \end{bmatrix}$. The eigenvector x associated with the eigenvalue λ is the solution to $Ax = \lambda x$. If $\lambda = 2$, this equation is

$$\begin{bmatrix} 4 & 2 \\ -5 & -3 \end{bmatrix}\begin{bmatrix} x_1 \\ x_2 \end{bmatrix} = 2\begin{bmatrix} x_1 \\ x_2 \end{bmatrix},$$

or

$$4x_1 + 2x_2 = 2x_1; \; -5x_1 - 3x_2 = 2x_2.$$

This pair of equation yields $x_1 = -x_2$. For the other eigenvector, associated with -1, $x_1 = -\frac{2}{5}x_2$. If $x_2 = 1$, then the eigenvectors have the form $x^1 = (-1, 1)^T$ and $x^2 = (-\frac{2}{5}, 1)^T$.

Consider what A does, as a transformation, to the eigenvectors:

$$\begin{bmatrix} 4 & 2 \\ -5 & -3 \end{bmatrix}\begin{bmatrix} -1 \\ 1 \end{bmatrix} = \begin{bmatrix} -2 \\ 2 \end{bmatrix}$$

$$\begin{bmatrix} 4 & 2 \\ -5 & -3 \end{bmatrix}\begin{bmatrix} -\frac{2}{5} \\ 1 \end{bmatrix} = \begin{bmatrix} \frac{2}{5} \\ -1 \end{bmatrix}$$

Thinking of A as a transformation of R^2, A sends the eigenvectors x^1 and x^2 to the vectors Ax^1 and Ax^2. Look at Figure 7.3. In pictures, A sends each of the vectors x^1 and x^2 to another vector on the same line as x^1 and x^2. Put another way, A sends an eigenvector to a scalar multiple of itself.

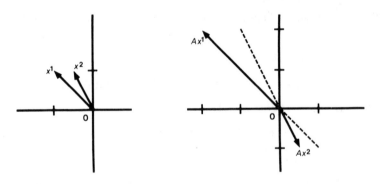

FIGURE 7.3

There is a general result here that is worth developing. Consider the plane R^2. Any linear transformation of R^2 to R^2, and any 2×2 matrix representing that transformation, certainly sends the origin to the origin and maps lines to lines. Thus, a 2×2 matrix A deforms R^2 into R^2, but not haphazardly. It cannot, for example, squoosh the top half plane to the left and the bottom half plane to the right, because a line then gets bent by the squoosh, and so on.

What kinds of deformations are allowed? Certainly a simple rotation of R^2 around the origin is allowed. Also allowed is a uniform stretching of the plane, sort of like grabbing it from the left and evenly squeezing it while forcing stuff to the right. Inversions are also allowed, such as flipping the plane around a line in the plane. Thus, an eigenvector has a geometric interpretation. It is simply a vector on a line that remains the same under the linear transformation.

For a 2×2 matrix A, there are two cases. Because the characteristic polynomial is of degree 2, either there are two real roots or there is a pair of complex roots. In the former case, there are two real eigenvalues. In the latter case, there are two complex eigenvalues. If the eigenvalues are real and distinct, the eigenvectors will be distinct (noncoincident) lines. If the real eigenvalues of A are not distinct, the matrix that diagonalizes A involves eigenvectors as columns. Those columns are dependent; so the diagonalizing matrix is singular.

Thus, suppose that the eigenvalues of A are distinct, and further suppose that the matrix A is symmetric. Then the eigenvectors are associated with real eigenvalues, and the eigenvectors lie along lines that are fixed under the transformation of space associated with A. This is why eigenvectors are important. For if the eigenvectors are chosen as the basis vectors, then these basis vectors are transformed, by A, only by a stretching, a scalar multiplication. Which scalar? The real eigenvalue associated with that eigenvector. Thus, given a linear transformation $L: R^2 \to R^2$, there are two natural bases to represent L in the form of a 2×2 matrix. Choosing the standard basis, the columns of A represent the images of $(1,0)^T$ and $(0,1)^T$ under L. Alternatively, choosing the basis to be the two eigenvectors associated with the two distinct eigenvalues of A, A is represented as the diagonal matrix

$$\begin{bmatrix} \lambda_1 & 0 \\ 0 & \lambda_2 \end{bmatrix}.$$

Picturing the determinant

Like eigenvectors, the determinant has a geometric interpretation. Recall that for $A = \begin{bmatrix} a & b \\ c & d \end{bmatrix}$, where A represents $L: R^2 \to R^2$, the determinant of A, written $\det A$, equals $ad - bc$. But $(a, c)^T$ and $(b, d)^T$ are the images of the standard basis vectors. Consider Figure 7.4. What is the area of the parallelogram determined by the sides (a, c) and (b, d)? The area is the base times the height. The height is certainly d. What is the base? Extend the line from $(a+b, c+d)$ through (a, c) to the x_1 axis to get $(x_1, 0)$; x_1 is the length of the base. To find x_1, note that it is on the constructed line, so that the slopes of the two parts separated by (a, c) are equal. Thus,

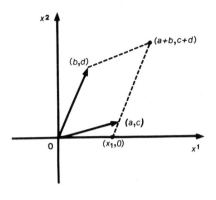

FIGURE 7.4

$$\frac{(d + c) - c}{(a + b) - a} = \frac{c - 0}{a - x_1}.$$

Hence, $d(a - x_1) = cb$; so $dx_1 = ad - bc$. Hence, $x_1 = (ad - bc)/d$. Thus, the area of the parallelogram is given by $d \cdot [(ad - bc)/d] = ad - bc$. The determinant of A is the area of the parallelogram spanned by the images of the standard basis vectors under A.

   This visualization suggests a further result. If $A = \begin{bmatrix} 4 & 2 \\ -5 & -3 \end{bmatrix}$, the determinant is equal to -2. How can an area be negative? Consider Figure 7.5. Certainly $(1, 0)^T \rightarrow (4, -5)^T$ and $(0, 1)^T \rightarrow (2, -3)^T$ under A. However, it is necessary to consider the orientation of the basis. If the second basis vector is found at an angle of less than $180°$ when proceeding counterclockwise from the first basis vector, the basis is said to have the usual orientation. Alternatively, the basis is a *positively oriented* set of basis vectors. If they are not so oriented, they are a *negatively oriented* set of basis vectors.

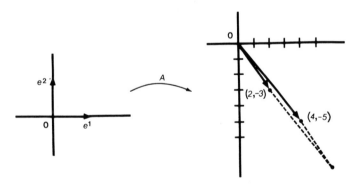

FIGURE 7.5

Now consider the columns of A, in order. They are the images of the positively oriented standard basis vectors. What is the orientation of this set of images? Going from $(4, -5)^T$ to $(2, -3)^T$ counterclockwise sweeps out an angle greater than $180°$. This pair of vectors, as a basis of R^2, has a negative orientation.

If the determinant of a matrix A is positive, then the orientation of the column vectors of A is positive. If $\det A < 0$, the column vectors (in order) form a negatively oriented set of basis vectors. Certainly if $\det A < 0$ for the 2×2 matrix A, switching the columns of A will yield a positively oriented pair of basis vectors. This helps to interpret the well-known property of determinants that interchanging adjacent columns changes the sign of the determinant.

One further point. Given a matrix A, if it is diagonalizable, then A is similar to the diagonal matrix $D = \begin{bmatrix} \lambda_1 & 0 \\ 0 & \lambda_2 \end{bmatrix}$, where λ_1, λ_2 are the eigenvalues of A. But similar matrices have the same determinant. The determinant of D is simply $\lambda_1 \lambda_2$, the product of the eigenvalues. Geometrically, it is just the area of the rectangle spanned by the column vectors $(\lambda_1, 0)$ and $(0, \lambda_2)$ along the x_1 and x_2 axes. The sign of the determinant is found by placing a plus or minus sign in front of the area by the orientation argument.

Certainly the trace of A equals the trace of D, because the trace is an invariant. But the trace of D equals $\lambda_1 + \lambda_2$. Thus, there is an especially simple way to calculate the eigenvalues of any 2×2 matrix A. If λ_1 and λ_2 are the eigenvalues, $\lambda_1 + \lambda_2 = \operatorname{trace} A$, and $\lambda_1 \lambda_2 = \det A$.

If $A = \begin{bmatrix} 1 & -3 \\ -3 & 4 \end{bmatrix}$, then $\operatorname{trace} A = 5$, and $\det A = -5$. Thus, $\lambda_1 + \lambda_2 = 5$, and $\lambda_1 \lambda_2 = -5$. Thus, $\lambda_2 = 5 - \lambda_1$; so $\lambda_1(5 - \lambda_1) = -5$, or $\lambda_1^2 - 5\lambda_1 - 5 = 0$. Thus,

$$\lambda_1 = \frac{5 \pm \sqrt{25 + 20}}{2}.$$

So

$$\lambda_1 = \frac{5 \pm \sqrt{45}}{2},$$

or

$$\lambda_1 = \frac{5 \pm 3\sqrt{5}}{2}.$$

Because of the symmetry of λ_1 and λ_2, $\lambda_1 = (5 + 3\sqrt{5})/2$, and $\lambda_2 = (5 - 3\sqrt{5})/2$.

EXAMPLE[4]

Suppose an economy uses n goods to produce those same n goods; so all means of production are themselves produced. Define the $n \times n$ matrix A as the input-output matrix, where the entry a_{ij} denotes the amount of input i needed to produce one unit of output j. Thus, column j of the matrix describes the input requirements, per unit of output, in the jth industry.

Suppose $x = (x_1, \ldots, x_n)^T$ denotes the gross output levels, where x_i is the gross output of good i. Then the vector Ax represents inputs required to produce gross output x. Hence, $x - Ax$ or $(I - A)x$ represents net output levels corresponding to x.

"A prime concern in input-output analysis is the question of whether or not a particular set of final demands can be satisfied. In other words, in what circumstances is the following 'weak solubility' condition satisfied?
(1) Weak Solubility: $(I - A)x \geq c$ has a solution $x \geq 0$ for *some* set of final demands $c \geq 0$.

It is also of interest to determine the conditions under which any set of final demands could be satisfied.
(2) Strong Solubility: $(I - A)x = c$ has a solution $x \geq 0$ for *any* $c \geq 0$.

A related issue involves the question of whether or not there exist prices at which all industries could operate profitably.
(3) Profitability: $p(I - A) > 0$ has a solution $p > 0$."
(pp. 115–16).

Graham showed that the appearance of a matrix like $I - A$, which suggests the connection with eigenvalues of A, is not accidental. Specifically, he demonstrated the geometric sense of the classical result: The statement "the largest eigenvalue of A is less than one" is equivalent to 1) or 2) or 3). That is, the solution to important input-output problems depends crucially on the size of the largest eigenvalue of the input-output matrix.

FURTHER READING

Lang's *Second Course in Calculus* and Hirsch and Smale's *Differential Equations, Dynamical Systems, and Linear Algebra* are worth consulting. There are many exercises, to increase computational facility, provided by

---

[4] This example is taken from "A Geometrical Exposition of Input-Output Analysis" by my colleague Dan Graham. The page reference is to quoted material from this paper.

Mills in his elementary *Introduction to Linear Algebra for Social Scientists.*
See also the math review chapters in Lancaster's *Mathematical Economics*
and Chapter 1 of Wilf's *Mathematics for the Physical Sciences.*

EXERCISES

7.1 Show (by means of a 2×2 example) that if A, B, and C are square
matrices, $AB = AC$ does not entail $B = C$.

7.2 Discuss the eigenvalues and eigenvectors of

$$A = \begin{bmatrix} 3 & 0 \\ 0 & 0 \end{bmatrix}$$

and

$$B = \begin{bmatrix} 3 & -1 \\ 1 & 0 \end{bmatrix}.$$

Interpret, geometrically, the associated linear transformations of
$R^2 \to R^2$.

7.3 An $n \times n$ matrix A is called nilpotent if there is some integer s such
that $A^s = 0$. Any matrix is called strictly triangular if all the entries on or
above the main diagonal are zero. Show that any strictly triangular
matrix is nilpotent.

CHAPTER 8

Stability of linear dynamic systems

*But an actual solution, when defined
changes take place continually over a
period, would involve complicated
analysis, and little progress has as yet
been made in such an investigation.*
                                    A. L. Bowley (1924)

Economic models frequently analyze rates of change of economic variables. In partial-equilibrium analysis the rate of change of the market price for commodity x is a function of excess demand (i.e., the demand quantity minus the supply quantity) for that commodity. Write the rate of change of price as dp/dt or as $\dot{p}$. The quantity demanded, q^D, is a function of price, as is the quantity supplied. This produces

$$\dot{p} = f(D(p) - S(p)).$$

Suppose f is the identity function. Then the model becomes

$$\dot{p} = D(p) - S(p).$$

If $D(p) - S(p)$ is positive, $\dot{p}$ is positive. Thus, p is increasing, because a variable that has a positive rate of change over time is increasing. If $D(p) - S(p)$ is negative, p is decreasing. This equation is the *Walrasian tatonnement* price adjustment mechanism.

Suppose $\bar{p}$ is the equilibrium price; so $D(\bar{p}) = S(\bar{p})$. The derivative is used to find the affine map that best approximates $D(p) - S(p)$ near $p = \bar{p}$. Define the linear map $L : R \to R$ by $[D'(\bar{p}) - S'(\bar{p})]p$. Thus, $A(p) = [D'(\bar{p}) - S'(\bar{p})](p - \bar{p})$ approximates $D(p) - S(p)$ near $\bar{p}$. If $\hat{p} = p - \bar{p}$, then $\hat{p}$ measures the deviation of price from the equilibrium price. Notice that $\dot{\hat{p}} = d\hat{p}/dt = dp/dt = \dot{p}$. Hence, the affine map on the right-hand side of

$$\dot{p} = [D'(\bar{p}) - S'(\bar{p})](p - \bar{p})$$

is identical with the linear map on the right-hand side of

$$\dot{\hat{p}} = [D'(\bar{p}) - S'(\bar{p})]\hat{p}.$$

108

Reinterpreting $\hat{p}$ as "price," let

(t) $\dot{p} = [D'(\bar{p}) - S'(\bar{p})]p,$

where $p=0$ is the equilibrium (because p is "really" $\hat{p}$, and $\dot{p}=0$ if and only if $p-\bar{p}=0$; so $p=\bar{p}$). Equation (t) is the usual linear form of the tatonnement. Because $[D'(\bar{p}) - S'(\bar{p})]$ is just a constant, a real number, equation (t) is an equation of the form

(1) $\dot{x} = ax,$ for $a \in R.$

This equation hides the fact that x is a function of time. If time is modeled by the real-number line, a solution of equation (1) is a function from R to R whose graph is pictured (for arbitrary $x(t)$) in Figure 8.1. In other words, a solution of equation (1) is a differentiable function x such that $dx/dt(t)$ equals $ax(t)$. Assume that there is a solution to this equation. With this assumption, how is it solved? Write

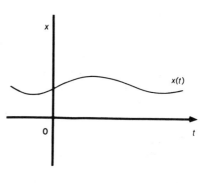

FIGURE 8.1

$$\frac{dx}{dt} = ax.$$

Now cross-multiply the dt and divide by x (somehow!) to get

$$\frac{dx}{x} = a\,dt.$$

Taking indefinite integrals of both sides yields

$$\int \frac{dx}{x} = \int a\,dt.$$

So

$$\log x = at + C,$$

where C is the constant of integration. Now take exponentials of both sides to get

$$\exp(\log x) = \exp(at + C)$$

or

$$x = e^{at+C}$$

or

$$x = e^{at} \cdot e^C.$$

Certainly, this x is a function of t, yielding

$$x(t) = e^C e^{at}.$$

If $t=0$, $x(0) = e^C$; so the solution is

$$x(t) = x(0)e^{at}.$$

A "solution" has been produced by an illegal operation, but is it the correct solution anyway? Does $x(t) = x(0)e^{at}$ solve $\dot{x} = ax$? Try to plug in. Compute $d/dt(x(0)e^{at})$ to get $a \cdot x(0)e^{at} = ax(t)$. Thus,

$$\dot{x}(t) = ax(t),$$

and so the solution of equation (1) is indeed $x(t) = x(0)e^{at}$.

What does the solution of $\dot{x} = ax$ look like? Consider Figure 8.2. Given $x(0) = \bar{x}$, the graph of $\bar{x}e^{at}$ has a different shape depending on whether $a \gtreqless 0$. Consider again the linearized Walrasian adjustment mechanism

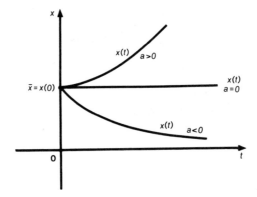

FIGURE 8.2

(t) $\dot{p} = [D'(\bar{p}) - S'(\bar{p})]p.$

Recall that $p=0$ for all t, or $p(t)=0$, is the equilibrium. If, at time $t=0$, $p(0) > 0$, will this adjustment rule force the market price close to equilibrium eventually? This is equivalent to asking whether or not

$$\lim_{t \to \infty} |(p(t) - 0)| = 0.$$

Because the solution of (t) is $p(t) = p(0) \exp[D'(\bar{p}) - S'(\bar{p})] t$, the question is whether or not

$$\lim_{t \to \infty} |p(0)| |\exp[D'(\bar{p}) - S'(\bar{p})] t| = 0.$$

Because $\lim_{x \to \infty} \exp(-x) = 0$, the solution of equation (t) aproaches zero eventually if $[D'(\bar{p}) - S'(\bar{p})] < 0$ (just consider the branch $a < 0$ in Figure 8.2). But $D'(\bar{p}) - S'(\bar{p}) < 0$ means that, at the equilibrium $\bar{p}$, the slope of the demand curve is less than the slope of the supply curve. In general, given the equation

(1) $\dot{x} = ax,$

the equilibrium $x = 0$ is asymptotically stable if, for any solution $x(t)$, $\lim_{t \to \infty} |x(t)| = 0$. The result is immediate that the equilibrium of equation (1) is asymptotically stable if and only if $a < 0$.

Multiple markets

Instead of a single market, consider a set of n markets. In this case the excess demand for commodity i is a function not only of the price of commodity i but of all other prices as well. Thus, if $q_i = E^i(p_1, p_2, \ldots, p_n)$ is the function that expresses the excess-demand quantity for good i,

(2) $\dot{p}_i = E^i(p_1, p_2, \ldots, p_n)$ for $i = 1, 2, \ldots, n.$

As a system, equation (2) can be written

$$\dot{p}_1 = E^1(p_1, p_2, \ldots, p_n)$$
$$\dot{p}_2 = E^2(p_1, p_2, \ldots, p_n)$$
$$\vdots$$
$$\dot{p}_n = E^n(p_1, p_2, \ldots, p_n).$$

Note that the right side of this system defines a function $E : R^n \to R^n$ by $E = (E^1, E^2, \ldots, E^n)^T$. Let $p_1 = p_2 = \cdots = p_n = 0$ be the equilibrium price by thinking of p as measuring deviations from equilibrium. If E is differentiable at $p = (p_1, p_2, \ldots, p_n)^T = 0$, then E can be approximated near $p = 0$ by a linear mapping from R^n to R^n.

This linear map is represented, in the standard basis of R^n, by the Jacobian of E at $p = 0$; this, recall, is the $n \times n$ matrix whose i, jth entry is $\partial E_i / \partial p_j$. This produces the linear system

$$\dot{p} = [J(E)]_{p=0}\,p,$$

where p is the column n-vector

$$\begin{bmatrix} p_1 \\ p_2 \\ \vdots \\ p_n \end{bmatrix},$$

$\dot{p}$ is the column n-vector

$$\begin{bmatrix} \dot{p}_1 \\ \dot{p}_2 \\ \vdots \\ \dot{p}_n \end{bmatrix},$$

and $[J(E)]_{p=0}$ is the $n \times n$ matrix

$$\begin{bmatrix} \dfrac{\partial E_1}{\partial p_1} & \dfrac{\partial E_1}{\partial p_2} & \cdots & \dfrac{\partial E_1}{\partial p_n} \\ \vdots & & & \\ \dfrac{\partial E_n}{\partial p_1} & \dfrac{\partial E_n}{\partial p_2} & \cdots & \dfrac{\partial E_n}{\partial p_n} \end{bmatrix}_{p=0}.$$

Writing the linear system out in full yields

$$\dot{p}_1 = \frac{\partial E_1}{\partial p_1}\,p_1 + \cdots + \frac{\partial E_1}{\partial p_n}\,p_n$$

$$\dot{p}_2 = \frac{\partial E_2}{\partial p_1}\,p_1 + \cdots + \frac{\partial E_2}{\partial p_n}\,p_n$$

$$\vdots \qquad\qquad\qquad \vdots$$

$$\dot{p}_n = \frac{\partial E_n}{\partial p_1}\,p_1 + \cdots + \frac{\partial E_n}{\partial p_n}\,p_n.$$

In general, then, consider systems of the form

(3) $\dot{x} = Ax,$

where $\dot{x}$ and x are column n-vectors and A is an $n \times n$ matrix of real numbers. As before, $x(t) = 0$ is the equilibrium of this system. [Because $\dot{x}(t) = 0$, clearly $\dot{x}(t) = Ax(t)$, and so $x(t) = 0$ is an unchanging function of t.]

The interesting question is whether any solution of the system $\dot{x} = Ax$ eventually gets close to $x = 0$, the equilibrium. If this happens, then no matter what $x(0)$ is, $x(t)$ gets to equilibrium eventually. Formally, a solution $x(t)$ of $\dot{x}=Ax$ is asymptotically stable if $\lim_{t\to\infty}\|x(t)\|=0$. Of course, $x(t)$ is a function from R^n to R^n; it is of the form $x(t)=(x_1(t),x_2(t),\ldots,x_n(t))^T$, where $x(t)$ is a column n-vector of real numbers for any $t\in R$.

The solution of equation (3) depends on the solution for $\dot{x}=ax$. Suppose A were in fact a diagonal matrix of the form

$$\begin{bmatrix} \lambda_1 & & & 0 \\ & \lambda_2 & & \\ & & \ddots & \\ 0 & & & \lambda_n \end{bmatrix}.$$

Then the system $\dot{x}=Ax$ would actually be

$$\dot{x}_1 = \lambda_1 x_1$$
$$\dot{x}_2 = \lambda_2 x_2$$
$$\vdots$$
$$\dot{x}_n = \lambda_n x_n.$$

Each of these equations is of the form $\dot{x}=ax$, where x is a function $x(t)$ from R to R. Hence, in this case,

$$x_1(t) = x_1(0)\exp(\lambda_1 t)$$
$$x_2(t) = x_2(0)\exp(\lambda_2 t)$$
$$\vdots$$
$$x_n(t) = x_n(0)\exp(\lambda_n t)$$

provides the solution.

If A is diagonalizable, then the elements of the diagonal matrix are the eigenvalues of A. This observation motivates the following result for the system (3) (provided A has distinct eigenvalues): The solution $x(t)$ of the system $\dot{x}=Ax$ is given by the function

$$x(t) = (x_1(0)\exp(\lambda_1 t), x_2(0)\exp(\lambda_2 t),\ldots,x_n(0)\exp(\lambda_n t))^T,$$

where $\lambda_1,\lambda_2,\ldots,\lambda_n$ are the distinct eigenvalues of the matrix A.

Under what circumstances will $\lim_{t\to\infty}\|x(t)\|=0$? If all eigenvalues are real numbers, and all those real numbers are negative, then certainly $\lim_{t\to\infty}|x_i(0)\exp(\lambda_i t)|=0$. Thus, a necessary and sufficient condition for asymptotic stability of equilibrium of equation (3) is that all real eigenvalues must be negative. If A is symmetric, then all eigenvalues are real. Under what conditions are those real eigenvalues negative? For the multimarket equilibrium problem, this question reduces to asking under what conditions the Jacobian of the excess-demand functions at equilibrium (a) will be symmetric and (b) will have negative eigenvalues.

Asymptotic stability of equation (2) can be obtained by making assumptions about the excess-demand functions that are strong enough to turn the Jacobian into a matrix with negative real eigenvalues. Because each entry of the Jacobian is of the form $\partial E_i / \partial p_j$, each entry has the interpretation as a change in excess demand for good i induced by a small change in the price of good j. If income effects are zero, then the Slutsky theorem ensures that $\partial E_i / \partial p_j = \partial E_j / \partial p_i$. So the Jacobian is symmetric.

Further, if the excess-demand functions are well-behaved (downward-sloping demand curves), then $\partial E_i / \partial p_i < 0$. Thus, the Jacobian matrix itself has a main diagonal composed of negative numbers. If $\partial E_i / \partial p_j > 0$, then an increase in the price of good j increases excess demand for good i, so that goods i and j are gross substitutes. Assuming gross substitutes and downward-sloping demand curves yields a sign pattern of the Jacobian matrix as

$$\begin{bmatrix} - & & & \\ & - & & + \\ & & - & \\ + & & & \ddots \\ & & & & - \end{bmatrix}.$$

However, if the matrix had the sign pattern

$$\begin{bmatrix} - & & & \\ & - & & 0 \\ & & \ddots & \\ 0 & & - & \\ & & & - \\ & & & & - \end{bmatrix},$$

then asymptotic stability would be immediate.

Imagine that it is possible to take some of the negative stuff from the diagonal element in the ith row of the J matrix and add it to all other positive elements in the ith row. This could produce a row with a negative number on the main diagonal and zeros everywhere else in that row. This mental experiment seems to require, for its success, that the negative diagonal element in row i be algebraically larger than the sum of the positive off-diagonal elements in row i. Does the Jacobian, in fact, have such a structure?

What economic assumptions about excess-demand functions can produce this property of J? It turns out that, besides gross substitutability, two other assumptions suffice. First, it is required that the excess-demand functions be homogeneous of degree 0 in prices, so that only relative prices affect demand. Second, it is necessary that Walras's law hold, so that the total value of purchases in the economy equals the value of sales in the economy. These assumptions suffice to ensure that the eigenvalues of J are negative. (These assumptions make sure there is enough "negativity" in the term $\partial E_i/\partial p_i$ to turn $\partial E_i/\partial p_j$ from positive to zero.)

What happens if J is not symmetric? In that case, the eigenvalues are not necessarily real numbers; they may be complex numbers, such as $\lambda_i = 2 + 3i$, where $i = \sqrt{-1}$. In general, any complex number z can be written as $z = x + iy$, where x is the *real part* of z, or $x = \mathrm{Re}\, z$, and y is the *imaginary part* of z, or $y = \mathrm{Im}\, z$. Thus, $z = \mathrm{Re}\, z + i(\mathrm{Im}\, z)$.

Without going into details, the eigenvalue condition that ensures that $\dot{x} = Ax$ is asymptotically stable can be generalized to the case in which the eigenvalues of A are complex. Instead of the requirement that the eigenvalues themselves be negative for stability, in the complex eigenvalue case the stability condition becomes that the real parts of all the eigenvalues must be negative for stability. Of course, if all eigenvalues are real, all eigenvalues equal their real parts; so this result indeed generalizes the usual condition.

EXAMPLE[1]

To illustrate how this kind of analysis is used in economics, consider the following problem. If an industry is composed of a lot of firms, and each firm can adjust its own output by hiring more labor (but not capital), what happens when unusual profits are being made in that industry? Intuitively, existing firms will increase output. But also, new firms will enter the industry. There is a long-run equilibrium number of workers per firm and number of firms determined by competition; if the firms and the industry are not initially in equilibrium, will they eventually get there? In other words, is the long-run competitive equilibrium asymptotically stable?

Consider the following model. Let $x = f(l)$ be any firm's production function, where x is output per unit of capital and l is labor per unit of capital. The demand curve faced by the industry relates unit price p to total industry output nx, where n is the number of firms. If w is the money wage rate of a unit of labor, competitive equilibrium factor hire requires $w = pf'(l)$, where $f'(l)$, the derivative of the production function, is the marginal product of labor.

[1] This analysis is based on the work of Myers and Weintraub, "A Dynamic Model of Firm Entry." *Review of Economic Studies* 38:127-9, 1971.

How do l and n evolve over time? Assume that if it costs $\bar{w}$ to hire a worker, the rate of change in the number of workers is proportional to $w - \bar{w}$, the difference between marginal revenue and cost per worker. This can be written as

$$\dot{l} = \alpha(w - \bar{w}).$$

Also assume that the rate of change in the number of firms in the industry is proportional to net revenues in the industry, or $px - (\bar{w}l + \bar{r})$, where $\bar{r}$ is the opportunity cost of capital. (Each firm uses one unit of capital.) Thus, write

$$\dot{n} = \beta[px - (\bar{w}l + \bar{r})].$$

The equations for $\dot{l}$ and $\dot{n}$ define the system

$$\dot{l} = \alpha(w - \bar{w})$$
$$\dot{n} = \beta[px - (\bar{w}l + \bar{r})].$$

Because $w = pf'(l)$, $p = g(nx)$, and $x = f(l)$, it is possible to substitute for w, p, and x in the system to get

$$\dot{l} = \alpha[g(nf(l))f'(l) - \bar{w}]$$
$$\dot{n} = \beta[g(nf(l))f(l) - \bar{w}l - \bar{r}].$$

The model consists of these two dynamic equations in the two unknowns n and l. Thus, the system is of the form

$$\dot{l} = H(l, n)$$
$$\dot{n} = G(l, n).$$

Assuming that an equilibrium exists at (l^*, n^*), linearize this system at the equilibrium. Thus, compute the Jacobian of this system at (l^*, n^*) and write

$$\begin{bmatrix} \dot{l} \\ \dot{n} \end{bmatrix} = J(l^*, n^*) \begin{bmatrix} l \\ n \end{bmatrix},$$

where $J(l^*, n^*)$ is the 2×2 matrix given by

$$\begin{bmatrix} \dfrac{\partial H}{\partial l}(l^*, n^*) & \dfrac{\partial H}{\partial n}(l^*, n^*) \\[2ex] \dfrac{\partial G}{\partial l}(l^*, n^*) & \dfrac{\partial G}{\partial n}(l^*, n^*) \end{bmatrix}.$$

In order to determine if this system is asymptotically stable, it is necessary to compute the eigenvalues of this 2×2 nonsymmetric matrix. But for 2×2 matrices, the sum of the eigenvalues is the trace of the matrix, and the product of the eigenvalues is the determinant of the matrix. Consider any 2×2 matrix. Either the matrix has two real eigenvalues or it has a pair of complex eigenvalues such as $z_1 = x + iy$ and $z_2 = x - iy$. For stability, it is necessary to show that both the eigenvalues have negative real parts. Note that in either the real or complex eigenvalue case, the sum of the eigenvalues is the sum of their real parts. Thus, for stability, the trace of the 2×2 matrix must be negative. The product of two real negative eigenvalues is positive. The product of two complex eigenvalues, a complex pair, is always positive, because $(x + iy)(x - iy) = x^2 - i^2 y^2$. But $i^2 = -1$; so $z^2 = (x^2 + y^2)$. Thus, the determinant of a stable 2×2 matrix must be positive.

Stability requires a negative trace of $J(l^*, n^*)$ and a positive determinant of $J(l^*, n^*)$. It is time to compute:

$$\text{trace } J(l^*, n^*) = \frac{\partial H}{\partial l}(l^*, n^*) + \frac{\partial G}{\partial n}(l^*, n^*)$$

and

$$\det J(l^*, n^*)$$
$$= \frac{\partial H}{\partial l}(l^*, n^*)\frac{\partial G}{\partial n}(l^*, n^*) - \frac{\partial H}{\partial n}(l^*, n^*)\frac{\partial G}{\partial l}(l^*, n^*).$$

Routine calculations show that

$$\text{trace } J(l^*, n^*) = \alpha(f')^2 g' \cdot n + \beta(f)^2 g' + \alpha f'' g$$

and

$$\det J(l^*, n^*) = \alpha\beta(f)^2 \cdot g' \cdot g \cdot f''.$$

Because g is the demand function, $g' < 0$. Because f' is squared, it is positive. Because f'' is the second derivative of a production function, $f'' < 0$. The model posits that $\alpha > 0$ and $\beta > 0$. Consequently,

$$\text{trace } J(l^*, n^*) < 0$$

$$\det J(l^*, n^*) > 0.$$

Thus, the eigenvalues of $J(l^*, n^*)$ all have negative real parts under standard economic assumptions. The industry approaches the competitive equilibrium eventually. The long-run industry equilibrium is asymptotically stable.

A cautionary introduction to comparative statics

Many economic problems can be reduced to questions about the effects on equilibrium of changes in certain parameters. Suppose equilibrium is characterized by the function ϕ, where $\phi: R^m \to R^n$ and $m > n$. Suppose, further, that ϕ has the form

$$\phi^i(x_1, \ldots, x_n; a_1, \ldots, a_l) = 0$$

for $i = 1, 2, \ldots, n$, where $n + l = m$. Thus, ϕ is a system of implicit functions ϕ^i. If the Jacobian of ϕ is nonsingular at a point $x^* \in R^n$, then the Implicit Function Theorem allows a solution of the form

$$x_i^* = \phi^i(a_1, \ldots, a_l)$$

for $i = 1, 2, \ldots, n$ in a neighborhood of x^*. The x_i^* usually are equilibrium values of the economic variables x_i, and the a_i are parameters, or exogenous or predetermined variables.

A typical economic question asks how the equilibrium position responds to changes in the parameters of the model. The question involves determining the effects of changes in the a_i on the x_i^*. If $f: R^n \to R$, then a common notation for differentials suggests that

$$(d) \qquad df = (\operatorname{grad} f) \cdot dx,$$

where $dx = (dx_1, dx_2, \ldots, dx_n)^T$. The notation dx_i is supposed to mean "a small change in x_i," and df is supposed to mean "a small change in f." Thus, applying the operator equation (d) to the point x^* yields

$$df(x) = (\operatorname{grad} f)_{x^*} \cdot dx,$$

which seems to express a change in $f(x)$ in terms of the gradient of f at x^* and changes in the variables x_i. This is sometimes written

$$df(x) = \frac{\partial f}{\partial x_1}(x^*) \, dx_1 + \cdots + \frac{\partial f}{\partial x_n}(x^*) \, dx_n.$$

It is no accident that equation (d), involving differential forms, played no role in earlier chapters. Indeed, such an equation is quite difficult to develop. Economists use this formalism continually, however, without much concern about its meaning. If this formalism makes sense, then it is possible to ask how the equilibrium values of economic variables change as parameters change by direct consideration of the implicit functions ϕ^i that characterize equilibrium. One simply "takes the total derivative of ϕ^i" using the formalism (d) to generate

$$d\phi^i = (\operatorname{grad} \phi^i) \cdot (dx, da)^T,$$

$i = 1, 2, \ldots, n$, where $dx = (dx_1, \ldots, dx_n)^T$ and $da = (da_1, \ldots, da_l)^T$. This yields the system

$$
\begin{bmatrix}
\dfrac{\partial \phi^1}{\partial x_1} & \cdots & \dfrac{\partial \phi^1}{\partial x_n} & \dfrac{\partial \phi^1}{\partial a_1} & \cdots & \dfrac{\partial \phi^1}{\partial a_l} \\
\vdots & & & & & \\
\dfrac{\partial \phi^n}{\partial x_1} & \cdots & \dfrac{\partial \phi^n}{\partial x_n} & \dfrac{\partial \phi^n}{\partial a_1} & \cdots & \dfrac{\partial \phi^n}{\partial a_l}
\end{bmatrix}
\begin{bmatrix}
dx_1 \\ \vdots \\ dx_n \\ da_1 \\ \vdots \\ da_l
\end{bmatrix}
=
\begin{bmatrix}
0 \\ \vdots \\ \vdots \\ \vdots \\ \vdots \\ 0
\end{bmatrix},
$$

where the matrix is $n \times (n + l)$. Thinking of the dx_i's and da_i's as "variables," the system defines a set of homogeneous linear equations in those variables. Thus, there are n equations in the n variables dx_i and the l variables da_i. Alternatively, the system can be split into two parts, involving dx_i's and da_i's, to yield

$$
\begin{bmatrix}
\dfrac{\partial \phi^1}{\partial x_1} & \cdots & \dfrac{\partial \phi^1}{\partial x_n} \\
\vdots & & \\
\dfrac{\partial \phi^n}{\partial x_1} & \cdots & \dfrac{\partial \phi^n}{\partial x_n}
\end{bmatrix}
\begin{bmatrix}
dx_1 \\ \vdots \\ dx_n
\end{bmatrix}
= -
\begin{bmatrix}
\dfrac{\partial \phi^1}{\partial a_1} & \cdots & \dfrac{\partial \phi^1}{\partial a_l} \\
\vdots & & \\
\dfrac{\partial \phi^n}{\partial a_1} & \cdots & \dfrac{\partial \phi^n}{\partial a_l}
\end{bmatrix}
\begin{bmatrix}
da_1 \\ \vdots \\ da_l
\end{bmatrix}
$$

or

$$
A \, dx = -B \, da,
$$

where A is $n \times n$, dx is $n \times 1$, B is $n \times l$, and da is $l \times 1$. This is a set of n nonhomogeneous linear equations in what may be considered the n "unknowns" dx_i's. Formally, the solution is

$$
dx = -A^{-1} B \, da,
$$

when A is invertible. Thus, the comparative static formalism requires that the matrix

$$
A =
\begin{bmatrix}
\dfrac{\partial \phi^1}{\partial x_1} & \cdots & \dfrac{\partial \phi^1}{\partial x_n} \\
\vdots & & \\
\dfrac{\partial \phi^n}{\partial x_1} & \cdots & \dfrac{\partial \phi^n}{\partial x_n}
\end{bmatrix}
$$

be nonsingular, which was precisely the condition for use of the Implicit Function Theorem.

The solution will express the dx_i's in terms of constants from the A and

B matrices (from the Jacobian of ϕ evaluated at equilibrium) and the variables da_i. The result is that changes in the equilibrium values of the x's are expressed in terms of changes in the paramater values. This is the comparative static formalism.

EXAMPLE

Consider a simple three-equation macroeconomic model:

$$Y = C + I$$
$$C = a + bY$$
$$I = I(r).$$

Set up this model in the form of implicit functions for the variables Y, C, and I and the parameters a, b, and r as

$$\phi^1(Y, C, I; a, b, r) = 0$$
$$\phi^2(Y, C, I; a, b, r) = 0$$
$$\phi^3(Y, C, I; a, b, r) = 0$$

where ϕ^2, say, is defined by $C - bY - a = 0$. Using the comparative static formalism involving the Jacobian, the system becomes

$$\begin{bmatrix} 1 & -1 & -1 \\ -b & 1 & 0 \\ 0 & 0 & -1 \end{bmatrix} \begin{bmatrix} dY \\ dC \\ dI \end{bmatrix} = - \begin{bmatrix} 0 & 0 & 0 \\ -1 & -Y & 0 \\ 0 & 0 & -\frac{\partial I}{\partial r} \end{bmatrix} \begin{bmatrix} da \\ db \\ dr \end{bmatrix}.$$

Thus, the solution is

$$\begin{bmatrix} dY \\ dC \\ dI \end{bmatrix} = \begin{bmatrix} 1 & -1 & -1 \\ -b & 1 & 0 \\ 0 & 0 & -1 \end{bmatrix}^{-1} \begin{bmatrix} 0 & 0 & 0 \\ 1 & Y & 0 \\ 0 & 0 & \frac{\partial I}{\partial r} \end{bmatrix} \begin{bmatrix} da \\ db \\ dr \end{bmatrix}.$$

Performing the indicated operations yields

$$\begin{bmatrix} dY \\ dC \\ dI \end{bmatrix} = \begin{bmatrix} \frac{1}{1-b} & \frac{1}{1+b} & \frac{1}{1+b} \\ \frac{b}{1-b} & \frac{1}{1+b} & -\frac{b}{1+b} \\ 0 & 0 & -1 \end{bmatrix} \begin{bmatrix} 0 & 0 & 0 \\ 1 & Y & 0 \\ 0 & 0 & \frac{\partial I}{\partial r} \end{bmatrix} \begin{bmatrix} da \\ db \\ dr \end{bmatrix}.$$

Thus,

$$
\begin{bmatrix} dY \\ dC \\ dI \end{bmatrix} = \begin{bmatrix} \dfrac{1}{1+b} & \dfrac{Y}{1+b} & \left(\dfrac{1}{1-b}\right)\left(\dfrac{\partial I}{\partial r}\right) \\[2ex] \dfrac{1}{1+b} & \dfrac{Y}{1+b} & \left(\dfrac{-b}{1-b}\right)\left(\dfrac{\partial I}{\partial r}\right) \\[2ex] 0 & 0 & (-1)\left(\dfrac{\partial I}{\partial r}\right) \end{bmatrix} \begin{bmatrix} da \\ db \\ dr \end{bmatrix}.
$$

It follows immediately that, for example,

$$
dY = \frac{da}{1+b} + \frac{Y}{1+b}\,db + \frac{1}{1-b}\,\frac{\partial I}{\partial r}\,dr.
$$

This answers the question "What is the effect on equilibrium real GNP if interest rates increase, *ceteris paribus*?" The *ceteris paribus* phrase means that neither a nor b changes; so $da = db = 0$. Thus,

$$
dY = \frac{1}{1-b}\left(\frac{\partial I}{\partial r}\right)dr.
$$

Consequently,

$$
\frac{dY}{dr} = \left(\frac{1}{1-b}\right)\frac{\partial I}{\partial r}.
$$

Usual theory interprets b as the marginal propensity to consume; so $0 < b < 1$. $\partial I/\partial r$ usually is assumed to be negative. Thus, $dY/dr < 0$. "If interest rates increase, equilibrium real GNP falls, *ceteris paribus*" is a prediction of the model.

However, there is a major conceptual difficulty with comparative static analysis. How is it known that when a parameter changes, a new equilibrium exists at all? Implicit in a comparative statics argument is a statement that the new equilibrium is asymptotically stable, at least in the neighborhood of the local (near equilibrium) approximation. That is, the old equilibrium position is the initial position for the system defined by the new parameter values. Stability means that starting from such an arbitrary position, the (new) equilibrium is reached eventually. Consequently, comparative static analysis, to be complete, requires a dynamic system that is stable.

All too often economists do not explicitly identify the dynamic system that underlies a comparative static proposition. Such inattention may lead to a nonsensical conclusion. If, for example, an exogenous variable shifts in a model that is based on an unstable dynamic structure, then no equilibrium can be attained. Doing a comparative static analysis to investigate the properties of the "new" equilibrium that results from such a change will lead to fantastic conclusions.

EXAMPLE

Consider, for a single market, a perfectly inelastic demand curve. Let this curve intersect a supply curve once on a backward-bending section of that supply curve. Ask the following question: "If demand increases, does the equilibrium price rise, fall, or remain the same?" If the original equilibrium is p^* in Figure 8.3, the new one appears to be p^{**}, which is less than p^*. But how could price change from p^* to p^{**}, in view of the fact that price p^*, with demand curve D^1, generates excess demand?

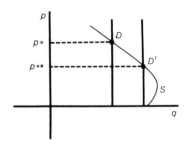

FIGURE 8.3

FURTHER READING

The best guide to dynamics is Hirsch and Smale's *Differential Equations, Dynamical Systems, and Linear Algebra*. For economists, Samuelson's *Foundations of Economic Analysis* is still worth reading, especially for its discussion of the "correspondence principle" relating dynamic stability to determinant comparative static results. For a more modern treatment, see also Quirk and Saposnik's *Introduction to General Equilibrium Theory and Welfare Economics*. Chapters 5 and 6 of this book provide a careful treatment of the interrelationships between stability and comparative statics for a general equilibrium system. A critical examination of these issues is presented by Fisher in a wonderful essay, "The Stability of General Equilibrium: Results and Problems," in Artis and Nobay's *Essays in Economic Analysis*.

EXERCISES

8.1 Consider the dynamic system, for x and $y \in R$,

$$\dot{x} = ax + by \quad \text{and} \quad \dot{y} = cx + dy.$$

Certainly, $(x, y)^T = (0, 0)^T$ is the (unique) equilibrium.

(a) What role does the assumption $ad - bc \neq 0$ play in describing the behavior of this system?

(b) Under what conditions will the equilibrium motion be asymptotically stable?

8.2 Suppose, for $a \in R$ and $x \in R$,

$$\dot{x} = ax.$$

Now suppose that a is a variable that moves, "slowly," from -1 to $+1$, as x moves "quickly" by $\dot{x} = ax$. Describe, in words and pictures, the behavior of x as time passes. (This is a simple "catastrophe" model. See O'Shea's "An Exposition of Catastrophe Theory, and Its Applications to Phase Transitions," 1976.)

CHAPTER 9

Quadratic forms

Mr. Cayley, who habitually discourses
pearls and rubies....
                    J. J. Sylvester (1852)

In old-fashioned algebra books, quadratic equations followed the discussion of linear equations. If $n=2$, a quadratic form is defined by

$$f(x_1, x_2) = ax_1^2 + dx_2^2 + 2cx_1x_2.$$

A quadratic form in n variables is a member of a subclass of functions from R^n to R. It is the sum of terms like $a_{ij}x_ix_j$ for $i,j=1,2,\ldots,n$; so $f(x_1, x_2, \ldots, x_n) = \sum_{j=1}^{n} \sum_{i=1}^{n} a_{ij}x_ix_j$, where $a_{ij} = a_{ji}$.

The presence of terms like a_{ij} in a quadratic form suggests that a matrix $A = (a_{ij})$ is present. In fact, if x is a column n-vector, and A is $n \times n$ and symmetric,

$$f(x) = x^TAx$$

defines a quadratic form. If $n=2$ and $A = \begin{bmatrix} a & b \\ c & d \end{bmatrix}$, then

$$f(x) = (x_1, x_2) \begin{bmatrix} a & b \\ c & d \end{bmatrix} \begin{bmatrix} x_1 \\ x_2 \end{bmatrix}.$$

So $f(x) = ax_1^2 + (b+c)(x_1x_2) + dx_2^2$. But $b+c=2c$, because $b=c$ when the matrix A is symmetric. Thus, the general quadratic form from R^2 to R is

$$f(x) = (x_1, x_2) \begin{bmatrix} a & c \\ c & d \end{bmatrix} \begin{bmatrix} x_1 \\ x_2 \end{bmatrix}.$$

There is a nice geometric interpretation of such forms. Because x^TAx is just another way of writing $x \cdot (Ax)$, the quadratic form $f(x) = x^TAx$ measures the dot (or scalar) product of the two vectors x and Ax. In other words, because $x \cdot y = \|x\| \|y\| \cos\theta_{xy}$, the quadratic form is related to the angle between the vectors x and Ax.

Consider the symmetric matrix A. As an $n \times n$ matrix, with real eigenvalues, A represents a uniform stretching or squeezing of R^n by the linear

124

transformation $L: R^n \to R^n$. A represents L in some choice of basis. Consequently, $f(x) = x \cdot Ax$ measures the angle between the vector $x \in R^n$ and the image of x, Ax, which is also a vector in R^n.

Definite forms

For a symmetric $n \times n$ matrix A, the quadratic form associated with A provides information about the geometric properties of the linear transformation L that is represented by A. Suppose $A = \begin{bmatrix} 3 & 2 \\ 2 & 6 \end{bmatrix}$. Then the quadratic form of A is

$$x \cdot \begin{bmatrix} 3 & 2 \\ 2 & 6 \end{bmatrix} x$$

for any vector $x \in R^n$, where $x \neq 0$.

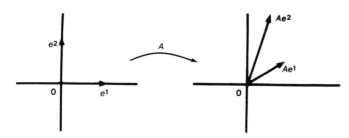

FIGURE 9.1

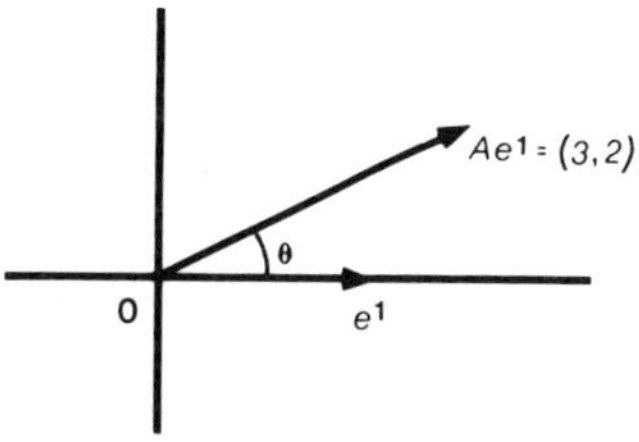

Consider this dot product by looking at x and Ax in Figure 9.1, where x is a standard basis vector e^1 or e^2. Now look just at e^1 and Ae^1 in Figure 9.2. Because the angle between e^1 and Ae^1 is acute, $\cos\theta > 0$, and so $e^1 \cdot Ae^1 > 0$. Similarly, $e^2 \cdot Ae^2 > 0$. Thus for any $x \in R^2$, because $x = x_1 e^1 + x_2 e^2$,

FIGURE 9.2

(1) $x \cdot Ax = (x_1 e^1 + x_2 e^2) \cdot A(x_1 e^1 + x_2 e^2)$.

Hence,

$$x \cdot Ax = x_1^2 e^1 \cdot Ae^1 + x_2^2 e^2 \cdot Ae^2 + x_1 x_2 (e^1 \cdot Ae^2 + e^2 \cdot Ae^1).$$

Certainly the first two terms on the right are positive. But what of the cross term?

The difficulty in "seeing" the angle between an arbitrary vector and its image vector under A is caused by the choice of bases. Is there a more convenient basis in which to visualize $x \cdot Ax$? If the real eigenvalues of A are distinct, then A is diagonalizable, so that $B^{-1}AB = D$, where D is an $n \times n$ diagonal matrix with the real eigenvalues of A arranged down D's main diagonal, and B is some nonsingular $n \times n$ matrix. B is, in fact, the matrix that has the eigenvectors as columns. Thus, consider $x \cdot Ax$. This is a scalar equal to y; so

$$x \cdot Ax = y.$$

Now, because $B^{-1}AB = D$, $A = BDB^{-1}$. Hence,

$$y = x \cdot Ax = x \cdot (BDB^{-1})x.$$

Rewrite this in transpose notation as

$$y = (x^T B)D(B^{-1}x).$$

Recall that B is the matrix whose columns are the eigenvectors of transformation. For such a matrix, called the *modal matrix*, it is a well-known fact that $B^{-1} = B^T$. Thus,

$$y = x^T BDB^{-1}x = (B^{-1}x)^T D(B^{-1}x).$$

But what is $(B^{-1}x)$? Because x is an arbitrary vector written using the standard basis, and B^{-1} changes the standard basis into the eigenvector basis of R^n, $B^{-1}x$ is simply the vector x written in terms of the new basis. Labeling $B^{-1}x = z$,

$$y = z^T Dz = z \cdot Dz.$$

But because z is an arbitrary vector,

$$x \cdot Ax = z \cdot Dz,$$

where D is the diagonalization of A. If D is the diagonalization of A, $x^T Ax = z^T Dz$ for any x and z; the sign of $z \cdot Dz$ is the same. Thus, for $A = \begin{bmatrix} 3 & 2 \\ 2 & 6 \end{bmatrix}$, compute A's eigenvalues in the usual way to find $\lambda_1 = 7$ and $\lambda_2 = 2$. Then A has the diagonal form

$$D = \begin{bmatrix} 7 & 0 \\ 0 & 2 \end{bmatrix}.$$

What is true of $z \cdot Dz$? Because the angle between e^1 and De^1 is zero, as is the angle between e^2 and De^2, $e^1 \cdot De^1 = 1$ and $e^2 \cdot De^2 = 1$. Thus, from equation (1), $x \cdot Ax = z \cdot Dz = z_1^2 + z_2^2 + z_1 z_2 (e^1 \cdot De^2 + e^2 \cdot De^1)$. But e^1 is perpendicular to e^2, and thus e^1 is orthogonal to De^2. Hence, $e^1 \cdot De^2 = 0$, and similarly for $e^2 \cdot De^1$. Thus,

$$x \cdot Ax = z \cdot Dz = z_1^2 + z_2^2.$$

Thus, $x \cdot Ax > 0$; the action of A on any vector x in R^2 is to send x to another vector, Ax, that makes an acute angle with x.

A quadratic form $x \cdot Ax$ is called *positive definite* if $x \cdot Ax > 0$ for any vector $x \in R^n$. Thus, an $n \times n$ symmetric matrix A, which gives rise to a positive definite quadratic form, has the property that the linear transformation L (which A represents) sends arbitrary vectors in R^n to new vectors at an acute angle to the original vector.

There is another result here. Because the distinct eigenvalues in the 2×2 example were both positive, the standard basis vectors were stretched or shrunk along the positive axes. Thus, the quadratic form $x \cdot Ax$ necessarily looked like $x_1^2 + x_2^2$, which defines a positive definite form. It can be shown that the converse is also true. Thus, $x \cdot Ax$, for A an $n \times n$ symmetric matrix, is a positive definite form if and only if the eigenvalues of A are positive numbers. The matrix A itself is called positive definite if $x \cdot Ax$ is a positive definite form.

EXAMPLE

Positive definite matrices appear frequently in econometrics. Suppose Y is a column n-vector of random variables with mean zero. The variance-covariance matrix of Y is defined as

$$\Omega = E[YY^T],$$

where E is the expectation operator. Suppose q is a scalar random variable defined by

$$q = x^T Y$$

for an arbitrary column n-vector x. What is the variance of q? By definition,

$$\mathrm{Var}(q) = E[qq^T].$$

But

$$E[qq^T] = E[x^T Y (x^T Y)^T].$$

So

$$\mathrm{Var}(q) = E[x^T Y Y^T x].$$

Because x is a vector, not a random variable, x can be pulled out of the expectations operator to yield

$$\text{Var}(q) = x^T E[YY^T]x.$$

So

$$\text{Var}(q) = x^T \Omega x.$$

But the variance of a nontrivial scalar random variable is always greater than zero; so $\text{Var}(q) > 0$ entails that

$$x \cdot \Omega x > 0,$$

and thus Ω is positive definite. The variance-covariance matrix is always positive definite.

Suppose that a quadratic form is not positive definite. Define a quadratic form $x \cdot Ax$ to be *negative definite* if, for any nonzero vector $x \in R^n$, $x \cdot Ax < 0$. This is equivalent to the statement that A comes from a linear transformation L that sends a vector x to a new vector that forms an obtuse angle with x. It is also equivalent to the statement that all the eigenvalues of A are negative.

Similar matrices having distinct eigenvalues have the same diagonal form. Thus, if A and $\hat{A}$ are similar, they each have the same diagonalization D; so $x \cdot Ax = z \cdot Dz = \hat{x} \cdot \hat{A}\hat{x}$. A matrix similar to a positive (negative) definite matrix is also positive (negative) definite. Positive or negative definiteness is an invariant.

A nonsingular $n \times n$ symmetric matrix that is neither positive definite nor negative definite is called indefinite.[1] Indefinite matrices represent linear transformations that send only some vectors x to vectors lying at an acute angle with x. As transformations, such indefinite matrices "mess up" space more than positive or negative definite matrices.

EXAMPLE

An interesting and nontrivial example of the use of quadratic forms in economics is based on the concept of asymptotic stability of a linear dynamic system. Consider the system, for x an n-vector and A an $n \times n$ matrix,

$$\dot{x} = Ax.$$

---

[1] Sometimes a symmetric $n \times n$ matrix A, such that $x^T Ax \geqslant 0$, is called *positive semidefinite*, whereas if $x^T Ax \leqslant 0$, A is called *negative semidefinite*.

Then $x(t)=0$ is the equilibrium path. At any time t, $\|x(t)-0\|$ measures the distance between the state variables of the system and their equilibrium positions. What, in general, does "distance" mean? The units that measure distance are arbitrary. Distance is really a function of the two points in question; call them x and y. As a function, "distance" has the property that it is always greater than or equal to zero, and it equals zero only when x and y coincide.

For the system $\dot{x}=Ax$, what is the distance between $x=x(t)$ and $x=0$ at time t? A Liapunov function for a system $\dot{x}=f(x)$ is a continuously differentiable function of x, denoted $V(x)$, that is always nonnegative and that is zero only when x is at equilibrium. $V(x)$ measures the distance between $x(t)$ and equilibrium. Now suppose that $x(t)$ satisfies $\dot{x}=Ax$; so $x(t)$ is a path of $\dot{x}=Ax$. It is obvious from Figure 9.3 (drawn for $A=a$, the one-dimensional case) that $x(t)$ approaches equilibrium if and only if $V(x)$ decreases over time. But a function decreases over time if and only if the time derivative of that function is always negative. Thus, compute the time derivative of $V(x)$, recognizing that x itself is a function of time:

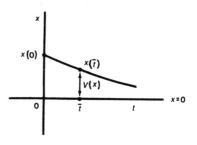

FIGURE 9.3

$$\frac{d}{dt}V(x(t)) = \frac{dV}{dx}\frac{dx}{dt}.$$

It is necessary to be a bit more specific about $V(x)$. What is a "good" function to represent the distance between x and 0? Certainly, if x is a vector in R^n, $x\cdot x$ represents distance (or the square of Euclidean distance) between x and 0 very nicely (because $x\cdot x>0$ for all $x\neq 0$, and $x\cdot x=0$ only when $x=0$). Thus, define $V(x)=x\cdot x$. This is a Liapunov function. What is dV/dt? A bit of computation shows that if x is $n\times 1$, and $x=x(t)$,

$$\frac{dV}{dt} = \frac{d}{dt}(x\cdot x) = \frac{d}{dt}(x^Tx) = x^T\dot{x} + \dot{x}^Tx.$$

Because $\dot{x}=Ax$,

$$\frac{dV}{dt} = x^T A x + (Ax)^T x.$$

Thus, $dV/dt = x^T A x + x^T A^T x = x^T (A + A^T) x$. Rewrite this as

$$\dot{V}(x) = 2x \cdot \left(\frac{A + A^T}{2} \right) x.$$

If A is symmetric, $A = A^T$; so $(A + A^T)/2 = A$. Thus, when A is symmetric,

$$\dot{V}(x) = 2(x \cdot Ax).$$

Stability of the system $\dot{x} = Ax$ requires that $\dot{V}(x) < 0$. It should be clear that $\dot{V}(x) < 0$ if and only if A is a negative definite matrix. This is true, of course, only when the eigenvalues of A are negative, which was the result suggested in Chapter 8.

Recalling the discussion of multimarket equilibrium from the last chapter, interpret x as the deviation of market price from equilibrium price, and interpret A as the Jacobian of the excess-demand functions. If the Jacobian is symmetric (i.e., ignoring income effects and concentrating on substitution effects), the stability of multimarket equilibrium is guaranteed provided the substitution matrix is negative definite.

Bowls

There is another useful geometric interpretation of a quadratic form. If A is a 1×1 matrix (i.e., a real number), the value of the quadratic form can be denoted $f(x)$; so $f(x) = ax^2$. The graph of this function is shown in Figure 9.4. If $a > 0$, the form is positive definite; if $a < 0$, the form is negative definite. The graph is like a bowl, with vertex at the origin, opening up if $a > 0$ and opening down if $a < 0$.

If A is a 2×2 symmetric matrix, define $f(x_1, x_2) = (x_1, x_2) \cdot A(x_1, x_2)$ to be the value of the form. Because A is symmetric, it is diagonalizable if its eigenvalues are distinct. Thus, if λ_1 and λ_2 are the distinct eigenvalues of A, there is a basis for R^2 in which

$$f(x_1, x_2) = (x_1, x_2) \begin{bmatrix} \lambda_1 & 0 \\ 0 & \lambda_2 \end{bmatrix} \begin{bmatrix} x_1 \\ x_2 \end{bmatrix} = \lambda_1 x_1^2 + \lambda_2 x_2^2.$$

The graph of this function appears in Figure 9.5. If $\lambda_1 > 0$ and $\lambda_2 > 0$, the form is positive definite, and the graph is a bowl (paraboloid) opening

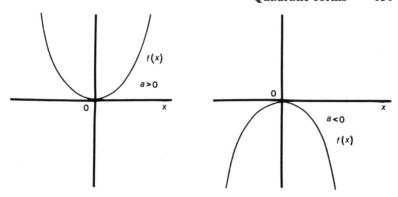

FIGURE 9.4

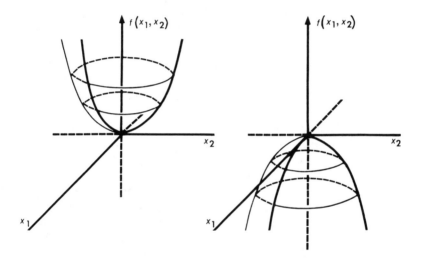

FIGURE 9.5

upward with vertex at the origin. If $\lambda_1 < 0$ and $\lambda_2 < 0$, the form is negative definite, and the bowl opens downward from the origin. A horizontal slice of the bowl, a cross section at $f(x_1, x_2) = a$, is a curve like $\lambda_1 x_1^2 + \lambda_2 x_2^2 = a$, which is an ellipse.

EXAMPLE

Recall that the Hessian matrix played an important role in the theory of the household. It has a square submatrix of the form

$$H = \begin{bmatrix} \dfrac{\partial^2 u}{\partial x_1^2} & \cdots & \dfrac{\partial^2 u}{\partial x_n \partial x_1} \\ \vdots & & \\ \dfrac{\partial^2 u}{\partial x_1 \partial x_n} & \cdots & \dfrac{\partial^2 u}{\partial x_n^2} \end{bmatrix}.$$

But $\partial^2 u/\partial x_i \partial x_j = \partial^2 u/\partial x_j \partial x_i$, because u is twice continuously differentiable. Thus, H is a symmetric matrix. This matrix has the property that all the elements on the main diagonal are negative, if the law of diminishing marginal utility is assumed.

If u is an additivity-separable utility function, so that $u(x_1, \ldots, x_n) = u^1(x_1) + \cdots + u^n(x_n)$, then $\partial^2 u/\partial x_i \partial x_j = 0$ for all $i \neq j$. In this case H is diagonal, with the negative diagonal elements $\partial^2 u/\partial x_i^2$. These elements are the eigenvalues of H, and so H is negative definite. But if H is negative definite, then H is nonsingular. Thus, because H is the Jacobian of the first-order (equilibrium) conditions for the household, the Jacobian of the implicit functions that characterize household equilibrium is nonsingular. Consequently, those implicit functions can be solved to get demand functions for commodity i.

It is, of course, unduly restrictive to assume that a utility function is additively separable. However, economists would like to be able to derive demand functions from first-order equilibrium conditions generated by utility functions. What assumptions about those utility functions permit the derivation? One assumption that certainly suffices is to suppose that the Hessian matrix of u at equilibrium is negative definite. For then, $H(u(\bar{x}))$ is nonsingular, and because H is the Jacobian of the first-order conditions, these equations can be solved to produce demand functions.

FURTHER READING

Traditional references include the books by Hadley, Gantmacher, and Frazer, Duncan, and Collier. See also the book by Herstein (Chapter 6, Section 11).

EXERCISES

9.1 If $f(x) = x^T A x$ for $x \in R^n$ and A $n \times n$ symmetric, show that

$$\operatorname{grad} f(x) = 2x^T A.$$

9.2 Redo Exercise 6.1(b) using the Liapunov function $V(x_1, x_2) = x \cdot x$. What does the assumption of asymptotic stability mean for the definiteness of the matrix $\begin{bmatrix} a & b \\ c & d \end{bmatrix}$?

CHAPTER 10

Concave, convex, and homogeneous functions from R^n to R

The effect of exclusive attention to those parts of mathematics which offer no scope for the discussion of doubtful points is a distaste for modes of proceeding which are absolutely necessary to the extension of the analysis.

Augustus deMorgan (1842)

This chapter examines some specific functions that have significant economic applications. A linear function $f: R^n \to R$ was defined by two conditions, additivity and homogeneity:

(1) $f(x + y) = f(x) + f(y)$ $x, y \in R^n$

(2) $f(\alpha x) = \alpha f(x)$ $\alpha \in R,\ x \in R^n$.

These properties, taken individually, define classes of functions that include linear functions. What functions satisfy equation (1) alone, or a generalization of equation (1)? What functions satisfy equation (2) alone, or a generalization of equation (2)?

Concave and convex functions

Recall that a convex set in R^n is a set of points in R^n such that a line segment drawn between any two of its points lies wholly within the set. That is, S is convex if $x, y \in S \subset R^n$, and $\alpha x + (1-\alpha)y = z$ for $0 \le \alpha \le 1$ implies that $z \in S$. There are several sets associated with functions from R^n to R. If some of those sets of points are convex, then the function has some useful properties.

Suppose $f: S \subset R^n \to R$, so that f is defined on the open set S, and suppose that S is a convex set; f is a *concave function* if, given any x and $\hat{x}$ in S, and for all $0 \le \alpha \le 1$,

(3) $f(\alpha x + (1 - \alpha)\hat{x}) \ge \alpha f(x) + (1 - \alpha)f(\hat{x})$.

Because $\alpha x + (1-\alpha)\hat{x} = z \in S$, inequality (3) means that the value of f at z,

134

or the value of f at some point between x and $\hat{x}$, is greater than or equal to the value of f represented by a point on the line connecting $f(x)$ and $f(\hat{x})$.

If $f: R \to R$, a concave function can be pictured by its graph, as in Figure 10.1. From the diagram, a concave function f from R to R has the property that the line connecting two separate points on the graph lies on or below the graph between those points. A function from R^n to R, defined on an open convex set S, is *strictly concave* if the inequality in (3) is a strict inequality. Intuitively, a strictly concave function has the property that a line joining two points on the graph lies below the graph between those

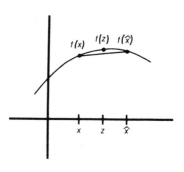

FIGURE 10.1

two points. It should be clear that a linear function is concave but not strictly concave. Thus, "concavity" generalizes the additivity property of linear functions.

A function $f: R^n \to R$, defined on an open convex set $S \subset R^n$, is *convex* if, for any x and $\hat{x} \in S$, and any $\alpha \in [0,1]$,

(4) $f(\alpha x + (1 - \alpha)\hat{x}) \leq \alpha f(x) + (1 - \alpha)f(\hat{x})$.

If the inequality sign in (4) is a strict inequality, f is *strictly convex*. A convex function has the property that a line drawn between two points on the graph lies on or above the graph between those two points. Thus, concave functions look like paraboloids opening downward, and convex functions look like paraboloids opening upward. Linear functions are certainly convex, but not strictly convex.

It is difficult to test a specific function $f: R^n \to R$ for concavity or convexity using the definition alone. Is there a simple test for convexity, an alternative characterization of convex functions? Suppose f is convex. Then

$$f(\alpha x + (1 - \alpha)\hat{x}) \leq \alpha f(x) + (1 - \alpha)f(\hat{x})$$

for all $x, \hat{x} \in S \subset R^n$ (S open and convex) and all $\alpha \in (0,1)$. Thus,

$$f[\hat{x} + \alpha(x - \hat{x})] \leq f(\hat{x}) + \alpha[f(x) - f(\hat{x})].$$

Define $v \equiv x - \hat{x}$, so that $x = \hat{x} + v$. Then, certainly,

$$f(\hat{x} + \alpha v) \leq f(\hat{x}) + \alpha[f(\hat{x} + v) - f(\hat{x})].$$

Subtracting $f(\hat{x})$ and dividing by α (because $\alpha \neq 0$) yields

$$\frac{f(\hat{x} + \alpha v) - f(\hat{x})}{\alpha} \le f(\hat{x} + v) - f(\hat{x}).$$

Because this inequality is true for all $\alpha \in (0, 1)$, in particular it is true in the limit as α approaches zero through positive numbers. Thus,

$$\lim_{\alpha \to 0^+} \left[\frac{f(\hat{x} + \alpha v) - f(\hat{x})}{\alpha} \right] \le \lim_{\alpha \to 0^+} [f(\hat{x} + v) - f(\hat{x})].$$

The limit as $\alpha \to 0$ on the left is simply the gradient of f at $\hat{x}$; so

$$\text{grad} f(\hat{x}) \cdot v \le f(\hat{x} + v) - f(\hat{x}).$$

If f is twice continuously differentiable, the Taylor-series expansion[1] of f, at $\hat{x}$, is given by

$$f(\hat{x} + v) \approx f(\hat{x}) + \text{grad} f(\hat{x}) \cdot v + \tfrac{1}{2} v \cdot Hf(\hat{x})v,$$

where $Hf(\hat{x})$ is the $n \times n$ (symmetric) Hessian matrix of second-order partial derivatives of f at $\hat{x}$. Thus, if f is convex and twice continuously differentiable at $\hat{x}$,

$$\text{grad} f(\hat{x}) \cdot v \le [f(\hat{x}) + \text{grad} f(\hat{x}) \cdot v + \tfrac{1}{2} v \cdot Hf(\hat{x})v] - f(\hat{x}).$$

So

$$0 \le v \cdot Hf(\hat{x})v,$$

or

$$v^T Hf(\hat{x})v \ge 0.$$

Because v is an arbitrary n-vector, it follows that if f is convex and twice continuously differentiable, then the Hessian of f near a point $\hat{x}$ is positive semidefinite. Analogously, it is locally true that concave functions have negative semidefinite Hessians. Strict concavity (convexity) is implied by, but does not imply, negative (positive) definiteness.

EXAMPLE

Recall that a utility function, a function from the (convex) non-negative orthant of R^n to R, might have a negative definite Hessian if such a Hessian represents the assumption of diminishing marginal utility.

---

[1] See the work of Apostol or Lang.

EXAMPLE

Suppose $f: R^n \to R$ is a production function. The problem of maximizing output (by choosing inputs $x_1, \ldots, x_n$) for a given total cost is solved by hiring inputs to the point where their marginal products are proportional to their prices. If the constant of proportionality equals λ, the equilibrium or first-order conditions for this problem have the form

$$\frac{\partial f}{\partial x_1} - \lambda p_1 = 0$$

$$\vdots$$

$$\frac{\partial f}{\partial x_n} - \lambda p_n = 0$$

$$C - p_1 x_1 - \cdots - p_n x_n = 0,$$

where x_i is the amount of factor i, $\partial f / \partial x_i$ is the marginal product of factor i, p_i is the price of factor i, and C is total cost. These $n+1$ equations can be written as

$$\phi^1(x_1, \ldots, x_n; p_1, \ldots, p_n; \lambda, C) = 0$$

$$\vdots$$

$$\phi^{n+1}(x_1, \ldots, x_n; p_1, \ldots, p_n; \lambda, C) = 0.$$

Thus, $\phi: R^{2n+2} \to R^{n+1}$; so there is a solution for the $n+1$ variables $(x_1, \ldots, x_n, \lambda)$ provided that the Jacobian of ϕ is of rank $n+1$. Some computation, holding $p_1, \ldots, p_n$ and C constant, shows that the Jacobian of ϕ is simply

$$J\phi(\bar{x}) = \begin{bmatrix} \frac{\partial^2 f}{\partial x_1^2} & \cdots & \frac{\partial^2 f}{\partial x_n \partial x_1} & -p \\ \vdots & & \vdots & \vdots \\ \frac{\partial^2 f}{\partial x_1 \partial x_n} & \cdots & \frac{\partial^2 f}{\partial x_n^2} & -p_n \\ -p_1 & \cdots & -p_n & 0 \end{bmatrix}.$$

If the Hessian of f at $\bar{x}$ is nonsingular, then $J\phi(\bar{x})$ will be nonsingular. Thus, $J\phi(\bar{x})$ has rank $n+1$, which allows a solution for x_i as

$$x_i = \theta^i(p_1, \ldots, p_n; C).$$

This is an input demand function. Consider the Hessian of f at $\bar{x}$:

$$\begin{vmatrix} \dfrac{\partial^2 f}{\partial x_1^2} & \cdots & \dfrac{\partial^2 f}{\partial x_n \partial x_1} \\[2ex] \vdots & & \\[1ex] \dfrac{\partial^2 f}{\partial x_1 \partial x_n} & \cdots & \dfrac{\partial^2 f}{\partial x_n^2} \end{vmatrix}$$

If f is twice continuous differentiable, then $Hf(\bar{x})$ is certainly an $n \times n$ symmetric matrix.

Diminishing marginal returns certainly mean that $\partial^2 f / \partial x_k^2 < 0$. If $Hf(\bar{x})$ is negative definite, then $Hf(\bar{x})$ is nonsingular, and there are diminishing marginal returns. For this reason it usually is assumed that production functions are at least strictly concave and twice continuously differentiable, although this does not suffice to conclude that the function has a negative definite Hessian.

Quasi convexity and quasi concavity

There are other sets associated with functions from R^n to R besides the graph, which is a set in R^{n+1}. Specifically, for $f: S \subset R^n \rightarrow R$, with S convex, consider the set

$$U(f, b) \equiv \{x \in S : f(x) \geq b\}.$$

$U(f, b)$ is a subset of S that consists of those points for which the value of the function exceeds or equals the real number b. Because the set of all points x in S that have the property that $f(x) = b$ is a level set of f at height b, $U(f, b)$ is sometimes called an *upper contour set* of f.

EXAMPLE

If f is a utility function defined on R^2, the set of points in the first quadrant for which $f(x_1, x_2) = b$ form the indifference curve at b "utils." $U(f, b)$ is then the set of all bundles $x = (x_1, x_2)$ that the individual judges to be at least as desirable as a bundle z yielding b "utils."

In an analogous fashion, define the set

$$L(f, b) \equiv \{x \in S : f(x) \leq b\}$$

to be a *lower contour set* of f. Notice that if

$$\hat{x} \in U(f,b) \cap L(f,b),$$

then $\hat{x}$ is in a level set of f for which $f(\hat{x}) = b$.

EXAMPLE

Let f be a production function defined on R^2; so there are two inputs. Then $L(f,b)$ is the set of all input combinations that yield an output level no greater than b.

If f is a utility function, a level set is an indifference curve. If f is a production function, a level set is an isoquant. Because indifference curves and isoquants are used frequently in economic analysis, and because they can be defined by upper and lower contour sets, it is important to characterize such sets as $U(f,b)$ and $L(f,b)$.

A function $f: S \subset R^n \rightarrow R$, for S convex, is *quasi-concave* if the set $U(f,b)$ is convex for all $b \in R$. Such a function is *quasi-convex* if $L(f,b)$ is convex for all $b \in R$. Define f to be *strictly quasi-concave* (*strictly quasi-convex*) if the set $U(f,b)$ ($L(f,b)$) is *strictly convex* for all $b \in R$.

EXAMPLE

Utility functions and production functions, which have diminishing marginal rates of substitution along indifference curves or isoquants, are functions that are quasi-concave.

The relationships between graphs and level sets, or graphs and projections of cross sections of the graph onto the domain space, suggest that quasi concavity is somehow related to concavity and that quasi convexity is associated with convexity. Specifically, it is true that a convex function is also quasi-convex; a concave function is quasi-concave. Suppose f is concave. Then if x and $\hat{x}$ are in $S \subset R^n$, $f(\alpha x + (1-\alpha)\hat{x}) \geq \alpha f(x) + (1-\alpha)(\hat{x})$. Is it true that $U(f,b) = \{x \in S : f(x) \geq b\}$ is a convex set? Take x and y in $U(f,b)$. The problem is to show that for any $\beta \in [0,1]$, $z = \beta x + (1-\beta)y$ is also in $U(f,b)$. That is, is it true that $f(z) \geq b$? Certainly,

$$f(z) = f(\beta x + (1-\beta)y) \geq f(x) + (1-\beta)f(y)$$

by concavity. But because, by construction, x and y are in $U(f,b)$, $f(x) \geq b$ and $f(y) \geq b$. Thus,

$$\beta f(x) + (1 - \beta)f(y) \geq \beta b + (1 - \beta)b = b.$$

Hence, $f(z) \geq b$, and so z is in $U(f, b)$, which is consequently convex. Thus, concavity of a function implies quasi concavity. The converse is not true. To see this, notice that for $f: R \to R$, any monotone decreasing function is quasi-concave, because for such a function $x_1 < x_2$ implies $f(x_1) > f(x_2)$. Thus, the upper contour sets are the intervals of the form $(-\infty, a)$, which are certainly convex. But look at Figure 10.2. This function has enough of a wiggle in its graph so that some chords drawn

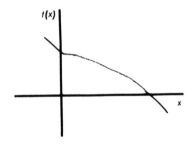

FIGURE 10.2

between points on the graph lie above the graph and other chords lie below the graph. The function is not concave.

A useful picture

Suppose a function $f: S \subset R \to R$, for S convex, is convex. Then if f is twice continuously differentiable, its second derivative is a nonnegative number. Now, f near $\bar{x}$ can be approximated by

$$f(\bar{x} + h) \approx f(\bar{x}) + f'(\bar{x})h + \tfrac{1}{2}f''(\bar{x})h^2.$$

Consequently, the left side is a function of h, as is the right side. The right side represents the sum of three functions: (1) a constant, representing the height on the graph; (2) a linear function through the origin; (3) a parabola opening upward, vertex at the origin, because $f''(x) \geq 0$. Thus, near $\bar{x}$, $f(x)$ is approximately the sum of a constant, a line, and an upward-opening parabola. Locally (near $\bar{x}$), it is useful to think of a convex function as a small tilted right-side-up bowl. This same kind of picture represents $f: R^n \to R$ when f is convex, because the positive semidefinite Hessian generates an upward opening paraboloid. In this case,

$$f(\bar{x} + h) \approx f(\bar{x}) + \operatorname{grad} f(\bar{x}) \cdot h + \tfrac{1}{2}h^T Hf(\bar{x})h.$$

Homogeneous functions

It is possible to use the second property of linear functions, equation (2), to create a further class of useful functions. A function $f: R^n \to R$ is homogeneous of degree m if $f(tx) = t^m f(x)$ for $t \in R$ and $x \in R^n$. Thus, linear functions are homogeneous of degree 1.

EXAMPLE

The log-linear utility function generates demand functions of the form

$$x_i = \frac{a_i y}{p_i},$$

where a_i is a constant, y represents household income, and p_i is the price of the ith good. Thus, the demand function D_i is of the form $x_i = D_i(p_i, y)$, a mapping from R^2 to R. It is homogeneous of degree 0 in prices and income, because $a_i(ty)/(tp_i) = x_i$.

EXAMPLE

The Cobb-Douglas production function is defined by

$$Q = AL^\alpha K^\beta,$$

where Q represents output, L and K represent labor and capital inputs, A is a constant, and α and β are constants that live in $[0, 1]$. The function maps $R^2 \to R$ as $f(L, K) = Q$. Because $A(tL)^\alpha(tK)^\beta = t^{\alpha+\beta}AL^\alpha K^\beta$, the Cobb-Douglas production function is homogeneous of degree $\alpha + \beta$. If $\alpha + \beta = 1$, the Cobb-Douglas function is homogeneous of degree 1 and represents constant returns to scale.

Because a homogeneous function of degree m is defined by

$$f(tx) = t^m f(x)$$

for any t, suppose x is fixed and t varies. Then, as a function of t, the equality may be differentiated to yield

$$\sum_{i=1}^n x_i D_i f(t, x) = mt^{m-1} f(x).$$

Setting $t = 1$ shows that

$$\sum_{i=1}^n x_i D_i f(x) = mf(x),$$

or, in classical notation,

$$x_1 \frac{\partial f}{\partial x_1} + \cdots + x_n \frac{\partial f}{\partial x_n} = mf(x)$$

when f is homogeneous of degree m.

This result, called *Euler's theorem,* is especially useful when f is homogeneous of degree 0 or 1. If f is homogeneous of degree 0,

$$\operatorname{grad} f(x) \cdot x = 0.$$

Thus, at x, the gradient of f at x is orthogonal to the vector x. If f is homogeneous of degree 1, then

$$\operatorname{grad} f(x) \cdot x = f(x).$$

Thus, f at x is represented by its gradient and the vector x. It is not difficult to see that if f is homogeneous of degree m, then each partial derivative of f, as a function, is homogeneous of degree $m-1$. Thus, Euler's theorem yields

$$x^T H x = m(m-1)f(x),$$

where H is the Hessian of f.

EXAMPLE

Consider again the Cobb-Douglas production function. Assume it is homogeneous of degree 1. The Euler theorem yields

$$\frac{\partial f}{\partial L} L + \frac{\partial f}{\partial K} K = Q.$$

Clearly, $\partial f/\partial L$ and $\partial f/\partial K$ are the marginal products of labor and capital. If competition assures that factors are paid their marginal products, then $(\partial f/\partial L)L$ is the wage bill and $(\partial f/\partial K)K$ is the capital bill. Thus, total output is fully accounted for by wage and capital payments. Economists call this result "the adding-up theorem."

EXAMPLE

In equilibrium for the firm, it must be the case that factor prices are proportional to marginal products. Thus, if $f: R^2 \to R$ is a production function, with factors x_1 and x_2, and p_1 and p_2 are the factor prices and λ is a constant,

$$\lambda \frac{\partial f}{\partial x_1} - p_1 = 0$$

$$\lambda \frac{\partial f}{\partial x_2} - p_2 = 0.$$

Suppose λ is the price of the output. Then the value of total output is $\lambda f(x_1, x_2)$. If f is homogeneous of degree 1, then

$$\lambda f(x_1, x_2) = \lambda \frac{\partial f}{\partial x_1} x_1 + \lambda \frac{\partial f}{\partial x_2} x_2,$$

and so

$$\lambda f(x_1, x_2) = p_1 x_1 + p_2 x_2.$$

But the left side is total revenue to the firm, and the right side is total cost; so equilibrium net revenue (or profit) is zero. Because this is true for any output, the idea of maximizing profit yields an indeterminate level of output for constant-returns-to-scale technologies.

A little thought suggests that this result comes directly from considering the equilibrium conditions as implicit functions, for in that case the determinacy of output levels is related to the nonsingularity of the Jacobian of those functions. But the Jacobian involves the Hessian of the production function f. Because f is homogeneous of degree 1, its Hessian has the property that $x^T H x = 0$; so H is singular.

FURTHER READING

The standard references for convexity issues include the famous "Fenchel notes," lectures by W. Fenchel at Princeton in 1951 entitled "Convex Cones, Sets, and Functions." See also Nikaido's *Convex Structures and Economic Theory* and Karlin's *Mathematical Methods*. For homogeneous functions, see Lancaster's *Mathematical Economics*.

EXERCISES

10.1 Suppose $f: S \subset R^n \to R$ is continuous and S is convex. Show that f is convex if and only if, for x and y in S,

$$f\left(\frac{x+y}{2}\right) \leq \frac{f(x) + f(y)}{2}.$$

10.2 A hyperplane in R^n divides R^n into two half spaces. Given a set $X \in R^n$ and a point $a \in X$, suppose there is a hyperplane passing through a such that all of X lies in, or on one side of, the hyperplane. Then that hyperplane is called a *supporting hyperplane* for X. Using the bibliographic references cited for this chapter, or Arrow and Hahn's book, prove the following *separation theorem*: Let X be a nonempty convex set. If a is a boundary point of X, then there exists a supporting hyperplane (for X) that passes through a.

10.3 Suppose $f: R^n \to R$, and f has the property that

$$f(tx) = \phi(t)f(x).$$

Then f is called *homothetic*.

  (a) Show that any function that is homogeneous (of degree m) is homothetic.
  (b) Show that a log-linear utility function is homothetic.
  (c) For a homothetic function, as defined, establish the generalized Euler equation

$$\phi'(1) \cdot f(x) = \operatorname{grad} f(x) \cdot x.$$

CHAPTER 11

Optimization (I)

Why not the best?
Jimmy Carter

Economic models often are based on the behavior of individual agents. A characteristic of such models is the assumption that agents make "rational" choices. Specifically, agents have well-defined objects of choice, have coherent rankings of those objects, and strive to choose the most preferred object available.

Earlier chapters have indicated how it is possible to rank bundles of goods, or input-output combinations, and to represent that ranking by a function from R^n to R. Possible objects of choice were n-vectors, defined by a set $S \subset R^n$. The choosing was defined by a function $f: S \to R$ that attached a real number to such a vector. The choice problem involves finding the point $x \in S$ such that $f(x)$ is as large (or small) as possible.

The optimization problem

Suppose there is a given function $f: R^n \to R$. The vectors $x \in R^n$ are called *instruments*. If the set $S \subset R^n$ defines feasible choices, then S is called the *opportunity set*. The function $f: R^n \to R$ is called the *objective function*. The general optimization (or programming) problem is to find an $x \in S$ such that $f(x)$ is as large as possible. Formally:

(O.P.) $\max_{x} f(x)$ subject to $x \in S \subset R^n$.

The structure of the analysis is contained in equation (O.P). The questions of interest are these: Does there exist any solution to equation (O.P)? What conditions on f and S guarantee solutions? How are solutions found under specifications of f and S? [Because maximizing a real-valued function is the same as minimizing the negative of that function, equation (O.P.) defines a class of minimization problems as well.]

145

EXAMPLE

Let p be output price and x be quantity of output. A sales-maximizing firm will want to solve

$$\max_{x} px$$

subject to a constraint that only some output levels are "sensible." Letting those outputs be denoted by $x \in S$, the firm will solve

$$\max_{x} px \quad \text{subject to} \quad x \in S.$$

What, in general, can be said about equation (O.P.)? Notice first that if x^* solves (O.P.), so that x^* is maximizing, then for any other $x \in S$, $f(x^*) \geq f(x)$. Such an x^* is a local maximum if for any $x \in S$ and $x \in N_\epsilon(x^*)$, $f(x^*) \geq f(x)$. Certainly a maximum is a local maximum. The issue of the existence of a solution to (O.P.) is partially settled by the *Weierstrass theorem*.

Suppose f is continuous. Then nearby points in S get sent to nearby points in R. If $f(x)$ lives in a bounded set in R, then there is some real number that $f(x)$ does not exceed. If, further, $f(x)$ lives in a closed set of R, any sequence of numbers $f(x)$ converges to an $f(x^*)$ that is also in that set. Thus, if $f(x)$ lives in a compact set, then there is a largest $f(x)$, and when f is continuous, it is possible to find the x^* that yields that largest $f(x^*)$. See Figure 11.1. But if f is continuous and S is compact, certainly $f(S) \subset R$ is a compact set. Thus, there is an $x^* \in S$ that maximizes f. The Weierstrass theorem states that a continuous function defined on a compact (opportunity) set achieves a maximum (and minimum) on that set.

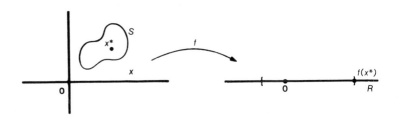

FIGURE 11.1

EXAMPLE

In economic analysis, the Weierstrass theorem is used in sometimes subtle ways. Suppose a consumer chooses goods bundles $x \in R^n$ to maximize utility U. Certainly, $x_i \geq 0$, but

$S = \{x \in R^n : x_i \geq 0\}$ is not compact. Thus, there may be no solution to $\max_x U(x)$ with $x \in S \subset R^n$. If goods are finite in amount, then S may be considered bounded. The solution then will exist, although for "sensible" utility functions the maximizing bundle might contain all the goods in the universe. It is the income constraint, of course, that forces a sensible solution. Affordability of bundles creates a compact feasible set of potential choosable bundles.

EXAMPLE

Suppose $f: R^2 \to R$ is defined by $f(x_1, x_2) = x_1^2 + x_2^2$, for $0 \leq x_i \leq 1$. Thus, S is the unit square in R^2, which is compact; f is clearly continuous, because it is differentiable. Hence, a maximum exists. Figure 11.2 shows the mapping. Certainly the point $(0, 0) \to 0$ and $(1, 1) \to 2$. Further, any point on the intersection of the circle $r = x_1^2 + x_2^2$ with the unit square gets sent to the point $r \in [0, 2]$; so the pre-images of points in R are quarter circles. The point $(1, 1)$ yields the largest-radius quarter circle that has a nonvacuous intersection with the unit square.

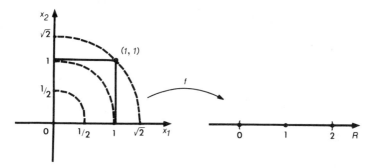

FIGURE 11.2

The Weierstrass theorem guarantees that a global maximum exists when S is compact and f is continuous. But such global maxima are difficult to find in the general case when S is complicated and f, as a map, pushes space around in a complicated fashion. The general strategy for solving equation (O.P.) in that case should by now be obvious. Restricting attention to a small subset of S, a neighborhood of $x \in S$, approximate f by a linear mapping using the derivative. Because linear maps have nice properties, it may be possible to characterize, with little trouble, a local maximum. Then compare all those local maxima to identify the global maximum for f.

A strong result, of special use to economists, makes this task feasible.

For suppose there is a procedure that identifies local maxima. If S is convex as well as compact, and f is a strictly concave function, then the graph of f looks like a bowl opening downward. Such a function has a unique global maximum value, and the only local maximum is, indeed, that global maximum. Thus, any procedure that identifies a local maximum for such a function will also have identified the global maximum. This result is called the *local-global theorem*. It is important in economic analysis because, as Chapter 10 suggested, the basic objective functions economists use are concave (or convex functions, which characterize local-global minima).

EXAMPLE

Utility functions, profit functions, and production functions that are strictly concave are all sensible objective functions for maximizing agents. Cost functions are strictly convex and are sensibly minimized.

Local maxima

The solution of the general problem (O.P.) frequently reduces to finding local maxima. What must be true at a point x^* when $f(x^*) \geq f(x)$ for all points x near x^*? The previous chapter showed that when f was twice continuously differentiable, then locally, near x^*,

$$f(x^* + h) \approx f(x^*) + \operatorname{grad} f(x^*)h + \tfrac{1}{2} h^T Hf(x^*)h,$$

when h is a "small" column n-vector. $Hf(x^*)$ is the Hessian of f at x^*. If x^* maximizes f,

$$f(x^* + h) - f(x^*) \approx \operatorname{grad} f(x^*)h + \tfrac{1}{2} h^T Hf(x^*)h \leq 0.$$

Let $h = \lambda x$, where λ is a scalar. Then

$$f(x^* + \lambda x) - f(x^*) \approx \operatorname{grad} f(x^*)\lambda x + \tfrac{1}{2} \lambda^2 x^T Hf(x^*)x \leq 0.$$

If $\lambda > 0$, divide the last inequality by λ and let $\lambda \to 0$ to yield

$$\operatorname{grad} f(x^*)x \leq 0,$$

where x is any small nonzero vector.

But λ could have been negative. In that case, dividing by λ and taking limits yields

$$\operatorname{grad} f(x^*)x \geq 0.$$

Thus,

$$\operatorname{grad} f(x^*)x = 0$$

for all nonzero x; at an x^* that locally maximizes f,

$$\operatorname{grad} f(x^*) = 0.$$

Consequently, at any maximizing x^*, for any small n-vector h,

$$f(x^* + h) - f(x^*) = \tfrac{1}{2} h^T Hf(x^*)h \le 0,$$

whereas at any minimizing x^*,

$$f(x^* + h) - f(x^*) = \tfrac{1}{2} h^T Hf(x^*)h \ge 0.$$

Thus, at a local maximizing x^* of f, it must be true that $\operatorname{grad} f(x^*) = 0$ and $Hf(x^*)$ is negative semidefinite. At any local minimizing x^* of f, it must be true that $\operatorname{grad} f(x^*) = 0$ and $Hf(x^*)$ is positive semidefinite. These two conditions characterize local optima. If x^* locally maximizes f, then it must be true that the gradient of f at x^* is zero and the Hessian of f at x^* is negative semidefinite. These are necessary conditions that f be locally maximized by x^*.

Unconstrained optimization

Consider again the general problem

(O.P.) $\max_{x} f(x)$ subject to $x \in S \subset R^n$.

Suppose that $S = R^n$, so that the opportunity set is all of R^n. Intuitively, there are no constraints at all on the choice of instruments to maximize the objective function f. R^n is certainly not compact; so there is no guarantee that equation (O.P.) has a solution even if f is twice continuously differentiable. But if f is maximized by $x^* \in R^n$, certainly x^* locally maximizes f near x^*. Thus, for given f, compute $\operatorname{grad} f(x)$. Then find all points $x^* \in R^n$ that satisfy $\operatorname{grad} f(x^*) = 0$. In other words, if $f: R^n \to R$, then as x^* varies over R^n, $\operatorname{grad} f(x^*): R^n \to R$, and $\operatorname{grad} f(x^*)$ is a linear mapping. The kernel of this mapping is precisely the set of points that potentially optimize f. If the kernel is the empty set, there is no optimum. If the kernel has a finite number of points x_i^* in it, check $Hf(x_i^*)$ to see whether x_i^* yields a local maximum or local minimum. The largest local maximum (minimum) is the global maximum (minimum). If the kernel contains an infinite number of points, it may be true that the subset of those points at which the Hessian of f is negative semidefinite is vacuous (so no maximum exists) or contains but one point x^*, in which case the global maximum is $f(x^*)$.

EXAMPLE

1. Suppose $f: R^2 \to R$, where $f(x_1, x_2) = x_1^2 + x_2^2$. Find the x^* that optimizes f over R^2. Certainly, $\text{grad} f(x^*) = (2x_1^*, 2x_2^*)$. Thus, the kernel of $\text{grad} f(x^*) : R^2 \to R$ is the set $(0,0)^T$, because only $(0,0)^T$ gets sent to zero by $\text{grad} f(x^*)$. But $Hf(x^*) = \begin{bmatrix} 2 & 0 \\ 0 & 2 \end{bmatrix}$, which is diagonal and strictly positive definite for any x^*, and particularly for $x^* = (0,0)^T$. Thus, there is only one local optimum, and it is a local, and thus global, minimum. There is no maximum.

2. Suppose $f: R^2 \to R$, where $f(x_1, x_2) = \sin x_1 + \cos x_2$. Find the x^* that optimizes f over R^2. Certainly, $\text{grad} f(x^*) = (\cos x_1^*, -\sin x_2^*)$. What is the kernel of the linear mapping $\text{grad} f(x^*)$? It is the set of points such that $\cos x_1^* = 0$ and $-\sin x_2^* = 0$. But $\cos x_1^* = 0$ for $x_1^* = ((2n-1)/2)\pi$, for integers $n = \cdots -2, -1, 0, 1, 2, \cdots$. And $-\sin x_2^* = 0$ when $x_2^* = (2m/2)\pi$, for integers $m = \cdots -2, -1, 0, 1, 2, \cdots$. Thus, the kernel of the gradient map is the set $\text{Ker grad} f(x^*) = \{(x_1^*, x_2^*) : x_1^* = (2n-1)(\pi/2)$ and $x_2^* = (2m)(\pi/2)$ for all (positive and negative) integers n and $m\}$. This set is certainly infinite. It has cardinality $\aleph_0$.

Consider the Hessian

$$Hf(x^*) = \begin{bmatrix} -\sin x_1^* & 0 \\ 0 & -\cos x_2^* \end{bmatrix}.$$

For any (x_1^*, x_2^*) in $\text{Ker grad} f(x^*)$, $-\sin x_1^*$ is either $+1$ or -1, and similarly $-\cos x_2^* = \pm 1$. Thus, the eigenvalues of $Hf(x^*)$ are never zero. They are both negative when $-\sin x_1^* = -1$ and $-\cos x_2^* = -1$, for then $Hf(x^*)$ is strictly negative definite. Thus, for n and m both odd, (x_1^*, x_2^*) defines a strict local maximum, and when n and m are both even, (x_1^*, x_2^*) defines a strict local minimum. If n is even (odd) and m is odd (even), (x_1^*, x_2^*) does not generate a local optimum. It is easy to see that at any maximizing x^*, $f(x^*) = 2$, and at any minimizing x^*, $f(x^*) = -2$.

Classical programming

Suppose the opportunity set is defined as the kernel of a mapping from R^n to R^m. That is, suppose

$S = \{(x_1, \ldots, x_n)^T \in R^n : g_1(x_1, \ldots, x_n) = 0, \ldots, g_m(x_1, \ldots, x_n) = 0\}.$

Then, if $g = (g_1, \ldots, g_m)^T$, the optimization problem becomes the classical programming problem

(C.P.) $\max_x f(x)$ subject to $g(x) = 0,$

where $x \in R^n$, $f: R^n \rightarrow R$, and $g: R^n \rightarrow R^m$. The study of equation (C.P.) proceeds by reducing (C.P.) to the unconstrained equation (O.P.). Notice that the opportunity set is defined by

$$g_1(x_1, \ldots, x_n) = 0$$
$$g_2(x_1, \ldots, x_n) = 0$$
$$\vdots$$
$$g_m(x_1, \ldots, x_n) = 0.$$

If g, as a mapping, has a Jacobian of rank m, and $n > m$, then the Implicit Function Theorem permits expression of exactly m of the x_i's as functions of the remaining $n - m$ of the x_i's. Thus, suppose $x^* \in R^n$ solves equation (C.P.), and assume that g is continuously differentiable near x^* and that the Jacobian of g has rank m. Then,

$$x_{n-m+1}^* = \phi^1(x_1^*, \ldots, x_{n-m}^*)$$
$$x_{n-m+2}^* = \phi^2(x_1^*, \ldots, x_{n-m}^*)$$
$$\vdots \qquad \vdots$$
$$x_n^* = \phi^m(x_1^*, \ldots, x_{n-m}^*).$$

Substituting these values of $x_{n-m+1}^*, \ldots, x_n^*$ into equation (C.P.) yields

$$\max f(x_1, \ldots, x_{n-m}; \phi^1(x_1, \ldots, x_{n-m}), \ldots, \phi^m(x_1, \ldots, x_{n-m})),$$

which is an unconstrained maximization problem for

$$(x_1, \ldots, x_{n-m})^T \in R^{n-m}.$$

At a local maximum, the gradient of f must be zero, and the Hessian must be negative semidefinite. This means that if $x^1 = (x_1, \ldots, x_{n-m})^T$ and $x^2 = (x_{n-m+1}, \ldots, x_n)^T$ is a partition of the original vector x,

$$\text{grad} f(x) = \text{grad} f(x^1, x^2) = \text{grad} f(x^1, \phi(x^1)).$$

Thus, in classical notation,

$$\text{grad} f(x^*) = \frac{\partial f}{\partial x^{1*}} + \frac{\partial f}{\partial x^{2*}} \frac{\partial \phi}{\partial x^{1*}} = 0$$

at any x^* that solves the problem (C.P.). But because the constraints, $g_i = 0$, must hold for all x, certainly for all x^1,

$$g(x^1, \phi(x^1)) = 0.$$

Thus,

$$\frac{\partial g}{\partial x^1} + \frac{\partial g}{\partial x^2}\frac{\partial \phi}{\partial x^1} = 0,$$

and hence

$$\frac{\partial \phi}{\partial x^1} = -\frac{\partial g}{\partial x^2}^{-1}\frac{\partial g}{\partial x^1}$$

for all x^1. Substituting this last expression, true for all x^1, into the gradient condition true at the optimum x^{1*} yields

$$\frac{\partial f}{\partial x^{1*}} + \frac{\partial f}{\partial x^{2*}}\left[-\frac{\partial g}{\partial x^{2*}}^{-1}\frac{\partial g}{\partial x^1}\right] = 0.$$

Now define the row vector $y = (y_1, \ldots, y_m)$ by

$$y = \left[\frac{\partial f}{\partial x^{2*}}\left(\frac{\partial g}{\partial x^{2*}}\right)^{-1}\right].$$

Thus, the gradient condition, which necessarily holds at an optimum, becomes

$$\frac{\partial f}{\partial x^1} - y\frac{\partial g}{\partial x^1} = 0.$$

Because it is always true that

$$\frac{\partial f}{\partial x^2} - \frac{\partial f}{\partial x^2}\left(\frac{\partial g}{\partial x^2}\right)^{-1}\frac{\partial g}{\partial x^2} = 0,$$

the gradient condition that must hold at an optimum can be written, finally, in terms of the original variable x as

$$\frac{\partial f}{\partial x} - y\frac{\partial g}{\partial x} = 0.$$

In modern notation, this gradient condition states that at an optimum x^* of (C.P.),

$$Df(x^*) = yDg(x^*),$$

where $y = (y_1, \ldots, y_m)$ is a real m-vector whose components are positive or negative.

EXAMPLE

Find $\max_{x_1, x_2} x_1^2 + x_2^2$ subject to $x_1 + x_2 = 2$. Certainly, $f(x) = x_1^2 + x_2^2$, and $g(x_1, x_2) = x_1 + x_2 - 2 = 0$. At an optimizing $x^* = (x_1^*, x_2^*)^T$, the condition

$$\frac{\partial f}{\partial x^*} - y \frac{\partial g}{\partial x^*} = 0$$

yields

$$\frac{\partial f}{\partial x_1^*} - y \frac{\partial g}{\partial x_1^*} = 0,$$

$$\frac{\partial f}{\partial x_2^*} - y \frac{\partial g}{\partial x_2^*} = 0,$$

and

$$x_1^* + x_2^* - 2 = 0.$$

Thus, at an optimizing x^*, it is true that

$$2x_1^* - y \cdot 1 = 0$$
$$2x_2^* - y \cdot 1 = 0$$
$$x_1^* + x_2^* - 2 = 0.$$

Consequently, it must be the case that

$$x_1^* = 1, \qquad x_2^* = 1, \qquad y = 2.$$

This problem is pictured in Figure 11.3.

The gradient condition, which necessarily holds at an optimizing x^* for equation (C.P.), may be produced by an alternative construction. If the problem (C.P.) is given, define the row m-vector $y = (y_1, \ldots, y_m)$ to be the *Lagrange multipliers*. Define the Lagrange function for (C.P.) or the Lagrangian by

$$L(x; y) = f(x) - yg(x).$$

Thus, L maps R^{n+m} to R.

Consider the unconstrained optimization problem (O.P.) for L as

$$\max_{x, y} L(x; y).$$

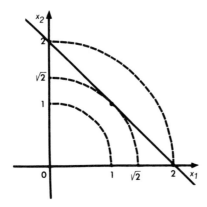

FIGURE 11.3

It is necessary, at an optimum, that

$$\text{grad}\, L(x^*; y^*) = 0.$$

But

$$\text{grad}\, L(x; y) = \left(\frac{\partial L}{\partial x}, \frac{\partial L}{\partial y} \right)_{x^*, y^*} = \left(\frac{\partial f}{\partial x} - y\,\frac{\partial g}{\partial x}, -g \right)_{x^*, y^*}.$$

Thus, the gradient condition defines the two equations

$$\frac{\partial f}{\partial x^*} - y^* \frac{\partial g}{\partial x^*} = 0$$

$$g(x^*) = 0,$$

and these conditions are identical with the gradient conditions that characterized an optimum x^* of equation (C.P.).

EXAMPLE

Consider the problem of maximizing the utility function $u: R^n \to R$ subject to the income constraint $p \cdot x = I$, where p is a given price vector, I is given household income, and x is a commodity bundle. Thus, consider the problem

$$\max_{x} u(x) \quad \text{subject to} \quad I - px = 0.$$

Define the Lagrangian

$$L(x; y) = u(x) + y(I - px)$$

for scalar y. Then, at an optimum, (x,y),

$$\frac{\partial u}{\partial x} - yp = 0$$

$$I - px = 0.$$

These $n+1$ equations, true at an optimum, are written out as

$$\frac{\partial u}{\partial x_1} - yp_1 = 0$$

$$\vdots$$

$$\frac{\partial u}{\partial x_n} - yp_n = 0$$

$$I - p_1 x_1 - \cdots - p_n x_n = 0.$$

Thus, in "equilibrium," that is, at a constrained utility maximum, the marginal utility of commodity i is proportional to the ith price, and the ratio of marginal utilities of goods i and j is equal to the ratio of their prices.

To distinguish among local optima, to find out whether optimizing x^* yields a maximum or a minimum, it is necessary to examine the Hessian of the Lagrangian. If the problem (C.P.) is given, and the Lagrangian is $L(x;y) = f(x) - yg(x)$, then

$$HL(x^*;y^*) = \begin{bmatrix} \dfrac{\partial^2 L}{\partial x^{*2}} & \dfrac{\partial^2 L}{\partial y^* \partial x^*} \\ \dfrac{\partial^2 L}{\partial x^* \partial y^*} & \dfrac{\partial^2 L}{\partial y^{*2}} \end{bmatrix}.$$

So

$$HL(x^*;y^*) = \begin{bmatrix} \dfrac{\partial^2 f}{\partial x^{*2}} - y^* \dfrac{\partial^2 g}{\partial x^{*2}} & -\dfrac{\partial g}{\partial x^*}^T \\ \dfrac{\partial g}{\partial x^*} & 0 \end{bmatrix}.$$

It is important to recognize the dimensions of the vectors and matrices that make up $HL(x^*;y^*)$: $(\partial^2 f/\partial x^{*2} - y^* \partial^2 g/\partial x^{*2})$ is an $n \times n$ matrix, and $-\partial g/\partial x^*$ is an $m \times n$ matrix, because $g: R^n \rightarrow R^m$; 0 is an $n \times m$ matrix of zeros. This dimensionality argument arises from the fact that all vectors are column vectors. Thus, if $f(x) = Ax$, grad $f(x) = A$, where A is $(m \times n)$ and x is $(n \times 1)$. Thus, if $g(x) = x^T A^T$, then grad $g(x) = A^T$.

The Hessian $HL(x^*; y^*)$ is sometimes referred to as a bordered Hessian, because the matrix $\partial^2 L/\partial x^{*2}$ is "bordered" by matrices that come from the constraints and by a zero matrix. The condition that (x^*, y^*) generate a maximum is the condition that $HL(x^*, y^*)$ be negative semidefinite. It is not difficult to establish that this condition on the bordered Hessian will be satisfied if, and only if, the matrix $(\partial^2 L/\partial x^{*2})$ is negative semidefinite.

EXAMPLE

Consider the gradient conditions, established in the previous example, for the constrained utility maximization problem. Do they define a maximum? Compute the Hessian of $L(x; y) = u(x) + y(I - px)$ as

$$HL(x^*; y^*) = \begin{bmatrix} \dfrac{\partial^2 u}{\partial x^{*2}} - p \\ p \qquad 0 \end{bmatrix}.$$

$HL(x^*; y^*)$ is negative semidefinite when $\partial^2 u/\partial x^{*2}$ is negative semidefinite. But this certainly occurs when the utility function is concave. Thus, if u is a concave twice continuously differentiable utility function, a solution to the constrained utility maximization problem is indeed a maximum, not a minimum.

EXAMPLE

There is an interesting problem that brings together a number of concepts in a single solution. Consider the problem

$$\max_x f(x) \quad \text{subject to} \quad g(x) = 0,$$

where x is an n-vector, $f(x)$ is the quadratic form $x^T A x$, and $g(x) = x^T x - 1$. If the sum of squares of the instrument vectors equals 1, how large can a given quadratic form be? Form the Lagrangian $L(x; y) = x^T A x + y(x^T x - 1)$ for A an $n \times n$ symmetric matrix. The gradient conditions, true at any optimum, are that

$$\frac{\partial L}{\partial x} = 2x^T A + 2yx^T I_n = 0$$

$$\frac{\partial L}{\partial y} = x^T x - 1 = 0.$$

If (x^*, y^*) solves these equations,

$$x^{*T}A + y^*x^{*T}I_n = 0$$

$$x^{*T}x^* = 1.$$

Multiplying the first vector equation on the right by x^* is equivalent to multiplying each of the first n of the $n+1$ gradient conditions by the appropriate x_i^* and summing. Performing this operation produces

$$x^{*T}Ax^* + y^*x^{*T}I_n x^* = 0,$$

so that

$$x^{*T}Ax^* = -y^*.$$

Thus, at any optimum, $f(x^*) = -y^*$.
   The condition $\partial L/\partial x = 0$ also entails that

$$x^{*T}A = -y^*x^{*T}.$$

But because $f(x^*) = -y^*$, $f(x^*)$ solves the equation

$$Ax = f(x^*)x.$$

Thus, $f(x^*)$ is an eigenvalue of A.
   Further, if $f(x^*)$ is maximal, then $f(x^*)$ is the largest eigenvalue of A. To see that x^* actually maximizes $f(x)$, compute the Hessian of L as

$$HL(x^*; y^*) = \begin{bmatrix} 2A^T + 2y^*I_n & (2x^{*T}I_n)^T \\ 2x^{*T}I_n & 0 \end{bmatrix}.$$

This bordered Hessian is negative semidefinite when $2A^T + 2y^*I_n$ is negative semidefinite. But $y^* = -f(x^*)$, and $f(x^*)$ is an eigenvalue of A. Thus, because $A^T = A$, the matrix

$$(A - f(x^*)I_n)$$

is singular. So $x^T(A - f(x^*)I_n)x = 0$, and thus the bordered Hessian is certainly negative semidefinite. Notice further that if $f(x^*) = 0$, then $y^* = 0$. So the presence of the constraint does not matter in the problem. If $y^* = 0$, the constraint is not binding.

The Lagrangian technique for solving optimization problem (C.P.) is especially useful in economics. Geometrically, the gradient conditions state that at an optimizing x^* the gradient of the objective function is a real n-vector that is a linear combination of the gradients of the constraint functions. Now suppose that the constraint functions g are of the form $g_i(x_1, \ldots, x_n) = b_i$ for a scalar b_i. So $g(x) = b$ defines the constraints, for b an n-vector. "Loosening" the constraint is modeled by changing the vector b. How does the value of the objective function change at an optimizing x^* as b changes? Consider the Lagrangian, at an optimum, as a function of b:

$$L(b) = f(x^*(b)) + y^*(b)[b - g(x^*(b))].$$

Here the Implicit Function Theorem has been used, in the gradient condition, to show that the optimizing vectors (x^*, y^*) are functions of b. Then,

$$\frac{\partial L}{\partial b} = \frac{\partial f}{\partial x^*} \frac{\partial x^*}{\partial b} - y \frac{\partial g}{\partial x^*} \frac{\partial x^*}{\partial b} + (b - g(x^*)) \frac{\partial y^{*T}}{\partial b} + y$$

$$= \left(\frac{\partial f}{\partial x^*} - y \frac{\partial g}{\partial x^*} \right) \frac{\partial x^*}{\partial b} + (b - g(x^*)) \frac{\partial y^{*T}}{\partial b} + y$$

$$= y$$

because the gradient conditions hold at (x^*, y^*). Thus, the Lagrange multiplier y_i measures the change in the value of the objective function L as the ith constraint is relaxed. If at an optimum the ith constraint function is nonbinding, y_i will be zero.

One additional feature of the Lagrange technique should be noted. Solving constrained optimization problems like (C.P.) may be very difficult. However, the Lagrange multiplier technique generates $n + m$ equations in the $n + m$ variables (the instruments and the multipliers). These gradient conditions define a mapping $\phi: R^{n+m} \to R^{n+m}$. Any optimizing (x^*, y^*) is, of course, in the kernel of this mapping, because $\phi(x^*, y^*) = 0$. It is sometimes possible actually to construct the kernel of ϕ, by solving the equations, if ϕ is linear. If ϕ is not linear, indirect techniques may sometimes help to characterize the equilibrium even when (x^*, y^*) cannot be found as a simple algebraic expression.

EXAMPLE

Consider the log-linear utility function defined by $u(x) = \sum_{i=1}^n a_i \log x_i$, where $0 < a_i < 1$ and $\sum_{i=1}^n a_i = 1$. Suppose it is desired to maximize $u(x)$ subject to the household budget constraint $px = I$. Form the Lagrangian $L(x; y) = \sum a_i \log x_i + y(I - px)$. Then the gradient conditions become

$$\frac{a_1}{x_1} - yp_1 = 0$$

$$\frac{a_2}{x_2} - yp_2 = 0$$

$$\vdots \qquad \vdots$$

$$\frac{a_n}{x_n} - yp_n = 0$$

$$I - (p_1x_1 + p_2x_2 + \cdots + p_nx_n) = 0.$$

These $(n+1)$ equations in the $(n+1)$ variables $(x;y)$ define a mapping $\phi: R^{n+1} \rightarrow R^{n+1}$ by

$$\phi = (\phi^1, \phi^2, \ldots, \phi^{n+1})^T,$$

where, for $i = 1, 2, \ldots, n$,

$$\phi^i(x_1, x_2, \ldots, x_n; y) = \frac{a_i}{x_i} - yp;$$

and

$$\phi^{n+1}(x_1, x_2, \ldots, x_n; y) = I - p \cdot x.$$

Certainly, ϕ is not a linear mapping.

How can the system $\phi(x;y) = 0$ be solved to find the optimum? There are two approaches. First, it is possible simply to assume that a solution (x^*, y^*) exists and then to use the Implicit Function Theorem to show that $x_i^* = \Theta^i(p_1, \ldots, p_n; a_1, \ldots, a_n; I)$ characterizes that optimum. This demand function Θ^i, which is the real object of the exercise, can be analyzed without having to produce Θ^i explicitly. However, if an explicit demand function is desired, x_i^* must be found by solving $\phi(x;y) = 0$. One useful technique involves multiplying each of the first n equations by x_i, yielding

$$\left(\frac{a_i}{x_i} - yp_i \right)x_i = 0$$

or

$$a_i - yp_ix_i = 0.$$

Summing these n equations gives $0 = \sum a_i - y \sum p_i x_i = \sum a_i - yI$, from the $n+1$th equation. Because $\sum a_i = 1$, $y = 1/I$. Substituting this value for the multiplier into the ith equation yields

$$\frac{a_i}{x_i} - \frac{p_i}{I} = 0$$

or

$$x_i^* = \frac{a_i I}{p_i} \ .$$

This demand function is homogeneous of degree 1 in prices and income and, for income fixed, has a constant elasticity of demand. Sometimes nonlinear equations do have nice solutions.

FURTHER READING

Economists will want to consult Intrilligator's *Mathematical Optimization and Economic Theory*, Frisch's *Maxima and Minima*, and Dixit's *Optimization in Economic Theory* for fuller treatment of the ideas presented in this chapter.

EXERCISES

11.1 Find the global maximum of the function $f: R^2 \to R$ when $f(x_1, x_2) = x_1 - x_1^2 - x_2^2$, where $0 \le x_2 \le 1$.

11.2 Maximize the output, subject to given factor costs, for the CES (constant elasticity of substitution) production function $q = a[bL^{-\beta} + cK^{-\beta}]^{-h/\beta}$. Here, a, b, and c are positive constants, L and K are flows of input services, $h > 0$, and $\beta \ge -1$. Let total costs, C, be $wL + rK$ for w and r fixed.

11.3 Borrowing from Intrilligator (p. 217), a monopolist faces a linear marginal revenue and a quadratic marginal cost curve

$$MR = a - bq$$

$$MC = c - dq - eq^2,$$

where fixed cost is f and parameters a to f are all positive.

(a) Find the revenue, cost, demand, and average cost.
(b) Find the profit-maximizing output and the maximized profits.
(c) Find the excise tax rate (tax per unit sold) that maximizes tax revenue.
(d) Find the price ceiling that maximizes output.

11.4 Let y be a dependent variable and x a k-vector of independent variables. Let there be n observations on the variables generating data points. Suppose there is a linear relationship $y = a \cdot x$. If a is chosen to minimize the sum of squared errors as $S(a) = \sum_{i=1}^{n} (y_i - a \cdot x_i)^2$, find the vector a.

CHAPTER 12

Optimization (II)

Everyone who invents linear
programming these days seems to be
charmed by it.
Robert M. Solow (1956)

Many of the variables that appear in economic models are sensibly modeled not on $(-\infty, \infty)$ but on $[0, \infty]$. Prices cannot be negative, nor can outputs take on negative values. Consequently, many of the optimization problems in economics require that the instruments be constrained to nonnegative values. In such a case, an optimization problem takes the form

(O.P.N.) $\max_{x} f(x)$ for $x \geq 0$,

where $x \in R^n$ and $f: R^n \to R$. Here $x \geq 0$ means that each $x_i \geq 0$ for $i = 1, 2, \ldots, n$.

There are only two possibilities: Either $x_i^* > 0$ or $x_i^* = 0$ at an optimizing x^*, if such exists. If x^* solves (O.P.N.), suppose that all $x_i^* > 0$. If f is twice continuously differentiable on the set $S = \{x \in R^n : x > 0\}$, then

$$\text{grad} f(x^*) = 0.$$

If, at x^*, $x_i^* = 0$, then certainly $(\partial f(x^*)/\partial x_i^*)x_i^* = 0$. Thus, at any solution x^* of (O.P.N.), it is necessary that

$$\text{grad} f(x^*)x^* = 0.$$

Because x^* is a column n-vector, this condition has the geometric interpretation that the vector $\text{grad} f(x^*)$ is orthogonal or perpendicular to the vector x^* at any solution x^* of (O.P.N.). Figure 12.1 describes the situation in the case $n = 1$. In panel (a), f is optimized at $x^* > 0$; so $Df(x^*) = 0$. In (b), f is optimized at $x^* = 0$, and, in fact, $Df(x^*) < 0$. In (c), $Df(x^*) = 0$, even though $x^* = 0$.

The case $Df(x^*) < 0$ at $x^* = 0$ is not accidental. Near any x^* where f is twice continuously differentiable, certainly (see Chapter 11)

$$f(x^* + \lambda x) - f(x^*) \approx \text{grad} f(x^*)\lambda x + \tfrac{1}{2}\lambda^2 x^T Hf(x^*)x \leq 0.$$

161

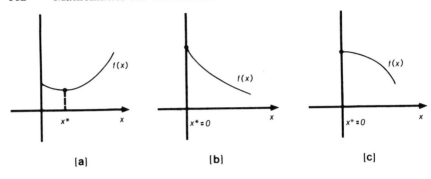

FIGURE 12.1

As before, if x^* maximizes f, and λ is a small scalar, then as $\lambda \to 0$,

$$\text{grad} f(x^*)x \le 0$$

for all $x \ge 0$ and $\lambda \ge 0$. If $x^* = 0$, λ cannot be negative. Thus, it is always true, at a solution x^* to (O.P.N.), that

$$\text{grad} f(x^*)x^* = 0$$

$$\text{grad} f(x^*) \le 0$$

$$x^* \ge 0.$$

Thus, the solution x^* to (O.P.N.) necessarily satisfies one equation and $2n$ equalities.

EXAMPLE

Consider the average cost function $c = q^2 - aq + b$. What are the solutions to

$$\min_q c \quad \text{with} \quad q \ge 0?$$

This is equivalent to solving

$$\max_q (-q^2 + aq - b); \quad q \ge 0.$$

The conditions that hold at any optimizing q^* are

$$(-2q^* + a)q^* = 0$$

$$-2q^* + a \le 0$$

$$q^* \ge 0.$$

If $q^* > 0$, then $-2q^* + a = 0$; so $q^* = a/2$. If $q^* = 0$, then the inequality $-2q^* + a \leq 0$ entails that $a \leq 0$. Thus, q^* is a cost-minimizing output at positive output levels when the average cost curve is U-shaped in the first quadrant. Zero output is cost-minimizing when the average cost curve is steadily increasing for nonnegative outputs.

The conditions that necessarily hold at a solution x^* to (O.P.N.) have an alternative form. Specifically, for all $i = 1, 2, \ldots, n$,

$$\frac{\partial f(x^*)}{\partial x_i} = 0 \quad \text{if} \quad x_i^* > 0$$

$$\frac{\partial f(x^*)}{\partial x_i} \leq 0 \quad \text{if} \quad x_i^* = 0.$$

Nonlinear programming

The two problems (C.P.) and (O.P.N) can be co-joined to create the general nonlinear programming problem (N.P.):

(N.P.) $\max\limits_{x} f(x)$ subject to $x \geq 0$ and $g(x) \leq b$.

Here, $f: R^n \to R$, $x \in R^n$, and $g: R^n \to R^m$; f and g are assumed to be twice continuously differentiable. In this problem, f is to be maximized by choice of nonnegative instruments that live in a set characterized by m inequalities. Because (N.P.) contains (O.P.N) as a special case where $g(x) = -x$ and $b = 0$, at any optimum x^* of (N.P.) it must still be true that

$$\text{grad } f(x^*)x^* = 0$$

$$\text{grad } f(x^*) \leq 0$$

$$x^* \geq 0.$$

What additional restrictions characterize the optimum? Consider the function, for a row m-vector y,

$$L(x, y) = f(x) - y(b - g(x)).$$

For a fixed y^*, if x^* solves (N.P.), certainly x^* maximizes $L(x, y^*)$. But for fixed x^*, consider the effect of changing y. Choosing y to maximize $L(x^*, y)$ for $y \geq 0$ produces a solution y^* such that for L a function of y,

$$y^* \operatorname{grad} L(x^*, y^*) = 0$$

$$\operatorname{grad} L(x^*, y^*) \leq 0$$

$$y^* \geq 0.$$

This has the interpretation that

$$\frac{\partial L}{\partial y_i} = 0 \quad \text{if} \quad y_i^* > 0$$

$$\frac{\partial L}{\partial y_i} \leq 0 \quad \text{if} \quad y_i^* = 0.$$

But because

$$\frac{\partial L}{\partial y_i}(x^*, y^*) = -(b_i - g_i(x)),$$

these conditions entail that

$$b_i - g_i(x^*) = 0 \quad \text{if} \quad y_i^* > 0$$

$$-(b_i - g_i(x^*)) \leq 0 \quad \text{if} \quad y_i^* = 0,$$

or

$$b_i = g_i(x^*) \quad \text{if} \quad y_i^* = 0$$

$$g_i(x^*) \leq b_i \quad \text{if} \quad y_i^* = 0.$$

In other words, at a y^* that maximizes $L(x^*, y)$, the ith constraint on x of (N.P.) is binding if $y_i^* > 0$, and the ith constraint on x is not necessarily binding if $y_i^* = 0$.

Consider the problem (N.P.) and the associated Lagrangian (with a plus sign in front of the row m-vector of y's)

$$L(x, y) = f(x) + y(b - g(x)).$$

The solution (x^*, y^*) to the problem

$$\max_{x, y} L(x, y) \quad \text{subject to} \quad x \geq 0, y \geq 0$$

must satisfy

(K–T) $$\frac{\partial L}{\partial x}(x^*, y^*) = \frac{\partial f(x^*)}{\partial x} - y^* \frac{\partial g(x^*)}{\partial x} \leq 0$$

$$\frac{\partial L}{\partial x}(x^*, y^*)x^* = \left(\frac{\partial f(x^*)}{\partial x} - y^* \frac{\partial g(x^*)}{\partial x} \right)x^* = 0$$

$$x^* \geq 0$$

$$\frac{\partial L(x^*, y^*)}{\partial y} = b - g(x^*) \geq 0$$

$$y^* \frac{\partial L(x^*, y^*)}{\partial y} = y^*(b - g(x^*)) = 0$$

$$y^* \geq 0$$

The first set of three conditions holds at any maximum x^* of $f(x)$ with $x^* \geq 0$. The second set of three conditions states that the constraints on x imposed in (N.P.) must hold in either a binding or nonbinding fashion. It ought to be clear that the second set of conditions also has the interpretation that y minimizes $L(x, y)$ for fixed x. Thus, these conditions define a saddle point for $L(x, y)$, where x^* maximizes L for choice of y, and y^* minimizes L for choice of x. Consequently, there are two equations and $2n + 2m$ inequalities that necessarily hold at any solution to (N.P.).

EXAMPLE

Consider the problem

$$\max_{x_1, x_2} x_2 \quad \text{subject to} \quad x_1 \geq 0, x_2 \geq 0$$

and

$$3x_1^2 + x_2^2 \leq 1$$

$$8x_2 - x_1 \geq 1.$$

The feasible set is the intersection of the positive quadrant with the interior of an ellipse and a half plane, as pictured in Figure 12.2. The level sets of the objective function $f(x) = (0, 1) \cdot x$ are straight lines in the (x_1, x_2) plane of slope equal to zero. They are drawn in Figure 12.3. Lines to the north represent larger values of $f(x)$. Notice that the gradient of f at any x^* is simply the vector $(0, 1)$. Vectors orthogonal to this gradient vector satisfy $(0, 1) \cdot x = 0$ and thus lie on the level sets. The gradient is perpendicular to the level set. It "points" in the direction of fastest increase of the values $f(x)$. At any solution $x^* = (x_1^*, x_2^*)^T$ of this problem, it must be true that

$$\frac{\partial L}{\partial x_1} = -6x_1 y_1 - y_2 \leq 0$$

$$\frac{\partial L}{\partial x_2} = 1 - 2y_1 x_2 + 8y_2 \leq 0$$

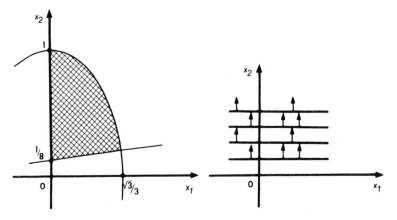

FIGURE 12.2   FIGURE 12.3

$$(-6x_1 y_1 - y_2)x_1 + (1 - 2y_1 x_2 + 8y_2)x_2 = 0$$

$$x_1 \geq 0, \qquad x_2 \geq 0$$

and

$$\frac{\partial L}{\partial y_1} = 1 - 3x_1^2 - x_2^2 \geq 0$$

$$\frac{\partial L}{\partial y_2} = -1 - x_1 + 8x_2 \geq 0$$

$$y_1(1 - 3x_1^2 - x_2^2) + y_2(-1 - x_1 + 8x_2) = 0$$

$$y_1 \geq 0, \qquad y_2 \geq 0.$$

Putting Figures 12.2 and 12.3 together, it appears that $x_1^* = 0$, $x_2^* = 1$ should be a solution. In that case, the constraint $x_1 - 8x_2 \leq -1$ is nonbinding, so that $y_2^* = 0$. Substituting these values in the first equation yields $y_1^* = \frac{1}{2}$. It is easily verified that these values satisfy the conditions.

There is a useful geometric interpretation of these conditions, called the *Kuhn-Tucker conditions* (K-T), which necessarily hold at any solution to (N.P.). Define the "outward-pointing normal" to a curve at a point as a vector orthogonal to the tangent plane at that point.

Consider the objective function f and its level sets; grad $f(x)$ is a vector that points in the direction of greatest increase of $f(x)$. This is easy to see because, for any x^*, $f(x^*) + \text{grad} f(x^*)(x-x^*)$ approximates $f(x)$ near x^*. Thus, $\{x: f(x) = a\}$, a level set of f, is approximated by

$$\{x: \operatorname{grad} f(x^*)(x - x^*) = 0\}.$$

Thus, $x - x^*$ is orthogonal to $\operatorname{grad} f(x^*)$. But $x - x^*$ is in the tangent plane of $f(x)$ at x^*. Because $\operatorname{grad} f(x^*)$ is perpendicular to all vectors in that plane, it points outward from $f(x^*)$ in the direction of increased value.

Consequently, the K–T conditions really state that the gradient of f at x^* is a weighted average, with nonnegative weights, of the outward-pointing normals to the constraint curves at x^*. Figure 12.4 provides an illustrative example. This argument also shows that the point of intersection of the two nonaxis constraints cannot be an optimum. See Figure 12.5. Here the gradient is not a weighted average, with nonnegative weights y_i^*, of the outward-pointing normals of the constraints at x^*. Similarly, if the objec-

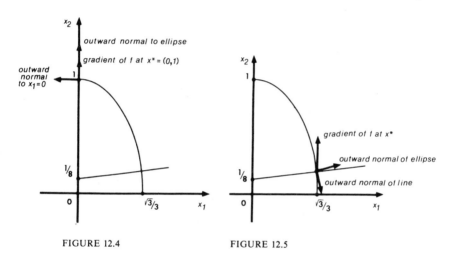

FIGURE 12.4   FIGURE 12.5

tive function to be maximized is $f(x) = x_2 - x_1$, the level sets will be 45° lines increasing in value to the northwest. At the point $x_1^* = 0$, $x_2^* = 1$, the gradient vector $f(x^*)$ is again a nonnegative weighted average of the outward-pointing normals of the constraints, as in Figure 12.6.

The K–T conditions, which necessarily are satisfied at a solution x^* to (N.P.), are also sufficient in a case of special interest to economists. If the objective function f is concave, and all the constraint functions are convex, then any x^* that satisfies the K–T conditions is a solution to (N.P.). Thus, if all the constraint inequalities are linear (defined by hyperplanes), so that the feasible set is the convex intersection of half planes, and f is concave, then the K–T conditions are necessary and sufficient for a solution to (N.P.).

EXAMPLE

In a utility maximization problem, where $u: R^n \to R$, suppose

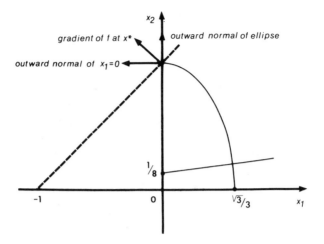

FIGURE 12.6

the constraints are $x_i \geq 0$ and $p \cdot x \leq y$ for given prices, $p \in R^n$, and income, $y \in R$. Thus, the problem is

$$\max_x u(x) \quad \text{subject to} \quad p \cdot x \leq y \quad \text{and} \quad x \geq 0.$$

Certainly the set $S = \{x \in R^n : x \geq 0 \text{ and } p \cdot x \leq y\}$ is convex. If u is concave, then the K–T conditions define a utility-maximizing bundle $x^* \in R^n$. (Because S is compact and U is certainly continuous, a solution x^* exists. The result means that the solution of the K–T conditions is the x^* sought.)

Linear programming

A particularly useful specialization of the nonlinear programming problem obtains when the objective function is linear (and hence concave) and the constraint set is bounded by hyperplanes. Thus, consider the problem[1]

(L.P.) $\max_x ax$ subject to $Ax \leq b$ and $x \geq 0$,

where a is a row n-vector of constants, b is a column m-vector of constants,

---

[1] For the sake of convenience, I here eschew the convention of this book that all vectors are column vectors. The "other" convention, that Lagrange multipliers are always row vectors, forces this abandonment of our sensible procedures.

$x \in R^n$, and A is an $(m \times n)$ matrix of constants. Simultaneously, consider the *dual problem*

(D.L.P.) $\quad \min\limits_{y} yb \quad$ subject to $\quad yA \geq a \quad$ and $\quad y \geq 0$,

where y is a row m-vector. The K–T conditions are necessary and sufficient for a solution to (L.P.), if ax is concave and $Ax \leq b$ and $x \geq 0$ define a convex constraint set. Form the Lagrangian

$$L(x,y) = ax + y(b - Ax),$$

where y is a row m-vector of Lagrange multipliers. Then the K–T conditions for (x^*, y^*) are

$$\frac{\partial L}{\partial x} = a - yA \leq 0$$

$$\frac{\partial L}{\partial x} x = (a - yA)x = 0$$

$$x \geq 0$$

$$\frac{\partial L}{\partial y} = b - Ax \geq 0$$

$$y \frac{\partial L}{\partial y} = y(b - Ax) = 0$$

$$y \geq 0.$$

However, if one had been interested in solving the dual problem (D.L.P.), the K–T conditions with a column n-vector of Lagrange multipliers x would have yielded exactly this same group of two equations and $2m + 2n$ inequalities. The Lagrangians for (L.P.) and (D.L.P.) are identical.

Now, if x^* solves (L.P.) and y^* solves (D.L.P.), certainly

$$(a - y^*A)x^* = 0 = y^*(b - Ax^*).$$

Thus, $ax^* = y^*b$, and so the values of the objective functions of the original problem, called the *primal*, and the dual problem, called the *dual*, are equal. It is also possible to show that if both the primal and the dual have feasible solutions (i.e., a solution that satisfies the respective constraints), then both primal and dual have optimal solutions.

Finally, the interpretation of the instruments y_i in the dual problem as Lagrange multipliers for the primal problem leads to the result that if the ith dual variable is zero at an optimal solution, the ith constraint of the primal is nonbinding. And if the jth instrument variable x_j of the primal is zero at an optimal solution, the jth constraint of the dual is nonbinding.

EXAMPLE

To appreciate the power of the solution techniques associated with the primal–dual relationship, consider the problem

$$\min_{y_1,y_2,y_3,y_4} \quad 6y_1 + 20y_2 + 3y_3 + 20y_4$$

subject to

$$3y_1 + 6y_2 - y_3 + 2y_4 \geq 4$$

$$-4y_1 + 2y_2 + y_3 + 5y_4 \geq 2$$

$$y_1 \geq 0, \qquad y_2 \geq 0, \qquad y_3 \geq 0, \qquad y_4 \geq 0.$$

Doing a direct graphic analysis would require a four-dimensional space. But writing this problem out as a (D.L.P.) yields

$$\min_{y}(y_1,y_2,y_3,y_4) \begin{bmatrix} 6 \\ 20 \\ 3 \\ 20 \end{bmatrix}$$

subject to

$$(y_1,y_2,y_3,y_4) \begin{bmatrix} 3 & -4 \\ 6 & 2 \\ -1 & 1 \\ 2 & 5 \end{bmatrix} \geq (4,2)$$

$$y_1 \geq 0, \qquad y_2 \geq 0, \qquad y_3 \geq 0, \qquad y_4 \geq 0.$$

Thus, the associated primal is

$$\max_{x}(4,2) \begin{bmatrix} x_1 \\ x_2 \end{bmatrix}$$

subject to

$$\begin{bmatrix} 3 & -4 \\ 6 & 2 \\ -1 & 1 \\ 2 & 5 \end{bmatrix} \begin{bmatrix} x_1 \\ x_2 \end{bmatrix} \leq \begin{bmatrix} 6 \\ 20 \\ 3 \\ 20 \end{bmatrix}$$

$$x_1 \geq 0, \qquad x_2 \geq 0.$$

The primal can be pictured in two dimensions, as in Figure 12.7, with the cross-hatched region as the feasible set. The objective function has level sets of the form $\{x: 4x_1 + 2x_2 = \text{constant}\}$; so the level sets are lines in the (x_1, x_2) plane of slope equal to -2. It is easy to see that an optimal solution occurs at the point where constraints 4 and 2 intersect. This point is $x_1^* = 30/13$, $x_2^* = 40/13$. At x^*, the constraints $3x_1 - 4x_2 \leq 6$ and $-x_1 + z_2 \leq 3$ are not binding. Thus, $y_3^* = y_1^* = 0$. Thus, the original problem reduces to

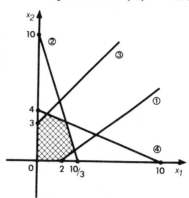

FIGURE 12.7

$$\min_{y} (y_2, y_4) \begin{bmatrix} 6 \\ 3 \end{bmatrix}$$

subject to

$$(y_2, y_4) \begin{bmatrix} 6 & 2 \\ 2 & 5 \end{bmatrix} \geq (4, 2)$$

$$y_2 \geq 0, \qquad y_4 \geq 0.$$

This is pictured in Figure 12.8, where again the cross-hatched portion of the plane represents feasible solutions. Because the level sets of the objective function are lines such as $\{(y_2, y_4): 6y_2 + 3y_4 = a\}$, of slope equal to -2, with lower values to the southwest, the solution is certainly at the intersection of the lines $6y_2 + 2y_4 = 4$ and $2y_2 + 5y_4 = 2$, or $y_2^* = 8/13$, $y_4^* = 2/13$. Thus, the original problem has the solution $y^* = (0, 8/13, 0, 2/13)$. It is easy to verify that

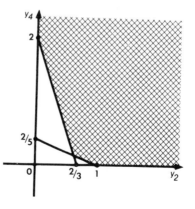

FIGURE 12.8

$$(0, 8/13, 0, 2/13) \begin{bmatrix} 6 \\ 20 \\ 3 \\ 20 \end{bmatrix} = (4, 2) \begin{bmatrix} 30/13 \\ 40/13 \end{bmatrix} = 200/13.$$

EXAMPLE

Consider a "two-sector" type of model, with markets for n final goods and m factors of production. Let the goods quantities be denoted by x_i and the factor quantities be denoted by r_i. Let the product prices be p_i and the factor prices be v_i. Let the technology be defined by an input-output matrix A, where the entry a_{ij} defines the quantity of factor j used to produce one unit of output i. Certainly, A is an $m \times n$ matrix. If the demand for good i is given by a demand function $D_i(p_1, \ldots, p_n; v_1, \ldots, v_m)$ and the supply of the jth factor is exogenously given as r_j, then it is certainly the case that

$$a_{1j}x_1 + a_{2j}x_2 + \cdots + a_{nj}x_n \leq r_j,$$

for $j = 1, 2, \ldots, m$. In words, the economy's requirements for factor j cannot exceed the total supply of factor j. In matrix notation,

$$Ax \leq r,$$

where x and r are column vectors. Further, under this constant-returns-to-scale technology, no firm can make a pure profit, because that profit-making firm could enlarge its scale then to generate infinite profits. Hence, unit costs cannot be less than unit price, or

$$a_{i1}v_1 + a_{i2}v_2 + \cdots + a_{im}v_m \geq p_i,$$

for $i = 1, 2, \ldots, n$. In matrix notation,

$$vA \geq p,$$

where v and p are row vectors. Because surely $x \geq 0$ and $v \geq 0$, these inequalities can be written as

$$Ax \leq r \quad x \geq 0$$

and

$$vA \geq p \quad v \geq 0.$$

These inequalities look like the constraint conditions for a primal-dual pair of linear programming problems, with primal objective function $p \cdot x$ and dual objective function $r \cdot v$.

Consider the problem

$$\max px \quad \text{subject to} \quad Ax \leq r \quad \text{and} \quad x \geq 0 \quad \text{and}$$
$$\min rv \quad \text{subject to} \quad vA \geq p \quad \text{and} \quad v \geq 0.$$

It is easy to see that both primal and dual have feasible solutions for given A, r, and p. Thus, both primal and dual have optimal solutions that can be denoted x^* and v^*. Further, $px^* = rv^*$; so total revenue equals total costs in this economy at the optimum. Also, if the ith constraint in the primal is non-binding at the solution x^* (so that there is an excess supply of factor i), then the ith dual variable is zero. (Hence the price of factor i is zero, and so factor i is a free factor.) The structure of the argument then entails that if the technology, factor supplies, and product prices are given, then factor prices and product quantities are determined. Solution of the problem, for given A and r, means that there is a function that maps $R^n \to R^{n+m}$ by $p \to (x; v)$.

Thus, pick a price vector p^1 and find the associated $(x^1; v^1)$ by solving the problem. Is it the case that $x^1 = D(p^1; v^1)$? If so, then the price vector that factors (households) and firms took as given generates market outcomes that produce goods quantities and factor prices that are consistent with the price vector. The system of markets is in equilibrium. However, if p^1 does not satisfy $x^1 = D(p; v^1)$, use the Implicit Function Theorem to find a p^2 satisfying $x^1 = D(p^2; v^1)$. Then use this p^2 to find the $(x^2; v^2)$ from the programming problem. Does this p^2 solve $x^2 = D(p; v^2)$? If so, then p^2 is an equilibrium price vector. If not, continue the procedure. Using a sophisticated result about fixed points of correspondences, it is possible to show that if the demand functions are "nice enough," this process must eventually produce a p^* such that $p^* \to (x^*; v^*)$ and $x^* = D(p^*; v^*)$. In words, under the assumptions made, there exists a competitive equilibrium price vector.

FURTHER READING

In addition to the readings noted for Chapter 11, economists ought to be familiar with Mangasarian's *Nonlinear Programming* and the classic *Linear Programming and Economic Analysis* by Dorfman, Samuelson, and Solow.

EXERCISES

12.1 There are n refineries with daily capacity D_i $(i=1,2,\ldots,n)$ and m oilfields with daily production rate Q_j $(j=1,2,\ldots,m)$. The value of sending one barrel of oil from the jth source to the ith refinery is p_{ij}. Assume that

$$\sum_{}^{n} D_i \geq \sum_{}^{m} Q_j.$$

Set up the linear programming problem determining the refining process on the daily oil yield that maximizes value subject to the natural constraints (adapted from Karlin, p. 153).

12.2 An important nonlinear programming problem is that of allocating a scarce resource, the total supply of which is b, to n given tasks with separable rewards:

$$\max_{x_1,\ldots,x_n} F_1(x_1) + F_2(x_2) + \cdots + F_n(x_n)$$

subject to

$$x_1 + x_2 + \cdots + x_n \leq b \quad \text{and} \quad x_1 \geq 0, x_2 \geq 0,\ldots,x_n \geq 0$$

(adapted from Intrilligator, p. 65). Find the Kuhn–Tucker conditions for this problem, and interpret them.

12.3 Consider a utility function U defined on $S \subset R_+^n$, where R_+^n is the nonnegative orthant. Let given income be y and given prices be $p \in R^n$. Maximize utility subject to $p \cdot x \leq y$ and $x \geq 0$. Carefully introduce whatever assumptions about U are necessary to develop the solution.

Additional exercises

1. Indicate which of the following adjectives (perhaps more than one) describe the sets listed below: open, closed, bounded, compact, countable, uncountable, convex.
   (a) $X = \{x \in R : 0 \leq x \leq 1\}$
   (b) $I = \{$irrational numbers between 3 and 5$\}$
   (c) $Z = \{\ldots -3, -2, 0, 1, 2, 3, \ldots\}$
2. Graph the following functions, from R to R, and state whether or not they are continuous:
   (a) $f: R \to R$ defined by $f(x) = \sin x$
   (b) $f: R \to R$ defined by $f(x) = 1/(1-x)$
3. Using the definition of continuity, show that the function f, defined by $f(x) = 2x$, is continuous at $\bar{x} = 0$.
4. Show that if f is defined by $f(x) = 3x^2 + 7$, $Df(1)$ defines the linear mapping $L(x) = 6x$. (Use the definition of differentiability.)
5. Let $B = \{x \in R^n : x_i \geq 0\}$ represent bundles of goods.
   (a) Is this set B compact or convex? Why or why not? Explain.
   (b) Construct a definition of "finiteness of resources" that makes B compact when resources are finite.
6. Suppose $f: R^2 \to R$ is defined by $f(x_1, x_2) = \exp(x_1)$. Show the action of f on R^2 as a mapping by identifying the sets in R^2 that get transferred to the points in R.
7. Construct the affine mapping that best approximates $f: R^3 \to R$ near $x = (1, 1, 1)$ when f is defined by $f(x_1, x_2, x_3) = x_1^2 + x_1 x_2 x_3$.
8. If $f: R^m \to R$ is linear, show that f is continuous at $x = 0$.
9. Let $U(X) = A X_1^{\alpha_1} X_2^{\alpha_2} \ldots X_n^{\alpha_n}$ define a Cobb-Douglas utility function. Compute grad $U(X^*)$.
10. Sketch the level sets of $U(x_1, x_2) = \frac{1}{2}\log(x_1) + \frac{1}{2}\log(x_2)$, for $x_i > 0$, $i = 1, 2$.
11. $L: R^3 \to R^4$ is defined by $L(x_1, x_2, x_3) = (0, 0, 0, x_1)$.
    (a) Show that L is a linear mapping.
    (b) Show that dim Ker L + dim Im $L = 3$.
    (c) If standard bases are chosen for R^3 and R^4, L is represented by what matrix A?
    (d) Using (b), what is the rank of A?
    (e) If the basis of R^3 is

175

$$\{a = \begin{bmatrix} 1 \\ 1 \\ 1 \end{bmatrix}, b = \begin{bmatrix} 0 \\ 1 \\ 0 \end{bmatrix}, c = \begin{bmatrix} 2 \\ 0 \\ 3 \end{bmatrix}\},$$

what matrix represents L if R^4 has the standard basis?

12. Consider the Cobb-Douglas production function $Q = AL^{\alpha}K^{\beta}$, where $0 < \alpha < 1$, $0 < \beta < 1$, and $A > 0$ are constants; so the function is like $f: R^2 \to R$.

    (a) What is the gradient?

    (b) What is the Hessian?

    (c) Evaluate the Hessian at $L = K = 1$.

    (d) What is the trace of the Hessian at $L = K = 1$?

    (e) What is the determinant of the Hessian at $L = K = 1$?

    (f) What are the eigenvalues of the Hessian at $L = K = 1$?

13. If n is the rate of growth (exogenous constant) of labor, and s is the fraction of output saved (exogenous constant), and q and k are output per head and capital per head, respectively, a neoclassical one-sector growth model is described by

$$\dot{k} = sf(k) - nk, \quad s > 0, \quad n > 0,$$

where $f(k)$ is a neoclassical production function $q = f(k)$ with $f' > 0$, $f'' < 0$, $f(0) = 0$, $f'(0) = +\infty$.

    (a) Does there exist an equilibrium k^*? Why?

    (b) Show that k^* may be stable under the given assumptions.

14. Consider Exercise 12.3. What assumptions about U guarantee that the induced demand functions will be homogeneous of degree zero in p and y?

15. Given a linear programming problem and its dual, suppose a unique solution exists. Show that the solution is a function of the constraining constants. Show that the solution values depend continuously on those constants.

16. Input demand functions may be obtained from a nonlinear programming solution to "maximize output subject to given factor costs." What needs to be assumed about the production function to so derive downward-sloping input demand functions?

Bibliography

Apostol, Tom M. 1957. *Mathematical Analysis.* Reading, Mass.: Addison-Wesley.
Arrow, Kenneth J., and Hahn, Frank H. 1971. *General Competitive Analysis.* San Francisco: Holden-Day.
Aumann, Robert J. 1964. "Markets with a Continuum of Traders." *Econometrica* 32:39–50.
Dieudonné, Jean. 1960. *Foundations of Modern Analysis.* New York: Academic Press.
Dixit, Avinash. 1976. *Optimization in Economic Theory.* Oxford: Oxford University Press.
Dorfman, Robert, Samuelson, Paul A., and Solow, Robert. 1958. *Linear Programming and Economic Analysis.* New York: McGraw-Hill.
Fenchel, Werner F. 1953. "Convex Cones, Sets, and Functions." Department of Mathematics, Princeton University (mimeograph).
Fisher, Franklin M. 1976. "The Stability of General Equilibrium: Results and Problems." In: *Essays in Economic Analysis,* edited by Michael Artis and Robert Nobay, pp. 3–29. Cambridge University Press.
Frazer, Robert A., Duncan, W. J., and Collier, A. R. 1950. *Elementary Matrices.* Cambridge University Press.
Freyd, Peter. 1964. *Abelian Categories.* New York: Harper & Row.
Frisch, Ragnar. 1966. *Maxima and Minima: Theory and Economic Applications.* Chicago: Rand McNally.
Gantmacher, F. R. 1959. *The Theory of Matrices, Vol. 1.* New York: Chelsea.
Georgescu–Roegen, Nicholas. 1966. *Analytical Economics.* Cambridge, Mass.: Harvard University Press.
Graham, Daniel A. 1975. "A Geometrical Exposition of Input-Output Analysis." *American Economic Review* 65:115–26.
Graham, Daniel A. 1980. *Microeconomics: The Analysis of Choice.* Boston: D. C. Heath.
Hadley, George F. 1961. *Linear Algebra.* Reading, Mass.: Addison-Wesley.
Halmos, Paul R. 1958. *Finite Dimensional Vector Spaces.* Princeton, N.J.: Van Nostrand.
Herstein, I. N. 1965. *Topics in Algebra.* New York: Blaisdell.
Hirsch, Morris, and Smale, Steven. 1974. *Differential Equations, Dynamical Systems, and Linear Algebra.* New York: Academic Press.
Intrilligator, Michael. 1971. *Mathematical Optimization and Economic Theory.* Englewood Cliffs, N.J.: Prentice-Hall.
Kamke, Erich. 1950. *Theory of Sets,* translated by Frederick Bagemihl. New York: Dover.

177

Karlin, Samuel. 1962. *Mathematical Methods and Theory in Games, Programming, and Economics, Vol. 1.* Reading, Mass.: Addison-Wesley.

Katzner, Donald. 1982. *Analysis without Measurement.* Cambridge University Press.

Lancaster, Kelvin. 1968. *Mathematical Economics.* New York: Macmillan.

Lang, Serge. 1964. *Second Course in Calculus,* 2nd edition. Reading, Mass.: Addison-Wesley.

Lang, Serge. 1964. *Calculus of Several Variables.* Reading, Mass.: Addison-Wesley.

Mangasarian, Olvi L. 1969. *Nonlinear Programming.* New York: McGraw-Hill.

Mills, Gordon. 1969. *Introduction to Linear Algebra for Social Scientists.* London: George Allen and Unwin.

Myers, Myron, and Weintraub, E. Roy. 1971. "A Dynamic Model of Firm Entry." *Review of Economic Studies* 38:127–9.

Nikaido, Hukukane. 1968. *Convex Strucures and Economic Theory.* New York: Academic Press.

O'Shea, D. 1976. "An Exposition of Catastrophe Theory, and Its Applications to Phase Transitions." Papers in Pure and Applied Mathematics, Number 47. Kingston, Ontario: Queen's University (mimeograph).

Piaget, Jean. 1970. *Structuralism,* translated by C. Maschler. New York: Basic Books.

Quirk, James, and Saposnik, Rubin. 1968. *Introduction to General Equilibrium Theory and Welfare Economics.* New York: McGraw-Hill.

Royden, H. L. 1966. *Real Analysis.* New York: Macmillan.

Samuelson, Paul A. 1947. *Foundations of Economic Analysis.* Cambridge, Mass.: Harvard University Press.

Spivack, Michael. 1965. *Calculus on Manifolds.* Menlo Park, Calif.: W. A. Benjamin.

Thom, René. 1975. *Structural Stability and Morphogenesis,* translated by D. H. Fowler. Reading, Mass.: W. A. Benjamin.

van der Waerden, Bartel L. 1953. *Modern Algebra, Vol. 1.* New York: Ungar.

Weintraub, E. Roy. 1980. "Catastrophe Theory and Intertemporal Equilibrium." *Economie Appliqueé* 32:303–15.

Wilf, Herbert. 1962. *Mathematics for the Physical Sciences.* New York: John Wiley.

Index

179